Revolutionary Pamphlets, Propaganda and Political Culture in Colonial Bengal

Shukla Sanyal

CAMBRIDGE
UNIVERSITY PRESS

CAMBRIDGE
UNIVERSITY PRESS

Cambridge House, 4381/4 Ansari Road, Daryaganj, Delhi 110002, India

Cambridge University Press is part of the University of Cambridge.

It furthers the University's mission by disseminating knowledge in the pursuit of education, learning and research at the highest international levels of excellence.

www.cambridge.org
Information on this title: www.cambridge.org/9781107065468

First published 2014

Digitally Printed at Replika Press Pvt. Ltd.

A catalogue record for this publication is available from the British Library

ISBN 978-1-107-06546-8 Hardback

Contents

Preface

The origins of the study lay in a chance visit to the *Smaraniya Bichar Sangrahalaya* (Museum of Memorable Trials) in the premises of the Alipore Sessions Court, Kolkata, which houses a valuable collection of records of the revolutionary nationalist (earlier known as the terrorist) movement in Bengal. In this museum, I came across a number of documents pertaining to the Alipore Bomb Trial of 1908 and a few pamphlets written and circulated by the revolutionary nationalists. Shri Anando Raha, the then Director of the Museum, was kind enough to let me have a closer look at the documents. My interest was aroused, and I followed up with further research in the West Bengal State Archives. When I first began to think of a book on the subject, it was conceived as a straightforward study of the role of propaganda in the dissemination of revolutionary nationalist ideas in Bengal. But as the work progressed, I realized that the subject held immense possibilities. It could help throw light on a number of issues that were of crucial importance to the shaping of nationalist consciousness in the early twentieth century in Bengal, issues that have generated important historiographical debates ever since. But I was ill-equipped to handle these questions at the time. In the course of the next few years, though sometimes distracted by my other research interests, I kept returning to this study that has, at last, been completed! This book, that has combined the study of pamphlet propaganda with political culture, tries to show that in the constitution of the public sphere, the ephemeral and the substantial, the religious and the secular, the spiritual and the material, the public and the private are inextricably linked. These categories are often mutually counterposed in historical studies, but they flow into each others' domains, embody different meanings in different historical epochs and for groups differently positioned in society so that historians willing to recognize the fluidity of these categories are empowered with new possibilities of interrogating the past. I should also make the point here that though I have used 'grand theory' as a beginning point from which to embark on analysis and interpretation, I have always tried to keep local contexts, both in terms of time and space in mind, while writing the text. I have consciously tried to steer a steady course between mind numbing empirical detailing or vacuous interpretation with not much historical content, dual pitfalls that can beset writing practices in history.

Over the years, I have learned a great deal from reading the works of outstanding scholars of Indian history, especially Sumit Sarkar, Rajat Kanta Ray, Tapan Raychaudhuri, Dipesh Chakrabarty, Partha Chatterjee, Gautam Bhadra and Mushirul Hasan. The new pathways of imagining, thinking and writing about history that the contributions of these scholars have opened up, have made it possible for me to even think of writing this book. I owe a special debt of gratitude to Professor Rajat Kanta Ray for some invaluable advice when I first embarked on this project. Professor Gautam Bhadra has provided constant encouragement, though he has frequently been critical of my observations. The three anonymous readers of the manuscript provided valuable new insights and raised important questions. I have tried to address the issues raised by them and hope that I have been able to provide at least partial answers to their queries. I am grateful to Professor Suranjan Das, member of the History Department and also Vice-Chancellor of the University of Calcutta for his unfailing support, which included allowing me to take a period of leave during a critical period in the writing of this book. I would like to thank my former colleagues in the History Department of Calcutta University for providing a stimulating academic environment which contributed to thinking through many of the ideas discussed in the book. A year of teaching a post-graduate course on revolutionary nationalism to a class of bright and exacting students in University of Calcutta in 2012–13 helped immensely in clarifying and reformulating my thoughts. A special note of thanks to Anasua Bagchi and Mimasha Pandit, once my students and now my academic comrades, with whom I have discussed my work over the years and who have unfailingly come to my aid whenever I needed it. A Minor Research Project Grant from the University Grants Commission for the period 2007–09 and travel grants from the History Department of University of Calcutta under the Centre for Advanced Studies Programme in 2003, 2007 and 2011 have helped in funding the research carried out for this book.

I have visited various libraries and archives during the period that I was writing the book, including the National Archives of India, the West Bengal and Maharashtra State Archives, the National Library in Kolkata, the Nehru Memorial Museum and Library in New Delhi, the library of the Cellular Jail in the Andamans and the Calcutta Police Museum. The staff of these various institutions has invariably been helpful in locating records and providing me with information. I am beholden to the Assistant Commissioner of Police I, Police Headquarters of Lalbazaar for giving me permission to photograph the rare pamphlets preserved in the Calcutta Police Museum and to Deepanjan Mukherjee for photographing these pamphlets with such care. Debjani Mazumdar, Rajesh Dey and Suvadip Bhattacharjee of Cambridge University Press have helped me at every stage in the process of publishing this book and I gratefully acknowledge this help. A section of Chapter III appeared in the *Journal of Asian Studies* in 2008. I am grateful to the publishers of this journal for giving me permission to republish this section in the book. I am indebted to Rajat Chanda (Rajat-da) for taking the trouble, many years ago, to send me much needed material from libraries in the United States.

Most of all, I am grateful to the members of my family for their encouragement and their confidence in me during the long years that it has taken to write this book. I discussed ideas with my husband and assured my children that this book would be completed some day. I am glad to have been able to keep the promise that I made them – that this book would not be a posthumous publication! This book is dedicated to the memory of my parents who would have been immensely happy had they been alive today to see the book in print.

Abbreviations

WBSA, WB	West Bengal State Archives, Writers' Building
WBSA, IB	West Bengal State Archives, Intelligence Branch
Serial Number	SN
File Number	FN

Glossary

Atri, Angira, Janak, Yajnavalkya, Vyas, Vasistha: Sages of ancient India.

Basav, Varuna, Vasudev: Warrior heroes of the Hindu pantheon.

Bhagavata Purana: One of the eighteen *Puranas*. The *Puranas* form part of the body of ancient Indian philosophical literature.

Khatriya, Kshatriya: The Hindu warrior castes.

Gita: A philosophical tract that was a part of the Indian historical epic, the *Mahabharata.*

Pandavas: One of the two warring group of cousins (the other being the *Kauravas*) who were the participants in the great battle of *Kurukshetra*, which forms the subject matter of the Indian epic, the *Mahabharata.*

Firinghi, firinghee, feringhee: A pejorative term used for people of mixed race and Europeans.

Koti: 10 million.

Lakh: Hundred thousand.

Lathi: Bamboo stave.

Introduction

The revolutionary nationalist movement in Bengal, or the terrorist movement as it was more popularly known till the term became embroiled in nasty controversies arising out of contemporary political developments, has fired the imagination of generations of Indians, and especially Bengalis. In the early twentieth century, the heroic actions of young men and women who selflessly sacrificed their lives in the service of the motherland touched a chord amongst a people who had grown steadily more restive under the patronizing tutelage of foreign rulers. Similarly, the narratives which detailed these actions of the men and women found deep emotional resonance among later generations who read their own frustrations and longings into a movement that seemed to echo their own idealism while at the same time appearing to aspire to utterly unattainable ends.

This book explores an aspect of the early revolutionary nationalist movement in Bengal that has been quite neglected in historical literature – that is, revolutionary propaganda. Revolutionary propaganda was mainly carried out through the medium of the underground pamphlet press. The pamphlet press has received considerably less attention than the newspaper press in the study of Bengal politics, perhaps because of its avowedly ephemeral character. Yet, historians working in pamphlet journalism have amply demonstrated the importance of the pamphlet press in furthering our understanding of the history of journalism. Through a close study of the pamphlet press of the early revolutionary nationalist movement in Bengal (1908–18), this work will illustrate the effectiveness of the pamphlet press in educating public opinion about the political aims and methods of the revolutionary militants, in mobilizing support and recruits for their efforts and in legitimizing their movement in the political arena. Historians of the nationalist movement in Bengal have been slow to realize the importance of propaganda as a discrete field of study. In concentrating on the study of nationalist institutions, ideologies and practices, historians have generally tended to overlook the processes through which the former were propagated to the mass public and made acceptable to them. It is this lacuna in historical literature that this work hopes to address.

Secondly, a study of revolutionary propaganda through the medium of pamphlets, throws light on certain under explored but critically important dimensions of the revolutionary nationalist movement and helps to underline its complexities which, in turn, open up avenues for new ways of analysing and understanding the political culture of late nineteenth and early twentieth century Bengal. The focus of this study is not 'revolutionary action' or 'terrorist activities' but rather the political ideas, value systems, hopes and aspirations of the revolutionaries that found expression through the medium of seditious pamphlets and that can best be understood within the context of the larger politico-cultural world that the revolutionaries inhabited at the turn of the twentieth century. The fulcrum around which this world revolved was the quest for a national identity and political destiny. The sense of personal identity and the self-worth of the revolutionaries were tied up with this quest. The revolutionaries, in their efforts to conceptualize and propagandize this identity, drew upon the resources that this world made available to them. This work aims to show how the revolutionaries attempted to negotiate the complex cross-currents of thought that appeared to make it seemingly impossible to take any clear-cut intellectual position. As thinking individuals they had to confront and assess the new intellectual and cultural challenges that the colonial encounter had unleashed under the rubric of 'modernity' and the necessity of confronting these new challenges involved radical engagements with their own cultural heritage. The complexities and contradictions of the cultural matrix within which the revolutionaries operated influenced the content of seditious pamphlet propaganda. In this study, this propaganda has been read as attempts to discursively frame the public meanings of colonial power and authority with the intention of subverting such meanings, and, in the process, shape an identity that would be radically different from that of the colonized subject. Intertwined with this study of revolutionary propaganda are the themes of governmental reaction and response to seditious propaganda that are analysed as attempts made by a colonial government to control the representations and dissemination of public meanings of power and dominance that were posing such serious challenges to their continued political control over the country.

The revolutionary nationalists, like their forbearers in the *swadeshi* movement in Bengal, realized, early on, the importance of building up a mass base of support among the population at large. This is not to say that the movement was a populist one. A reading of the revolutionary propaganda makes it apparent that the movement aimed to recruit from among educated young men of the upper castes, that is, from among the *bhadralok* class. But for the revolutionary movement to achieve any degree of success, it had to have the support of the larger population. The broad objective of revolutionary propaganda was to mobilize support for the militant nationalist movement. At the turn of the century Bengal, several nationalist political groups which advocated different political ideologies ranging from loyal support to the British government to its violent overthrow, began to compete for public attention and support. In order to influence public opinion these nationalist groups had to publicize their political programmes and ideologies and open up channels of communication with the masses. Hence, *propaganda* emerged as a powerful new weapon in the political arsenal.

The early revolutionary leaders like Aurobindo Ghose and his brother Barindra Ghose claimed at different times that terrorist violence could not achieve any long term aims and that the true purpose of the revolutionary movement was to prepare the country, through examples of heroism and supreme sacrifice, for the larger war against colonialism that was to follow.[1] Terrorism was not an objective in itself. Rather, it was the means to an end. In the long run terrorism was to develop into a revolution that would bring independence – social, political and economic – in its wake.[2] The immediate goal was for terrorist violence to shatter the aura of invincibility that enveloped the ruling class, thus ridding the subject people of their fear and awe of the colonial power and drawing them into the revolutionary movement. In this sense, terrorist action in the early period was itself a form of propaganda or 'propaganda by deed'. But simply to commit acts of terrorist violence was not enough to mobilize support for the revolutionary movement. The violence of terrorism had also to be legitimized. The revolutionary nationalists were faced with the problem of having to integrate the idea and practice of violence into a political culture that was quite unexposed to this phenomenon. The heroism and selflessness of a band of revolutionaries might evoke admiration but admiration alone could not assure the success of the movement. Violence had to be projected as a viable and legitimate political technique if the support required to sustain the movement in the long run was to be garnered from the general population and continued recruitment for the revolutionary cause assured. From the very beginning of the movement, the revolutionary terrorists or militant nationalists concentrated as much on propaganda as they did on terrorist action. The character of this propaganda was necessarily polemical – its purpose was not the rectification or redress of an unjust state of affairs. Rather, it was to persuade its targeted audience that the prevalent state of affairs was so unacceptable and so irremediable that the only available course of action was to put an end to it through revolution. The revolutionary nationalists turned to pamphlet propaganda which served as the means to disseminate arguments justifying the use of violence as a method of attaining independence. Revolutionary pamphlet propaganda thus became a means of explaining, rationalizing and legitimizing violence to the general public.

It is merely a truism to point out that acts of violence elicit different reactions from the various parties that are involved in it since they are affected differently by it. Violence may be represented as a triangle with the perpetrators at one axis, the victims at another and the witnesses occupying the third axis. Revolutionary violence also involved three parties, the revolutionary nationalists, the colonial government and the public. While the militant nationalists justified terrorist violence as a legitimate way of attaining independence, the colonial government denounced it as sedition. The same point may be made about revolutionary propaganda. Propaganda may be defined as a form of communication that seeks to influence the thought and behavior of persons to which it is addressed in favour of the desired intent of the propagandists. To those who are sympathetically inclined to a particular line of propaganda, it is legitimate communication that aims to persuade. To those who are hostile towards such propaganda, it is a form of manipulative communication that rests on deceit and lies.[3] So also in early twentieth century Bengal, there were contrasting views of the nature of revolutionary pamphlet literature. While the revolutionaries looked upon propaganda as a legitimate means of influencing public opinion,[4] the colonial government castigated revolutionary pamphlet propaganda as seditious literature that aimed to spread disaffection and defiance against the rulers and embarked on a policy of suppressing and stamping out this literature on a warlike footing. Aware of the importance of keeping public opinion on its side, the government, in its turn, sporadically attempted to counter revolutionary propaganda with propaganda of its own. Propaganda thus became yet another site of conflict between imperialism and nationalism.

This tussle between the revolutionary endeavour to disseminate propaganda on a large scale and the government's determination to suppress it points to the importance of the third party, i.e., the public, towards which this propaganda was directed. The growing importance of the public was connected to two other interlinked phenomena whose importance could not be ignored in early twentieth century Bengal: one was the growing power of print journalism and the other was the entry of the masses, though on a limited scale, into the arena of nationalist politics. Both brought about a sea change in the way politics was conceptualized and organized in early twentieth century Bengal.

Two well known theoretical works provide important starting points for historical inquiry into the kind of changes mentioned above. The first work is Jürgen Habermas's, *The Structural Transformation of the Public Sphere: An Inquiry into a Category of Bourgeois Society.*[5] According to Habermas, the closing years of the eighteenth century witnessed the emergence of a 'bourgeois public sphere' in various western European nations which indicated an intellectual realm within which educated individuals, using their reason and logic, could exchange information and discuss issues free from state interference and control. The 'political public sphere' or 'public sphere in the political realm' was an extension of the 'literary public sphere' that had emerged earlier and was devoted to a reasoned discussion of political matters. Institutions of sociability like coffee houses and salons as well as print matter like newspapers and pamphlets became the instruments for the exchange of ideas. Habermas's theory has been criticized on various grounds, but his concept of the 'public sphere' has proved extraordinarily useful in providing a theoretical framework for understanding the evolution of public communication and intellectual exchange in the modern world. This study of propaganda too utilizes the category of the 'public sphere' while remaining fully aware that the public sphere in a colonized society functioned in a way that was fundamentally different from Habermas's normative public sphere. In a colonized society there could be no public sphere that was completely free of intrusion or control by state power. This study uses the category in a limited sense to indicate a social space for informed discussion of various subjects by an educated public where the printed word served as the primary vehicle of communication.

Benedict Anderson's *Imagined Communities: Reflections on the Origin and Spread of Nationalism* underlines the contribution of the printed word to the formation of a national identity. Benedict Anderson connected the rise of modern nationalisms with the formation of 'imagined communities', made up of individuals inhabiting particular territorial units who had never met each other but yet developed a shared sense of community based on their reading of the same newspapers, pamphlets, novels and other print material. Nationalism thus involved the prior rise of 'print capitalism' that was made possible by the invention of the printing press and the subsequent emergence of print as a commodity that helped in the dissemination of the written word through novels, newspapers and books. Print capitalism further led to the rise of written vernacular languages and to the creation of reading publics who read in the vernacular.[6] Benedict Anderson has laid particular emphasis on the role of newspapers in the creation of the 'imagined community'. He compares the act of reading newspapers to 'a mass ceremony' for every reader is aware that there are numerous others who are reading the same thing and this leads to a sort of communion among readers.[7] Though Anderson's work provides valuable insights into the process of formation of national identities through the medium of the printed word, scholars have questioned his theoretical framework including his claim that European nationalism served as the model for subsequent nationalist movements.[8] Though nationalism as an ideology was imported into the colonies in the nineteenth century, the anti-colonial nationalist movements sought distinctive identities that would set them off from nationalist movements elsewhere. Moreover in a colonial setting, the threatening spectre of the 'other', that is, the colonizing power is as important a force in holding together the different groups that go to make a nation as a common identity or commonality.

The printed word played a critical role in the formation of public opinion and national consciousness in Bengal in the nineteenth and twentieth centuries. Any account of the associations between language, literature and the politics of nationalism must begin with a reference to the works of Bankimchandra Chattopadhyay, one of the foremost Bengali literary scholars of the nineteenth century. Bankimchandra spoke of *jati-pratishttha* (or the establishment of national consciousness) in his writings and turned to history and culture in his explorations of the origins of a 'Bengali' identity. The sheer beauty of Bankimchandra's language, as well as the lucidity and clarity of his Bengali prose, which expressed the deepest human emotions as well as the most difficult philosophical ideas with equal felicity, have led scholars to argue that he created the modern Bengali language. His writings helped to forge an emotional connect among his readers who began to feel that they formed a part of a shared community, on the lines theorized by Benedict Anderson. For example, his novel, *Anandamath* inspired his many readers as an ode to 'Bengali-

Hindu' nationalism and was to have a tremendous impact on the revolutionary terrorists.[9] The role of Bankim's pen in inspiring generations of nationalists was recognized by Aurobindo Ghose, the 'spiritual' leader of the revolutionaries in Bengal. Aurobindo Ghose spoke of the 'awakening and stimulating influence of Bankim on the national mind.' In Aurobindo's words,

> Young Bengal gets its ideas, feelings and culture not from schools and colleges, but from Bankim's novels and Rabindranath Tagore's poems; so true is it that language is the life of a nation.[10]

With his intense awareness of the power of language and particularly the power of the vernacular in disseminating nationalist ideas and building up public opinion, Aurobindo, along with several illustrious contemporaries, developed a particular brand of political journalism in the Bengali language that was appropriate for the spread of radical nationalist ideas in Bengal. Because the intended audience of these writers were their compatriots, rather than the English in India or Britain, it seemed perfectly rational for them to use the vernacular as the medium of communication. The reception of their works illustrates how printed matter, particularly print journalism, played an important role in the dissemination of revolutionary political ideas and the formation of radical public opinion in Bengal.

In order for print journalism to have an impact on public opinion, certain sociological conditions have to be fulfilled. Literacy levels and economic conditions have to be such that sufficient numbers of people buy newspapers, pamphlets and other periodical literature to make the publication of such material a viable concern. Though levels of literacy were low and the general population was abysmally poor in early twentieth century Bengal, sufficient numbers of people had access to periodical literature for the latter to function as an effective and popular medium for the communication of news. This accounted for the fact that political newspapers and pamphlets emerged as important tools for the dissemination of political news during this period. But their function was not restricted to mere reportage. Political newspapers and pamphlets aimed to influence the public just as they claimed to represent the public will through its columns. In recognition of this dual function, it has been pointed out that in their reportage of political events, newspapers claim both a descriptive or mimetic, and a prescriptive or instrumental relationship; in other words, they describe events and also attempt to influence the future course of events by shaping public opinion and policy. Journalists thus interpret their role both as provider of the information (that has to be accurate) upon which the public formulates its will and the instrument through which the public exercise their informed will.[11] In the world of print journalism, 'public opinion' thus emerges as an important, though abstract category that is frequently evoked as an expression of the collective will of a people that is well-informed in public affairs. Public opinion has often been described as a popular tribunal which could confer legitimacy on social and political practices.[12] By claiming to represent public opinion, newspapers and pamphlets could also lay claim to this power to confer legitimacy.

There is a fine line of difference however, at least in theory, between journalism and propaganda. Political reporting can be tendentious and inflected with the reporter's views and opinion on events that are unfolding on the political scene but journalistic integrity is perceived to be dependent on the degree that journalism delivers on the claim to present a neutral and, therefore, 'true' view of events. There is therefore a tension between the journalistic claim to record events and the journalistic desire to influence the course of events. But ultimately, news reporting operates on the implicit understanding that 'views' should not override 'news'. Propaganda has no such pretensions to neutrality. Its aim is to persuade its intended audience to accept a particular viewpoint with the result that mimetic representation of news is subordinated to the need to influence opinion. The effectiveness of propaganda is measured by the success of the rhetorical strategies employed in swaying public opinion in favour of the propagandists' point of view. The reach and persuasive power of propaganda is determined by the skill of the propagandists in wielding the written word.

The importance of print journalism in early twentieth century Bengal was enhanced by the political developments in the province during this period. The early twentieth century was a critical turning point in the history of the nationalist movement in Bengal. The partition of Bengal in 1905 marked the culmination of a series of measures that had progressively opened up a wide gulf between the rulers and the ruled in the course of the last half-century.[13] Curzon's imperious attempts to reverse the nationalist gains made in the direction of participatory government, as evidenced by the passing of the *Calcutta Municipal Amendment Act* of 1899 and the *Indian Universities Act* of 1904 that increased official control over these institutions, vitiated the political atmosphere. Matters were made worse by the increasing racial animosity between Indians and Europeans that was expressed most vocally in Indian complaints of partiality towards Europeans at all levels of the judicial system, so that Europeans escaped with light sentences in cases where Indians would have received much more severe punishment for similar violations of the law. During these troubled times, political leadership was assumed by a middle-class intelligentsia which was drawn mainly from the ranks of English educated professionals of the Hindu higher castes like Brahmins, Kayasthas and Baidyas and who were collectively known as the *bhadralok* (gentlefolk). The *bhadralok* mostly belonged to the small rural gentry whose landed incomes had dwindled as a result of the increasing pressure of population on land that had led to increasing subdivision of land and excessive sub-infeudation. The *bhadralok* had sought to supplement their inadequate landed incomes by getting an English education and moving into the professions such as government services. They were also the most affected by the economic crisis of the late nineteenth and early twentieth centuries. Rising prices, stagnant rents and increasing difficulty in finding employment because of overcrowding in the lower rungs of government service and professions bred frustration and unhappiness in their ranks. Those who were fortunate enough to find employment in government service soon felt stifled by the regimented routine of a clerical job and humiliated in an environment that gave them no respect and afforded no outlet for their creative energies. *Chakri* or salaried service became a metaphor for drudgery at work and created widespread resentment in a generation of Bengalis who had expected much more from a colonial education. The all encompassing sense of gloom found expression in the trope of *kaliyuga*, an age of darkness and degeneracy when the norms that structured the social order were overturned leading to a pervasive feeling of anomie among those who lived during those times.[14]

Nor was the situation more encouraging elsewhere. The British monopoly of modern business and industry which made it next to impossible for Indians to enter these fields, thus narrowing economic opportunities, and a growing understanding of the mechanisms of colonial expropriation as expressed in doctrines of the 'drain' helped them to connect their personal situations with the general conditions that prevailed under colonialism. Their English education had also given the *bhadralok* exposure to western ideas of liberalism and western representative institutions and the disjunction between these ideals and imperialist practices added to their discontent. When Curzon proclaimed the superiority of western values and ideals of truth in an address to Calcutta University, the hypocrisy and arrogance of the pronouncement outraged educated opinion. The outrage was all the more because the victory of Japan over Russia in 1904–05 exploded the myth of Western superiority and renewed the confidence of the *bhadralok* in their indigenous culture and achievements. Thus, was born cultural nationalism that found expression in a growing pride in the intellectual and cultural achievements of Bengalis, (and by extension of Indians) and a commensurate refusal to humbly accept the colonial aspersions of effeminacy and cowardice on the Bengali character and of debauchery and degeneracy on Bengali culture. This was accompanied at the political level by a growing determination to confront the injustices of colonial rule.

In this politically and racially charged atmosphere, the Partition of Bengal provided the proverbial spark that ignited a conflagration. The Partition of Bengal triggered waves of protest across Bengal and developed into a mass movement known as the *swadeshi* (indigenous) movement. Beginning with the limited aim of boycotting foreign goods and developing indigenous products the movement came to encompass a wide variety of social, political and economic aims.[15] But most importantly perhaps, stirred by the inspirational writings of the philosopher-poet, Rabindranath Tagore, the Bengalis began to lay great store by *atmashakti* or self-help in all spheres of life.[16] A new self-confidence pervaded all spheres of Bengali life. An example may be found in the s*wadeshi* songs whose lyrics were true reflections of the new spirit of the times. While in their earlier songs, the Tagore brothers, Rabindranath and Satyendranath had compared the poverty and misery of the country with the happiness, wealth and civilization of foreign lands and written with regret 'The sadness of your face, *Bharat*' (*moline mukhchandroma bharot tomari*) and 'what darkness in this land of *Bharat*' (*eki andhokar, e bharotbhumi*), Rabindranath now sang on a happier note of the beauty and bounty of the land with these famous lines, 'Today from the heart of Bengal, you have emerged on your own in all your beauty, o mother , I cannot turn my eyes away after gazing on you…' (*aji bangladesher hridoy hote kokhon aponi tumi ei aporup rupe bahir hole jononi, ogo ma tomae dekhe dekhe aankhi na phire…*)[17]

This same spirit was also evident in the sphere of politics. In the post partition period, the trend in Bengal politics was to move away from the old style politics of 'prayers and petitions' that was now contemptuously dismissed as political mendicancy. Instead, a number of Bengal politicians began to challenge the British claim to rule Bengal and began to stake claims to political rights and even political independence. These claims to political sovereignty marked a fundamental break in Bengali political thought. Under the aegis of the Indian National Congress, founded in 1885, most Bengali politicians had aspired to limited constitutional and administrative reforms. These limited political aspirations had provoked increasing impatience among groups of nationalists even within the Congress in the late nineteenth century. During the *swadeshi* era from 1905 to 1911, moderate Congressmen often clashed with their more radical colleagues who had begun to agitate for *swaraj* or self-rule. The extremists, as these radical politicians were known, desired political autonomy and sought to obtain it through methods such as passive resistance and boycott and through attacks on British rule in the press and on the platform.[18] Despite their differences, moderates and extremists in Bengal were united in their opposition to the Partition of Bengal and their support of *swadeshi*. But the ugly events of the Surat Conference which dissolved in chaos in December 1907 amidst the fighting between the moderate and extremist politicians of the Indian National Congress made an impact on Bengal politics. The extremists were manoeuvred out of the Congress and their institutional weakness at the grassroots level became apparent with their loss of power inside the Congress.[19] With the extremists marginalized, the radical element in Bengal politics was now represented by the revolutionary terrorists, armed groups of educated, mostly upper caste young men who advocated the cause of political independence that was to be achieved through a violent revolution. The organizational base of the revolutionary nationalist movement was made up of underground revolutionary cells, many of which had their origins in the *samitis* or volunteer associations of the *swadeshi* period that had engaged in picketing, political propaganda and constructive social work.[20] As mentioned above, the ultimate aim of the revolutionaries was to free the country from British rule, but their more immediate goal was to destabilize and defy the administration through a programme of political terror whose main planks were the assassinations of high-placed public officials and political *dacoities* (gang robberies) on the one hand and the dissemination of revolutionary propaganda on the other.

The novelty of the *swadeshi* movement rested on the fact that it first laid the foundation for a mass movement in Bengal and indoctrinated large sections of the Bengali population in the nationalist, or *swadeshi* philosophy. During the course of the *swadeshi* movement the Bengali nationalists began to make use of a wide range of innovative techniques to reach out to the masses and draw them into the movement. Both print and performative media were used to spread the *swadeshi* message. Under the circumstances, books, newspapers, pamphlets were published in profusion, patriotic songs were written and then sung in public places and *jatra* and theatre were performed as increasing numbers of Bengalis were caught up in the upsurge of emotions that went a long way in welding them into a nation. Many political commentators of the period remarked on the important role that newspapers played in the political life of Bengal during this period. Within a few days after the proposal for the transfer of Chittagong and Dacca Division to Assam was published in the *Government of India Gazette* of 12 December 1903, four leading Calcutta dailies viz. the *Amrita Bazar Patrika, Bengalee, Indian Mirror* and the *Hindu Patriot* and two principal vernacular papers *Sanjibani* and *Bangabasi* 'protested against the division of the Bengali race and expressed unwavering hostility to any partition in general terms.' Thus the *Amrita Bazar Patrika* in its issue of 14 December 1903 called on the people of East Bengal 'to hold protest meetings in towns and villages and prepare monster petitions signed by *lakhs* of people for submission to the government.'[21] When the government went ahead with the partition plan in 1905, the agitation was taken up by almost all newspapers. Surendranath Banerjee's newspaper *Bengalee* described it as a 'grave national disaster.'[22] Such comments indicate that the newspapers were attempting to take an active role in fashioning a political community that would transcend narrow ties of family, caste and region and instead seek to identify itself with the larger national community. Many newspapers claimed to speak for a powerful, if totally abstract new political force labeled 'public opinion' which emerged as an important source of legitimizing political action and competed among themselves to represent political reality to the public with a view to influencing public opinion. Aurobindo Ghose wrote about this new power of public opinion in his newspaper *Bande Mataram.*

> Half the battle of freedom in India will be won the day when a measure that the Government had set their hearts on, as they clearly had done in the present case, is subverted and repealed by pressure of organized and resistful popular opinion in the country.[23]

The more radical leaders like Aurobindo believed that the locus of legitimate political power clearly resided in the political community constituted by the people and not in an alien despotism and he saw it as his role to educate the people 'to an intelligent understanding of all public questions.'[24] The radicalization of the movement as reflected in the adoption of boycott and passive resistance owed a great deal to the anti-partition propaganda in the dissemination of which the newspapers played a leading role. Most disturbing from the government's point of view was that a section of the extremist press began to propagate the cause of revolution that was to be achieved by violent means. Government reports also noted that the circulation figures of newspapers rose steadily upwards as their tone became more seditious.[25] Not soon after, the government initiated legal proceedings against a number of newspapers like the *Jugantar*, the *Sandhya* and *Bande Mataram* which, the government claimed, were functioning as the propaganda arm of the militant nationalist movement in India. Most newspapers backed down in the face of governmental repression though the *Jugantar* remained defiant right till the very end. But governmental repression could not bring to an end the propaganda offensive launched through the medium of the printed word. The initiative now shifted to a new genre of printed material: the political pamphlet that made its entry into the sphere of Bengali political culture in the early twentieth century.

The political pamphlet has received little attention from historians who have chosen instead to concentrate on less ephemeral literary forms. Yet the political pamphlet emerged as an extraordinarily important political force during this period of political flux, when events moved rapidly and different political groups competed among themselves to ascribe meaning to these changes. Political pamphlets, which have been described as the 'most direct and immediate form that the printed word can take'[26] serve as critically important sources of information regarding contemporary political opinion. The pamphlets, which usually appeared close on the heels of important political events, tell us how different political actors understood and interpreted those events and how they aimed to intervene to influence their course. Aptly described as literature of the instant, the pamphlets provide us with a feel of the particular political moment as no other genre of print can. This study of revolutionary pamphlet propaganda underscores this point by demonstrating the importance of these pamphlets in furthering our understanding of the intricacies of a particularly complex political conjuncture. But pamphlet literature can provide the historian with far more than insights into contemporary events. For informing the political commentary in the pamphlets are the aims and aspirations, values, anxieties and prejudices of the pamphleteers that owe a great deal to the social and cultural indoctrination of the pamphleteers and which, when taken into account, provide new and exciting ways of reading the pamphlets. A careful reading of the revolutionary pamphlets, for instance, can enable the historian to delve beyond the surface commentary and form an idea of the political, social and cultural context within which the pamphleteers were operating. This is not to argue that the pamphlet propaganda of the revolutionary nationalists merely mirrored the dominant cultural discourses of the period. Rather, this study seeks to analyse the dynamics of the relationship between revolutionary propaganda and the political culture of Bengal. It is from this cultural environment that the pamphleteers drew the raw material that they then shaped into propaganda. It also influenced the ways in which the pamphleteers interpreted the material to which they gave form in the shape of propaganda. The pamphleteers, in their turn, worked upon this material and manipulated it in ways that best served their objectives. Exploring this complex process of negotiation by focusing on the meaning of the idioms, motifs and arguments used by the pamphleteers, involves placing these texts within diverse contexts. These include the ideological contestations between imperialism and nationalism, the competition among manifold nationalist groups for public acceptance and the attempts of the nationalists to forge a common cultural identity in contrast to that of the colonial rulers. Through an analysis of the content of seditious pamphlets and the rhetorical strategies adopted, the study hopes to open up innovative new ways of studying political propaganda.

The chapters are not arranged in the form of a chronological narrative. But there is a thematic logic in the way that they have been arranged. The first chapter of this book traces the history of seditious propaganda from its emergence during the tumultuous days of the *swadeshi* agitation right down to 1916 when a British crackdown brought about a temporary suspension of revolutionary terrorist action. The chapter explores how a section of the Bengali newspaper press came around to the idea that revolutionary violence was the only way of liberating Bengal from colonial rule. It argues that revolutionary propaganda carried on through the pamphlet press was the logical progression of the propaganda carried on through the columns of the most radical section of the extremist newspaper press. There was a close connection between these two forms of print literature in the kind of ideas they propagated, the political rhetoric that they employed and in the nature of the response they evoked from their audience and from the government. The chapter explores the reasons behind the emergence of pamphlet propaganda as the most important vehicle for the propagation of revolutionary ideas in the early twentieth century. It argues that in the context of the political circumstances prevailing in early twentieth century Bengal, the pamphlet was the most effective and efficient form of disseminating ideas considered seditious by the state.

The focus of the study then shifts to an exploration of the political ideology of the revolutionary nationalists through a content analysis of the revolutionary pamphlets. The early twentieth century was a period of political flux and contestation and a critical period for the formation of political attitudes. The focus of the political imagination was the 'nation'. A host of political narratives bore testimony to competing ideological visions of the future, visions that were sometimes complementary and sometimes conflictual. Chapter II enters this world of ideas and proceeds to analyse the particular political vision that the pamphleteers sought to articulate through their discourse of the 'nation'. Though seditious pamphlet literature represents only one narrative voice among the many that fed into the body of nationalist thought at the turn of the twentieth century, the pamphlets, when studied in the context of the political and cultural world of early twentieth century Bengal, reveal their kinship with and connections to the larger body of literary and political thought that contributed to the shaping of the national identity. The narratives reveal the various efforts being made by a people, divided though they might have been by class, gender, region and religion, to fashion an identity that would embrace a collectivity called the nation.

Historians are now familiar with theories that reject the idea that nationalism is somehow latent in the consciousness of peoples and that nations are natural entities that have existed since primordial times.[27] Rejecting the primordial or essentialist theories, the constructionists argue that nations are constructed in actual historical time and space by a people who decide, at a particular historical juncture, that they are part of the same collectivity by dint of shared ties of blood, history or culture and are thus entitled to self-determination. The nation is thus not a given, but rather a cultural construction that has to be brought into existence through an act of political will. 'The national project' embodies the beliefs, values, hopes, interests and ambitions of a political community and all of the latter are connected with a people's self-definition at a particular historical juncture. The nation that is imagined is thus a people's collective representation of itself.

Chapter II explores the political imagination and the self-representation of the revolutionaries as revealed in the pamphlets. It seeks to understand the type of nation envisioned by the pamphleteers through an analysis of the language of the revolutionary pamphlets. The immediate concern of the pamphleteers was with advancing arguments that would secure the acceptance of the idea of a violent revolution and rally the Bengali youth to the cause. But these arguments were inscribed in an intellectual fabric woven together with themes and ideas that were an integral part of the political culture of early twentieth century Bengal. The political language that the revolutionaries employed in order to make their arguments persuasive provides us with insights into the nature of the ideal polity that they envisioned. This reading of the pamphlets aims to historicize the arguments advanced by the pamphleteers and argues that the logic underlying the 'religionized' political language employed by the pamphleteers had as much to do with the nature of their brief, that is the need to persuade their audience, as with their efforts to negotiate the cultural environment at a critical historical juncture marked by flux and change. There is an attempt to interrogate the category of religion and explore the many meanings surrounding this category in different historical contexts. The chapter argues that a study of the history of seditious pamphlet propaganda is necessarily intertwined with an understanding of broader questions such as the ambiguity latent in concepts like religion which are apparently universal and timeless, but whose meaning is also contingent in time and place. Such questions are relevant for a historical study that deals not only with the complexities and intricacies of political culture in the context of the volatile situation in early twentieth century Bengal but also points towards the problems that the polity that was then in the making would face in the future.

Chapter III continues the focus on the political imaginary and argues that the efficacy of pamphlet propaganda had much to do with the skill of the pamphleteers in influencing the political imagination of its targeted audience. This chapter goes to the heart of this study as it takes up the question of violence. Violence may be defined as the use of force to achieve objectives that override the wishes and desires of others. But violence is not just instrumental behaviour. It has a symbolic aspect as well. Messages of power and political opposition are latent in acts of violence. Though people, otherwise divided by conflicting interests and values, may agree on the meaning that particular acts and images of violence are intended to convey, they are bound to contest their legitimacy if their material interests are adversely affected and values offended by such acts and images. The possibility as well as the actuality of such contestation leads the perpetrators of violence to seek legitimacy for their acts as a way of securing the acceptance of the larger community. This chapter attempts to analyse the meaning of revolutionary violence and describes the rhetorical strategies through which pamphleteers set about legitimizing the ideology and practices of terrorism. The effectiveness of pamphlet propaganda was largely attributable to the propagandists' skillful use of rhetorical mechanisms to establish an emotional connection with the targeted audience. Because violence is a historically situated and culturally mediated practice, the means of legitimizing violence have also to draw upon the cultural resources of the community.[28] All past experiences of violence and the meaning drawn from such experiences become a part of the cultural repertory of a community and are stored in cultural texts like theology, literature, philosophy and folklore. This constitutes an important resource that may be drawn upon to understand and legitimize violence in the future. Drawing on this insight, this chapter also argues that the representations of past experiences of violence were a very important rhetorical tool for the pamphleteers as they set about legitimizing the idea of revolutionary violence. In the process of framing public meaning for the political beliefs they sought to propagandize, the pamphlet writers made clever use of cultural symbols such as stories, images, and figures that had immediate resonance in Bengali society. These cultural symbols, in turn, provided the bases of the national identity that the pamphleteers sought to fashion through the medium of their propaganda. Paradoxically, this process of politicization, through the reinforcement of cultural identity, deepened cultural and political divisions in Bengal.

The next chapter focuses on the struggle between the pamphleteers and the state to control the production and dissemination of seditious propaganda. This chapter demonstrates how propaganda emerged as a site of ideological contestation between imperialism and nationalism through competing efforts to form, control and manipulate public opinion which had emerged as the locus of legitimacy in early twentieth century Bengal. Thus, Chapter IV explores both the pathways and the strategies through which the militant revolutionaries sought to disseminate their ideas as well as the response of the imperialist government to the emergence of this form of political propaganda. It documents the efforts of the British government to put in place an effective system of surveillance that would track, gather, analyse and if necessary, suppress propaganda that sought to propagate seditious ideas. It demonstrates how the government built up a model of sedition informed by racial assumptions of the Bengali character as well as the supposed inability of Bengalis to appreciate the benevolent dimensions of colonial rule. These assumptions were built into the policies formulated by the government to track and check the dissemination of seditious propaganda in early twentieth century Bengal.

The last chapter ties together the threads of some ideas that have made fleeting appearances in the earlier chapters in order to delineate how the pamphleteers scripted the *revolutionary nationalist* identity. The figure of the ideal revolutionary was inseparable from its political destiny. This figure was moulded by the fire of battle and melted down in martyrdom so that the entire trajectory of the revolutionary enterprise was mapped well in advance. The constitution of the revolutionary self can only be understood in the context of the historical conditions in which the revolutionaries found themselves. The chapter aims to show how the individual and the collective self, the private and the public spheres, emotions and ideology became fused in the construction of the revolutionary identity as the revolutionaries sought to negotiate a world structured by unequal power relations between the colonizers and the colonized with the aid of the resources bequeathed to them by their culture.

In conclusion, it may be pointed out this work operates on two levels. At one level it is a study of propaganda through the medium of the pamphlet press. It documents the history of the emergence and dissemination of pamphlet literature in the political life of Bengal and in the process underlines the power of the printed word in an age very different from the present one, where the printed media as the vehicle of mass communication and propaganda is being rapidly eclipsed in importance by the electronic media and most notably by the Internet. Simultaneously, by studying pamphlets as important cultural documents, the work aims to throw light on various aspects of the cultural and intellectual life of Bengal in the early twentieth century. It will become evident from this study that the subject of the seditious pamphlet press at the turn of the twentieth century is situated at an intellectual intersection where several important themes coalesce. An exploration of these themes which are interconnected and interdependent have been undertaken with the aim of presenting a wider perspective on Bengali political culture in the late nineteenth and early twentieth centuries.

A large part of the material used in this study has been drawn from the records of the Intelligence Branch of the West Bengal State Archives and also the branch housed at Writers' Building. The British government prepared detailed lists of seditious pamphlets together with their English translations. These lists and specimens of numerous pamphlets are to be found in the files preserved at the West Bengal State Archives, Intelligence Branch. I have found only translated versions of these leaflets for the period 1908–11 in the WBSA-IB, but a few original Bengali language versions still survive in the National Archives of India, New Delhi, the Maharashtrian State Archives in Mumbai and in the *Smaraniya Bichar Sangrahalaya* (Museum of Memorable Trials, hereafter SBS), at Alipore, Kolkata. The original pamphlets are available in the WBSA-IB from 1912 onwards. I have used the original Bengali versions whenever available but I have relied on the official translated versions when the original in Bengali was unavailable. Unless otherwise indicated by the words 'official English translation' all translations of the pamphlets are mine. The official lists of seditious pamphlets and their English translations have now been published in Amiya K. Samanta, ed. *Terrorism in Bengal: a Collection of Documents*, 6 vols. (Government of West Bengal, Kolkata, 1995).

I have also come across other valuable records at the National Archives (New Delhi). The Police Museum in Kolkata houses a small but invaluable repository of pamphlet literature. These records have been supplemented by the personal memoirs, biographies and correspondence of the revolutionary nationalists. A notable collection of memoirs and biographies is to be found in the Cellular Jail, Andaman, where many among the early revolutionaries were forced to spend a good many of the prime years of their lives. Another source of great value is the records of the trials of the revolutionary nationalists. A valuable collection of such trial records is to be found in the *Smaraniya Bichar Sangrahalaya* (Museum of Memorable Trials) housed in the Alipur Sessions Court, Kolkata.

And now, to turn to the inevitable question of the use of the term 'terrorist' in the text. I have used the term 'revolutionary terrorist' and 'revolutionary nationalist' interchangeably in the text, though I do feel that for the period that the book is dealing with, the term 'revolutionary terrorist' is most appropriate. The official records of the period 1908–18 use the term 'anarchist' most frequently, though 'terrorist' is also sometimes used. The term 'anarchist' as Sumit Sarkar, has pointed out, is meaningless in this context, because the people concerned were definitely not fighting for a stateless society. The terms 'terrorism' and 'terrorist' represent the official perspective on the events and individuals in question but the fact remains that the individuals did want to strike 'terror' into the heart of the colonial structure, and to that extent they may be termed 'terrorists'. But 'terrorism', was only the preparatory first stage in the general revolution that was to follow and the pamphleteers also make this same point. Therefore, the use of the term 'terrorist' without the prefix revolutionary, does not tell us the whole story of the revolutionary enterprise. Also, the aim of the revolutionaries was to establish an independent nation that was to be brought into existence through a violent revolution. Hence the term 'revolutionary nationalist' is also appropriate.

A final few words on the transliterations. In my own translations from Bengali texts, I have spelt words the way they are pronounced in Bengali, with a few exceptions which have been determined by the context. For instance, when translating from passages where the language is highly Sanskritized, I have retained *Lakhsmi*, the Sanskrtized form, rather than *Lokhhi*, as Bengalis would pronounce it. In the bibliography and references, I have retained the spellings of the original.

Endnotes

1 Peter Heehs, *The Bomb in Bengal: The Rise of Revolutionary Terrorism in India, 1900–1910* (Oxford University Press, New Delhi, 1993), p. 86.

2 Mallikarjuna Sharma, *Role of Revolutionaries in the Freedom Struggle: A Critical History of the Indian Revolutionary Movements, 1918–34,* (Marxist Study Forum, Hyderabad, 1987), p. 23.

3 Recognizing this distinction, Aristotle had contrasted rhetoric which could be ethical and rational with sophistry that was immoral. For studies of propaganda, see Ted J. Smith, ed., *Propaganda: A Pluralist Perspective* (Praeger, London, 1989); Garth S. Jowett, Victoria O'Donnell, eds., *Propaganda and Persuasion* (Sage Publications, New Delhi, 2012, fifth edition); Jacques Ellul, *Propaganda: The Formation of Men's Attitudes* (Knopf, New York, 1965).

4 For example, in an article titled *Biplab Tattva* (*Theory of Revolution*) the *Yugantar* newspaper mentioned propaganda along with revolutionary organization as the principal means of building up the revolutionary nationalist movement. This article has been reproduced in *Mukti Kon Pathe* (*Which Way Lies Liberty*), a collection of seditious *Jugantar* articles in Ashoke Kumar Mukhopadyay ed. *Mukti Kon Pathe* (Punascha Publications, Kolkata, 2006).

5 Jürgen Habermas, *The Structural Transformation of the Public Sphere: An Inquiry into a Category of Bourgeois Society,* Thomas Burger, trans. (1962, Cambridge, Massachusetts, 1989).

6 Benedict Anderson, *Imagined Communities: Reflections on the Origin and Spread of Nationalism* (Verso, London, 1983).

7 Ibid., p. 37–40.

8 Partha Chatterji 'Whose Imagined Community' in *The Nation And Its Fragments: Colonial and Post Colonial Histories* included in the *Partha Chatterjee Omnibus* (Oxford University Press, New Delhi, 1999), p. 3–13.

9 See Chapter II.

10 Sri Aurobindo, *Bankim Chandra Chatterji* (Sri Aurobindo Ashram, Pondicherry, 1995), p. 36. Also see, '*Aurobindor Bangla Charcha*' in Ramkrishna Bhattacharya, *Bangalir Natun Atmaparichoy: Samajsamskar Theke Swadhinata* (*The New Identity of the Bengalis. From Social Reform to Independence*) *Abobhash*, 2005, p. 103–13.

11 William Ray, *The Logic of Culture: Authority and Identity in the Modern Era* (Blackwell Publishers, Oxford, 2001), p. 42–3.

12 Keith Michael Baker, 'Public Opinion as Political Invention' in *Inventing the French Revolution: Essays in French Political Culture in the Eighteenth Century* (Cambridge University Press, Cambridge; 1990), p. 204–46; Jeremy Popkin, 'The Prerevolutionary Origins of Political Journalism' in Jack Censer ed., *The French Revolution and Intellectual History* (The Dorsey Press, Chicago, 1989); Robert Darnton, *The Forbidden Best-Sellers of Pre-Revolutionary France* (Norton and Company, 1996), p. 227.

13 The following account of Bengal politics is based on Rajat Kanta Ray, *Social Conflict and Political Unrest in Bengal: 1875–27* (Oxford University Press, 1984), p.

1–224 and Sumit Sarkar, *The Swadeshi Movement in Bengal: 1903–08* (Permanent Black, Raniket, 2010, second edition); See also Rajat Kanta Ray, 'Moderates, Extremists and Revolutionaries: Bengal, 1900–08' in Richard Sisson and Stanley Wolpert ed. *Congress and Indian Nationalism: The Pre-Independence Phase* (OUP, Delhi, 1988), p. 62–89 and idem. 'Land, Religion and Political Culture: The Militant Hindu Gentry of East Bengal 1905–17', paper presented at the Bicentenary Evaluation Seminar on the Permanent Settlement Organized by Bangladesh Itihas Samiti in November 1993.

14 For more on this theme see Sumit Sarkar, 'Kaliyuga, Chakri and Bhakti: Ramakrishna and His Times' in *Writing Social History* (Oxford University Press, New Delhi, 1997), p. 282–387, especially. 309–10.

15 Sumit Sarkar, *The Swadeshi Movement in Bengal.*

16 A key text is Rabindranath Tagore's 'Swadeshi Samaj', originally delivered as an address in 1904 in Kolkata. Reproduced in *Rabindra Rachanabali* (*Collected Works of Rabindranath,* Kolkata, 1368 B.E), p. 683–702.

17 This point was made by Nalinikishore Ghose, one of the early revolutionaries of Bengal, in his memoirs *Banglay Bipabbad* (Mitram, Calcutta, 2012), p. 44.

18 Amalesh Tripathi, *The Extremist Challenge* (Orient Longmans, Calcutta, 1967).

19 Rajat Kanta Ray, *Moderates, Extremists and Revolutionaries,* p. 79

20 Rajat Kanta Ray, *Social Conflict and Political Unrest,* p. 157–63.

21 From *State Committee for Compilation of 'History of Freedom Movement in India' Bengal Region,* Paper No. 47, Bundle No. 15, *Anti partition agitation. Swadeshi and Boycott.* West Bengal State Archives, Writers' Building.

22 Ibid.

23 Aurobindo, 'Partition and the Government', in *Sri Aurobindo: On Nationalism* (Sri Aurobindo Ashram, Pondicherry, 1996), p. 90.

24 Ibid., p. 91.

25 *Report on Native Owned Newspapers published in Bengal in 1907.* West Bengal State Archives, Political Department (Political), Confidential, File No. 44/8.

26 Harvey Chisick, 'The Pamphlet Literature of the French Revolution: An Overview', *History of European Ideas,* Vol. 17, (2/3), (1993): p. 150.

27 Benedict Anderson, *Imagined Communities: Reflections on the Origins and Spread of Nationalism* (London, 1991); E. J. Hobsbawm, *Nations and Nationalism since 1780: Programme, Myth, Reality* (Cambridge, 1990); Roger Grigor Suny 'Constructing Primordialism: Old Histories for New Nations' *The Journal of Modern History,* Vol 73 (4) (Dec., 2001): p. 862–96.

28 My understanding of violence as historically situated and culturally mediated practice is indebted to two studies, Bettina E. Schmidt and Inge W. Schroeder eds. *Anthropology of Violence and Conflict* (Routledge: Taylor and Francis Group, London and New York, 2001) and David E. Riches, *The Anthropology of Violence* (Basil Blackwell, Oxford, 1986).

1

The Origins of an Idea, 1905–18

By the turn of the twentieth century, there was a well defined public sphere in Bengal within which politics was conducted. A number of developments over the past century contributed to the evolution of this public sphere. The steady development of Bengali as a literary language in the course of the nineteenth century as a result of the efforts of litterateurs like Rammohun Roy, Pandit Ishwar Chandra Vidyasagar, Bankimchandra Chattopadhyay and Michael Madhusudan Dutt led to the emergence of a literary realm within which ideas and opinions on literary subjects were freely exchanged. The Bengali language came to be regarded as an indispensable instrument for the building of a nation as it was widely accepted that the 'enrichment of the mother tongue is closely associated with the overall development and enrichment of the whole nation.'[1] The nation-building project became the site for the fusion of literature and politics. Writers like Bankimchandra Chattopadhyay, Hemchandra Bandopadhayay, Akshaykumar Dutt, Ramesh Chandra Dutt and Nabinchandra Sen gave expression to the vision of the nation through their novels, plays, poems and historical fiction. Their writings embodied their longing for a nation that was united, glorious and strong. The literary public realm thus became closely related to the formation of national identity.

A more concretely political realm emerged with the formation of political associations like the Students' Association, the Indian Association and the Indian National Conference, a process that culminated in the formation of the Indian National Congress in 1885. The leadership in the public sphere was assumed by the intelligentsia which was mainly drawn from the male upper caste middle classes comprising lawyers, teachers, doctors and students, collectively designated as the *bhadralok*. The intelligentsia received, in the main, an English education which, in turn, served as a medium to introduce them to liberal ideas then prevalent in Britain. An increasing awareness that the political ideas, institutions and practices then accepted as normative in the metropolis were totally absent in the colony helped shape the content of institutional politics during this period. The political leadership began to voice, albeit timidly, the need for the development of responsible government in India. A 'public sphere in the political realm' thus emerged as its members began to give expression to their political desires before the state.

But the real turning point in the political life of the province came with the Partition of Bengal in October 1905. As a result of the Partition a new province of 'Eastern Bengal and Assam' was carved out of the old province of Bengal. The Partition, implemented by a high-handed British administration in total disregard of the intense opposition that the proposed plan had provoked among important sections of Bengalis, triggered an intense anti-partition movement in Bengal. An oppositional political realm now emerged in Bengal whose attitude towards colonial rule was contestatory. Sumit Sarkar, in his magisterial study of Bengal politics during this era, *The Swadeshi Movement in Bengal,* [2] has shown how the anti-partition movement gradually moved beyond its initial objective of reversing the partition and began to challenge the British claim to rule Bengal. His study makes evident how the trend in Bengal politics in the post-partition period was to move away from the old-style politics of 'prayers and petitions' that was contemptuously dismissed as political mendicancy and instead to build up a broad based movement that drew on the support and participation of the masses. New organizational forms and communication techniques were developed in order to involve the masses in the movement.[3]

However, the *swadeshi* movement was not a unitary phenomenon based on a single ideology and method. It is possible to discern several discrete trends within the movement. In his analysis of the trends within Bengal politics during the *swadeshi* age, Professor Sarkar has shown that they ranged from the moderate approach which was based on making appeals to the British liberal conscience, through non-political constructive work or constructive *swadeshi* and its radical counterpart, political extremism, based on extended boycott or passive resistance and finally terrorism or militant nationalism. These were distinct trends based on competing ideals and techniques though there was considerable overlap between moderate and extremist trends in the course of the movement. But broadly speaking, the dominant trend after 1905 was political extremism whose aim became the attainment of *swaraj* or political independence and its technique total non-cooperation with the British government known as the technique of passive resistance. With the waning of political extremism in 1907, terrorism emerged as a dominant trend with the immediate aim of destabilizing the British administration through acts of terror in preparation for the ultimate revolution that would put an end to British rule in India.

With the emergence of a public political realm that was oppositional in character during the *swadeshi* age, the character of politics also changed in Bengal. The moderates within the Congress movement had relied mainly on making appeals to the British government through pamphlets and petitions that were written in English with the aim of initiating political change that would make the government more representative. Their general lack of success made moderates the object of ridicule of a more radical group of politicians led by Bipin Chandra Pal and Aurobindo Ghose who came to be known as the extremists as they favoured a more confrontational approach in their dealings with the government. The extremists criticized the moderates as westernized, deracinated individuals who were quite out of touch with the common people. Instead of addressing petitions to the government, the extremists turned their attention to influencing public opinion in order to build up support for their brand of politics. In place of English, the extremists laid stress on the use of the vernacular as the medium of communication with the people. Their efforts at establishing contact with the masses paid rich dividends during the anti-partition movement. In the immediate aftermath of the partition, a common sense of outrage brought nationalists of all ideological hues closer together. The nationalists sought to put increased pressure on the government by mobilizing public support in favour of the anti-partition movement. But in order to mobilize public opinion the nationalists needed a public forum from which to publicize their views and influence public opinion. This need to disseminate news and views led to the rapid development of the political newspaper which was a powerful political tool because it could report and comment on political events that were still in the making and influence their outcome. The newspaper press thus emerged as an extraordinarily important tool of communication that served both to relay information to the public and also to represent public opinion that was held up as a fount of legitimacy and authority.

Even in the nineteenth century there had been occasions when newspapers had clashed with the colonial state when they had spoken out against abuses perpetrated by the colonizers in India. Skilled journalists had played a leading role in representing, organizing and influencing public opinion when they took up the cause of the protestors in the course of the indigo and *Santal* uprisings.[4] Nearer to our times, the native press played an important role in mobilizing public opinion in the course of the Ilbert Bill Controversy[5] as well as in the debates over the local self-government and municipal bills of 1883. This tradition of contestatory journalism came to the fore in the course of the *swadeshi* movement. But now specifically political issues such as the political future of the colonized nation were taken up and debated in newspapers. The new interest in politics led to an exponential rise both in the number of newspapers and of newspaper readership in both the vernacular and English languages during the *swadeshi* era.[6] It should be noted however, that newspapers were far from emerging as mass media in the early years of the twentieth century in Bengal. The low rates of literacy and the high rates of poverty ensured that large sections of Bengalis were deprived of access to the printed word. On the other hand, lack of access to a newspaper did not necessarily imply political ignorance. Government records mention that the politically informed read out the news from the vernacular newspapers to their less literate brethren who were often well-informed of political developments and that this was a feature of the social life of remote villages as well.[7] Newspapers thus served as the medium through which an informed public began to participate in a collective political life and came to share a sense of oneness as part of the same political community. In seeking to define the principles that should shape the outlook and guide the workings of this community, newspapers helped shape the public understanding of the nature of this political community and gave them a specific identity as members of this community.

Benedict Anderson connected the rise of modern nationalisms with the formation of 'imagined communities', made up of individuals inhabiting particular territorial units who had never met each other but yet developed a sense of shared national identity based on their collective experience of reading the same newspapers, books and other print material. Nationalism thus involved the prior rise of 'print capitalism' that was made possible by the invention of the printing press and the subsequent emergence of print as commodity. Coupled with this was the emergence of a reading public together with the development of communicative networks that facilitated the circulation and exchange of ideas.[8] A study of newspaper writings in early twentieth century Bengal provides us a rare insight into this process through which a political community was sought to be forged by journalists who, on the one hand, provided commentaries and interpretations of political events through which they sought to influence public opinion, and on the other, tried to present the views of the public through the columns of their newspapers.

In the aftermath of the Partition, the newspapers raised a cry for the revocation of the measure which was uniformly portrayed as unfair and unconstitutional. Taking note of the intensely unpopular nature of the act that had shown a 'contemptuous disregard' for public opinion, the *Bengalee*, a moderate English language newspaper edited by Surendranath Banerjee, the most well known Congress politician from Bengal advised,

> Prestige will not be lost but enhanced by deference to the public and by a reversion to the ancient principles of justice and fair play which have contributed so largely to the strength and the greatness of the British Empire.[9]

'Public opinion' was portrayed as a kind of watchdog of governmental activities whose function was to keep arbitrary acts in check. *The Daily Hitavadi* pointed out that that the Bengalis, as well as the Biharis and the Uriyas, had, by dint of their education, intellect and unity grown powerful in the field of Indian politics and that the Bengalis led public opinion in India. This had alarmed the British who had tried to shatter the strength of the Bengalis by partitioning the province.[10] By thus striking at the unity of the Bengalis, the newspapers argued, the British had unwittingly facilitated the formation of a larger unity: the nation, which was an entity that transcended petty ties of language and nation. Thus the *Bengalee* in its edition of 28 January 1906 agreed with a report that had appeared in the *Times* for the 30 December 1905 and which had claimed that the people had 'grown into something like a nationality.' This view was backed up by the *Charu Mihir* of 27 March 1906 which claimed that 'wider conceptions of nationality are being gradually generated as a consequence of this measure. They are no longer contented to look upon themselves as Bengalis or Biharis only. Their idea now is that they are all Indians.'

Within a short period, the movement proceeded beyond the demand for the revocation of the Partition and began to voice claims to *swaraj* (self rule). Politicians of different persuasions had varying interpretations of the meaning of *swaraj* with the moderates interpreting the demand as self-rule or autonomy within the framework of the Empire while the extremists held out for full independence. But what is striking is the gradual radicalization of the political tone after the early months of 1906. The increased stridency in journalistic tone had much to do with the incidents that marred the Bengal Provincial Conference that was held at Barisal in April 1906. The government's repressive attitude as manifested in the gratuitous use of force against the delegates to the conference together with the imprisonment of Surendranath Banerjee, led to an outpouring of anger against the government.[11] This anger found immediate voice in the newspapers which interpreted governmental action as an attack on the right of free speech. The newspapers also began to express the opinion that the use of brute force by the government could only trigger retaliatory violence within the province. Even moderate newspapers like the *Bengalee*, the *Daily Hitavadi* and the *Sanjivani* wrote about the loss of faith in British rule and warned about the dire consequences of British policy. Thus the *Sanjivani* wrote that news of the atrocities at Barisal had 'kindled a frightful fire of hatred and indignation' throughout the country, while the *Daily Hitavadi* claimed that had it been any other nation than the Bengalis, the severed head of Emerson, the Magistrate at Barisal would have been found rolling in the streets.[12] The paper concluded that even though it did not want an insurrection, the possibility was there that 'arms will at last be used against arms and the white man's blood will atone for the blood drawn from the persons of inoffensive boys.'[13]

The *Bengalee* expressed understandable outrage at the treatment meted out to its editor and proclaimed in apocalyptic tones

> ....On the action that Government takes in regard to the notorious outrage depends the future of political agitation in India. Whatever be the action a 'revolution' is inevitable, as it is impossible to transform the present form of government in which the people have no share into a 'system of national autonomy' except through the medium of a revolution. The revolution may be 'silent and bloodless' or it may not, but this rests with the government.[14]

While the moderate newspapers limited themselves to issuing veiled warnings of imminent bloodshed, the extremist newspapers were more direct. Thus, while the *Amrita Bazar Patrika* expressed the opinion that since the rule of law was at an end in the new province the people, in order to defend themselves, had to take the law into their own hands; the *Sandhya* put it bluntly when it wrote that 'revenge is the one unfailing healer of national humiliation.'[15]

This new and threatening tone gradually became the standard of political discourse in the newspapers of Bengal proper and, in fact, reached a higher pitch the following year. It should be mentioned here that the tone of the Bihari and Uriya papers, and those of the organs of the Muslim community with the exception of the *Mussalman* and the *Sultan* generally remained moderate and loyal but the attitude of the Hindu newspaper press of Bengal proper was one of unrelenting hostility towards the government.[16] The Punjab riots and the subsequent deportation of Lala Lajpat Rai and Ajit Singh as well as legislative measures like the *Regulation of Meetings Ordinance* and the *Seditious Meetings Act* provoked critical comments from the newspapers. But above all it was the widespread communal riots in Comilla and Mymensingh, which broke out in April and May 1907, that caused an outpouring of hostile sentiments in the newspapers of which the primary target was the colonial government. The prevalent line of interpretation in the native press was that the Mogra Bazaar, Jamalpur and other disturbances in Mymensingh was the result of the 'Mephistophelian policy' of 'divide and rule' being pursued by the colonial government which was showering undue favours on the Muslim community in order to incite them to turn against the Hindu community.[17] Nawab Salimullah of Dacca was said to be acting as a stooge of the government and it was alleged that he had let his goons loose on the Hindus with express instructions to commit rapine and pillage. All this was part of a governmental conspiracy, the newspapers alleged, to undercut the *swadeshi* and boycott movements. The press accounts repeatedly mentioned that governmental instigation accounted for the fact that the police with the help of goons were unleashing a reign of terror on the Hindu community while ignoring Muslim atrocities. The more radical or extremist newspapers expressed the opinion that the disturbances had taught the Hindu community that since they could not expect protection from the government they had to arm themselves in self-defence.[18] The *Bande Mataram* of 13 May 1907 summed up the situation:

> The *Bande Mataram* praises the government for its vigorous and unselfish efforts to turn all India into a nation of extremists. Its methods far excel what the leaders can do, and the policy of leaving the Muhammadans to inflict the utmost horrors of rapine and brigandage on a Hindu Population, sedulously disarmed and terrorized by official severity, has convinced the country that Pax Britannica is an illusion, and there is no peace worth having which is not maintained by the strengthened manhood of the people.

The call to arms in self-defence, the threats of retaliatory violence, the emphasis on 'strengthened manhood' introduced a new political language in Bengal and added a new and hitherto unfamiliar dimension to the political culture of the province. This language centred around the ideology of violence and concerned itself with a host of issues regarding the ethical, legal and practical implications of the use of violence as a technique for the fulfillment of political goals.[19] These questions would continue to be debated throughout the period of the nationalist struggle. For the time being these questions found expression in the columns of newspapers like *Jugantar, Bande Mataram, Sandhya* and *Navasakti.*

The newspaper that became the most closely identified with this discourse on violence was the *Jugantar,* described by the Government of Bengal as 'perhaps the most violent, bitter, and seditious of the vernacular papers.'[20] The story of the origins of the *Jugantar* newspaper illustrates the close associations between the two branches of the revolutionary movement, namely, revolutionary action and propaganda. The personalities most closely associated with the founding of the *Jugantar* newspaper namely, Barindra Kumar Ghose, Debabrata Basu, Abinash Bhattacharya and Bhupendranath Dutt were all members of a revolutionary secret society that had been set up in Calcutta around 1902 under the Presidentship of the barrister P. Mitter and the Vice-presidentship of C. R. Das and Aurobindo Ghose. Its aim was to impart physical and spiritual training to patriotic youths of the educated classes to prepare them for participation in the coming revolution. Over the course of the next few years, this society became the nodal point of a web of secret societies loosely known as *anushilan samities* that were scattered over Bengal.[21]

The *swadeshi* movement provided a much needed boost to the morale of the societies and the revolutionary leadership began to ready itself for revolutionary 'action'. But before such action could be undertaken a suitable atmosphere had to be created by building up public opinion in favour of revolutionary activities through the media of newspapers, songs and literature. At this juncture, Barin Ghose advocated the need for a newspaper that would spread the revolutionary message among a wider audience and help mobilize their sympathy for the cause. In March 1906, the *Jugantar* newspaper was founded as a weekly with Abinash Bhattacharya at the helm of affairs.[22] The name *Jugantar* was inspired by Shibnath Sastri's novel that had advocated the cause of social revolution. The *Jugantar's* message was that the immediate political goal should be the achievement of independence and this goal could only be realized through a violent struggle. The ideological message and political rhetoric as well as the linguistic style and idiom that were later to become the trademarks of the seditious pamphlet press were all prefigured in the *Jugantar.*

In an important article that detailed the outlines of the revolutionary programme, the *Jugantar* put forward its views on the importance of political propaganda for the dissemination of revolutionary ideas. According to the *Jugantar* there were preparatory stages for carrying out a successful revolution that involved the building up of public opinion and the acquisition of brute strength. It was the task of a morally and intellectually equipped revolutionary elite to prepare the general public for revolution. Citing the examples of the Russian revolutionaries, the French philosophers like Voltaire and Rousseau and the leaders of the Italian Carbonari like Mazzini, the *Jugantar* maintained that only a small number of skilled and dedicated leaders could assure the success of the Revolution. Turning to the importance of building up public opinion, the *Jugantar* expressed the view that the inhabitants of a colonial society suffered from low self-esteem and a lack of creative ability. The minds of such a people had to be infused with patriotic ideas in order to be awakened to patriotic consciousness. Once the minds of the people had been captured, they could then be moved to action. Among the means that the *Jugantar* proposed the formation of public opinion, pride of place was given to newspapers. It was pointed out that newspapers could influence public opinion with a speed that no other medium could. Therefore it was the responsibility of the editors of newspapers to build up public opinion through discussion on independence and revolution. As the writer put it 'Their (editors') pens would function as thunderclaps from which lightning would shoot through the minds of people.'[23] The *Jugantar* also pointed to the importance of song, literature, folk-theatre and the stage and secret societies as media for the propagation of revolutionary ideas.

The *Jugantar*'s own columns provided searing examples of the message that it preached. The articles repeatedly made the point that since British rule in India lacked moral and legal foundations, the Indians were not under any compulsions to obey it. That the British in India could wield power over millions of Indians was due to the pusillanimity and cowardice of the latter that prevented them from realizing that British rule rested on weak foundations. Since the failure of the Congress policy of 'prayers and petitions' had made it abundantly clear that the British would not willingly yield power or even share power with the Indians, the only recourse left was a violent revolution through which the Indians would seize power from the British and become masters of their own destiny.[24]

The *Jugantar*, may be said to have inaugurated a new era of political journalism in India. Bankimchandra Chattopadhyay had earlier demonstrated through his novels and articles that literary Bengali could be used effectively to disseminate nationalist ideas and build up nationalist sentiments. Aurobindo Ghose, the spiritual leader of the revolutionary nationalists had beautifully summed up the debt that the Bengali nationalists owed Bankim, the poet and stylist.

> No nation can grow without finding a fit and satisfying medium of expression for the new self into which it is developing – without a language which shall give permanent shape to its thoughts and feelings and carry every new impulse swiftly and triumphantly into the consciousness of all. It was Bankim's first great service to India that he gave the race which stood in its vanguard such a perfect and satisfying medium. He gave us a means by which the soul of Bengal could express itself to itself.[25]

The *Jugantar* writers followed ably in Bankim's footsteps and in the hands of *Jugantar* writers such as Bhupendranath Dutt, Debabrata Basu, Upendranath Bandopadhyay, Barindra Kumar Ghose and Aurobindo Ghose, Bengali emerged as an important vehicle for the conduct of revolutionary nationalist politics. The *Jugantar* writers were masters of Bengali prose and their articles combined searing satire with deep sadness, intense emotionalism and lilting lyricism with precise detached analysis and their writings had just the intended effect on the targeted audience. The *Jugantar* articles provided blazing proof of the fact that the Bengali language, when used effectively, could be wielded as a weapon of war.[26]

The success of the *Jugantar* newspaper in disseminating revolutionary propaganda was enhanced by an effective rhetorical technique, that is, the use of cultural symbols such as stories, images and figures that had immediate resonance in Bengali society. Because the *Jugantar* writers themselves came from Bengali Hindu backgrounds, such cultural symbols tended to be overwhelmingly Hindu. For example, the *Jugantar* writers imagined and represented the nation as a mother who had been made prisoner by demons. The revolutionaries were then represented as sons whose duty it was to free the suffering mother from her chains even at the cost of sacrificing their lives. This central idea was then buttressed by stories and metaphors drawn from the Hindu religious pantheon. This cultural insularity did not mean that the *Jugantar* writers were deliberately exclusionary. On the contrary, the *Jugantar* repeatedly called upon all Indians, both Hindus and Muslims to rise united against the British and a close reading of *Jugantar* articles makes it immediately apparent that the nation that it envisioned would be a unity based on plural foundations.[27] But some of the revolutionaries felt that the Hindu religious idiom that characterized the language of some of the *Jugantar* writers was merely a shallow technique or 'shortcut' to secure the adherence of people steeped in religion. It bred a narrowness of outlook and kept non-Hindu communities from joining the movement.[28] Nevertheless, this propaganda technique was widely used by the later pamphlet writers in order to strengthen the emotional connect with their readers.

Bracketed with the *Jugantar* by the Government of Bengal, was the *Sandhya,* that had been founded in December 1904 by Brahmabandhav Upadhyay. The *Sandhya* was described as being 'almost equally violent and seditious, while it eclipses the Yugantar in the extreme vulgarity of its abuse.'[29] The *Sandhya* soon became immensely popular not only among the educated elite but also among the lower middle classes of artisans and small shopkeepers. Its satirical editorials written in a folksy language that often bordered on the risqué, passed into popular folklore. The *Sandhya*'s particular contribution to Bengali political life was to transform nationalism into a popular sentiment, in the sense that people outside the narrow elite comprising the educated, Hindu male upper castes began to take an active interest in and express their views on politics.[30]

The *Navasakti,* which was owned by Manoranjan Guha and edited by Bipin Chandra Pal, both well known extremist leaders, was not less radical than the *Sandhya* in the policies that it advocated, 'though it was more guarded in its language.' The *Bande Mataram* described in a governmental report as the 'most ably conducted native paper published in Bengal'[31] was started as an English daily by Aurobindo Ghose, together with Subodh Chandra Mullik, Shyamsundar Chakrabarty, Bipin Chandra Pal and others. It advocated *Purna Swaraj* or complete independence and though it avoided open calls to violence, its allusive language could be interpreted as advocating the overthrow of British rule through violent methods. The *Bande Mataram* and the *Jugantar* were closely connected both in regard to the ideology they promoted and the people who worked for them and frequently the *Bande Mataram* republished articles 'from its more disreputable vernacular contemporary'.[32]

The colonial government that was used to dealing with the prayers, petitions and petulant protests of moderate politics, was seriously discomfited by the new tone in Bengal politics that found eloquent expression in the columns of extremist newspapers. Moreover a series of attacks on government officials carried out in late 1907 and early in 1908 by the militant revolutionaries made the government especially sensitive to the writings of the political press. Government reports began to draw connections between the writings in the revolutionary press and the influence that it had on revolutionary activities and public opinion.[33] A government report drawn up in a later period was to summarize the connection in the following words,

> Nothing is more noticeable in the history of the revolutionary movement than the causal connection between the recrudescence of violent propaganda in the press and of terrorism. Normally prone to unrestrained criticism of government action the press has allowed itself to be used by terrorist leaders for their own ends. The natural consequence of the daily poisoning of the minds of the credulous public was to create a mentality which believed that there was no enormity of which Government was not capable, and the mischief caused did not end with the generation, for the children of those whose minds were warped in their youth grew up in an atmosphere of hostility, suspicion and ill-will to the Government. Every subversive movement, therefore, met with the open and tacit approval of large sections of the people.[34]

In an attempt to subdue the revolutionary press the government instituted proceedings against a number of newspapers on the grounds of sedition. The *Jugantar* suffered a series of prosecutions in the course of 1907 and 1908. The *Bande Mataram* suffered two prosecutions in the course of 1907 and 1908 and Bipin Chandra Pal was imprisoned for six months on charges of contempt of court. Brahma Bandhab Upadhyay, editor of the *Sandhya* was charged with sedition and died in course of his trial in 1907. Both the *Bande Mataram* and the *Sandhya* had their presses confiscated. In Eastern Bengal and Assam, the government instituted judicial proceedings against the *Barisal Hitaishi,* edited and owned by Durga Mohan Sen and the *Rangpur Vartavaha,* edited and owned by Joy Chandra Sarkar in 1907, as a result of which both the editors suffered terms of imprisonment.[35]

The last straw, from the governmental point of view, was a bomb attack in Muzaffarpur carried out by two youths, Khudiram Basu and Prafulla Chaki in April 1908. The intended target of the attack was Kingsford, the District Magistrate of Muzaffarpur and former Chief Presidency Magistrate of Calcutta, who had earned the ire of the militants for the draconian punishments that he dealt out to political activists brought before him in court. Tragically, the bomb missed its target and killed two European women. The government swung into action and in the course of a raid in a garden house in Muraripukur, near Maniktala in North Calcutta, arrested several revolutionaries for involvement in the conspiracy including members associated with the *Jugantar* newspaper.

Shortly before these arrests, there had been a change in the management of the *Jugantar* newspaper. Apparently, Barindra had felt that the repeated prosecutions of the *Jugantar* were drawing unwelcome police attention to the entire revolutionary organization centred round the newspaper. Barin wanted the paper to be closed down and the emphasis shifted to revolutionary action once again. Not everyone connected with the paper agreed with this view and this disagreement led to Barin's exit from the organizational nucleus of the *Jugantar* newspaper. Consequently, Nikhileswar Ray Maulik took over the management of the newspaper under the patronage of Abinash Chakrabarti and Annada Prasad Ray, while Abinash Bhattacharya, former manager of the *Jugantar*, took over the then defunct *Navasakti* under the guidance of Aurobindo in an attempt to breathe new life into it. In May 1908, the *Jugantar* press was housed at No. 68 Maniktala Street where Nikhileswar Ray Maulik together with Kartik Dutta, one of the major writers for the newspaper, also lived. The arrests at Manicktala failed to dampen the spirit of the *Jugantar* for the articles became increasingly defiant in tone. Further prosecutions brought about its financial ruin and it finally collapsed in June 1908. On 23 June 1908 Nikhileswar himself was arrested in connection with the Alipore Bomb case. The arrest of Nikhileswar effectively put an end to the organization that had been built up for the publication of the *Jugantar*.[36]

Subsequent governmental action made it amply clear that revolutionary propaganda in newspapers had become as much a target of governmental repression as revolutionary action. The government was intensely aware of the fact that the revolutionaries were deploying against the state a weapon that was no less lethal than the bomb or the pistol. This was the power of the printed word. Thus, the *Criminal Law Amendment Act* of December 1908 that cracked down on terrorist organizations was preceded by a *Newspaper (Incitement to Offenses) Act* that was passed in June 1908. But the extremist press had blazed a trail that could not be extinguished easily. Over the years, the revolutionaries sedulously built up a propaganda network that the government found impossible to penetrate or control effectively. At the centre of this web of propaganda was a new literary genre: the revolutionary pamphlet.

The revolutionary pamphlet was a natural outgrowth of the revolutionary newspaper. In order to publish with any degree of regularity, newspapers needed to have at their disposal the services of an established press and printer. Colonial laws demanded that before publication all newspapers had to declare the identity of the printer and publisher and furnish a security deposit.[37] In order to make a profit, newspapers also required regular subscribers. In order to operate then, the newspaper press required a permanent establishment. Correspondingly, these conditions made it impossible to maintain anonymity. Yet, anonymity was essential for any printed medium that aspired to challenge the government and consequently laid itself open to charges of sedition. Here the pamphlet or leaflet had an edge over the newspaper. Political pamphlets typically appeared in flurries during times of political crisis and disappeared soon after. Since pamphlets did not appear regularly, their publication did not require the services of any particular press. Anonymous and fleeting, pamphlets were much more difficult to track down and suppress than the revolutionary newspaper. Unlike periodicals, the sole function of revolutionary pamphlets was the dissemination of propaganda. They were not concerned with reportage or provision of news except in so far as the latter served to further their ideological position. Their functions were limited to comment, criticism and persuasion. Their brevity demanded that their political message be put across as clearly, explicitly and persuasively as possible. Pamphlets were thus eminently suited for the dissemination of revolutionary propaganda. The distribution of revolutionary seditious leaflets became an established feature of the militant nationalist movement. British reports frequently pointed out that the appearance and widespread dissemination of pamphlet propaganda in a particular area was an indication of the increasing vitality of the 'anarchist' movement in this region.[38]

During the early years of the *swadeshi* movement, a number of seditious Bengali leaflets began to be circulated in Bengal. One of the first of such pamphlets was *Raja Ke* (*Who is the King?*) whose appearance on the political scene, towards the end of July 1905, was described by one British police official as 'the public commencement of the propaganda of murder and outrage.'[39]

The pamphlet, whose heading began with an allusion to the Partition of Bengal described, in blunt and colourful language, the economic wrongs perpetrated on the inhabitants of Bengal by the colonial rulers and expressed the opinion that such uncaring and ruthless rulers did not deserve the title of King.

> *Ami boli, amader raja nai. Amader raja thakile amader aaj e durabostha kokhonoi hoito na. Amra ei nirdoe hridoiheen probonchok mithyabadi o abishsvashi jatike raja boliya moha bhrom koriyacchi.* (Translation: I say, we have no King. Had we a King, we would not have been in such distress today. We have made a mistake by calling a cruel, heartless, deceitful, lying, unbelieving race our king.)

In language very reminiscent of that of the *Jugantar*, the pamphlet then called on all 'Hindu and Muslim brothers' to protect the honour of their suffering Mother Bengal.

> *Hindu o Musulman Bhatrigan. Ei doshyu jati sath samudro, tero nadi par hoiya ashiya amader sonar janani bango matake apamanito koritechhe, aar tomra nirabe shojhyo koritechho? ... . Bhai esho. Ekbar buk phulaiya, hridoyer shonite tarpan koriya jananike rakkha kori o jananir upojukto santan boliya porichoi dan kori.* (Translation: Brothers, Hindu and Mohammedan! This race of demons has come across the seven oceans and thirteen rivers and is humiliating our dear golden mother Bengal and you are quietly looking on? ... ... Brother, come, come for once with expanded chest[40] and by offering the blood of the heart, in saving the mother, be our mother's worthy sons.)[41]

In February 1906, a young boy named Khudiram Bose was caught distributing copies of this leaflet on the occasion of an Industrial Exhibition in Midnapur in February 1906. Khudiram was reputed to be a close follower of Satyendranath Bose, a close relative of Barin and Aurobindo and a leader of the Midnapore Revolutionary Society. A case was instituted against Khudiram, 'the first sedition case which had been tried in Bengal for many years' but later withdrawn because of his extreme youth.[42]

At about the same time, another pamphlet, *Sonar Bangla* or *Golden Bengal* also circulated in Bengal. Bhupendranath Dutt, one of the early revolutionary leaders has mentioned in his memoirs that several editions of the *Sonar Bangla* were issued. One such edition was distributed in large numbers in a meeting summoned at the Calcutta Town Hall on 7 August 1905 to protest against the Partition of Bengal.[43] Its message was very similar to that of *Raja Ke*. These leaflets were sent out in ordinary envelopes, addressed to students and to pleaders of Bar Libraries and according to a police report, 'were widely circulated among immature youths and the half-educated people in the mufassil, who devoured their contents with avidity.'[44] Apparently, the appearance of the *Sonar Bangla* pamphlet in August 1905 was the first sign of the anti-government movement in Dacca town, which subsequently emerged as a strong centre of the *swadeshi* movement and then, with the foundation of the Dacca Anushilan Samiti in September 1906, of the revolutionary terrorist movement.[45]

In the following years pamphlets and booklets like *Arya Bhumi* and *Lakhya* also circulated locally in certain districts of Bengal. Unlike most other 'seditious' pamphlets these were not anonymous and their content earned jail terms for their authors, publishers and writers. Thus, the *Aryabhumi* (*Aryan Land or Fatherland*), authored by Jadu Gopal Dhar, called upon all Bengalis to 'die smilingly for our wives, sons, parents, self-respect, and manliness'. This was circulated in Banwaripara of Barisal district in 1907. Described in a government report as a 'more direct and violent incitement to open and armed rebellion than has yet been circulated in this province', the publication of this pamphlet led to the institution of a case against its author.[46] Surendra Mohan Some, Surendra Kumar Bandopadhyay and Pyari Mohan Rai, respectively the author, publisher and printer of a seditious pamphlet styled *Lakhya* that was published in Madaripur in the district of Faridpur were prosecuted by the government and brought to trial in 1909.[47]

Despite the appearance of a few such pamphlets during the *swadeshi* age, it was really the *Jugantar* group that took the lead in fully exploiting the possibilities for revolutionary terrorist propaganda latent in the pamphlet. Before it was shut down, the *Jugantar* press had time to run off a pamphlet where it audaciously proclaimed,

> The *Jugantar* is not a paper, but a revolutionary idea, which, however persecuted and prosecuted, can never be suppressed. Try to check the progress of the idea and it develops into action. ... With the progress of time and events, *Jugantar* must appear in a neater and better form. This time, it is to be written on the breast of the damned British bureaucracy with letters of blood by the mighty strokes of the sword of the sturdy sons of Bengal. .... The murder of English devils is the incarnation of the *Jugantar*, and an insurrection would be the vivid personification of it.

It is evident from the language of this pamphlet that violent action was perceived by the revolutionaries as a logical and inevitable extension of revolutionary propaganda. The foregoing passage was followed by another that detailed the intricacies of making a bomb with picric acid. The pamphlet ended with the PostScript that the editor desired that revolutionaries all over the country would print it secretly in different languages and distribute it in millions.[48] This pamphlet was the first of a series from 1908 through 1916 that came to be known as the *Jugantar* pamphlets as they all began with the header

Om Jugantar. Not much information is available about these pamphlets, though police reports from 1908 mention that a number of *Jugantar* articles had been compiled into a pamphlet titled *Mukti Kon Pathe* that had been published in four parts and was being widely, though, secretly circulated in several districts.[49] An extract from the diary of a police inspector mention that the books *Mukti Kon Pathe* and *Matripuja* (*Worship of the Mother*) 'have been read by almost all of the young men of Khulna who had no occasion to read'.[50] Thus, was initiated a tradition of revolutionary political propaganda in Bengal carried out through the medium of pamphlets, propaganda that the government described as 'elaborate, persistent and ingenious'[51] and that it struggled to suppress and stamp out, mostly unsuccessfully, as part of the war that it waged against the revolutionary nationalist movement in Bengal.

During the years 1909–16, the revolutionary nationalist movement came to occupy a significant space within the arena of the multi-pronged Indian nationalist struggle against British rule. The split between the Moderates and the Extremists that lasted till 1916, led to a weakening of the nationalist movement on the constitutional front and the slack was taken up, to a certain degree, by the revolutionary movement.

However, in 1908–09 the revolutionary movement itself reeled under the impact of a series of reverses that it suffered during this period. The Alipore Bomb Case (1908–10), in the course of which the revolutionaries arrested in the Muraripukur Garden House were brought to trial, ended with long terms of imprisonment and exile being handed down to several revolutionaries including many who had been closely associated with the *Jugantar* Press like Barin Ghose, Upen Banerjee, Abinash Bhattacharya and Debabrata Bose. Aurobindo himself escaped imprisonment, but subjected to the dual push and pull of the continuing police investigations and his own awakening spiritual consciousness, left for Pondicherry in 1910 to pursue the Life Divine. But the successors of the first generation of revolutionaries soon regrouped and prepared the ground for a revolutionary movement to be organized along more ambitious lines.

According to a government report, an important revolutionary centre emerged in Bengal proper around a nucleus formed by Kartik Dutt and his band of co-revolutionaries. Kartik Dutt was a close friend of Barin Ghose and closely identified with the *Jugantar* group. Like the earlier revolutionaries associated with the *Jugantar* group, Kartik Dutt was active both in revolutionary propaganda and action. Most of the early *Jugantar* pamphlets were supposedly the handiwork of Kartik Dutt who composed them with the help of other revolutionaries like Runkhini Ray, Kiran Mukherjee and Panna Lal Chatterjee. With the exception of a couple of leaflets composed by Kiran Mukherjee and Probhash Deb that were supposed to have been printed at 68 Manicktola, and a third one composed by Kartik Dutt that was printed secretly at Barranagar, these leaflets were printed on a small hand press that was housed at 28 Shampukur Street where the *Jugantar* press had moved after the arrests at Manicktola. Closely associated with Kartik Dutt was the Sanskrit scholar and revolutionary Pandit Mokkhoda Samadhyayi who had shouldered much of the responsibilities involved in the publication of the *Sandhya* newspaper after the death of Brahmabandhab. It was Pandit Mokkhoda who allegedly helped Kartik Dutt with the publication of the *Jugantar* leaflets. Kartick Dutt was convicted and sentenced in March 1909 to six years rigorous imprisonment for his role in the Bighati dakaiti (robbery) case, though Mokkhoda, sent up for trial in the same case, was acquitted for lack of evidence. The same government report also mentions that Kartik Dutt had maintained two separate establishments for carrying out revolutionary activities. The centre at 28 Shampukur Street was used to carry out the activities of the underground press while another establishment at Chetla served as party headquarters.[52] Since *Jugantar* pamphlets continued to circulate in the two Bengals even after the arrest of Kartik, it may safely be concluded that Kartik had handed over the baton to other capable hands.

By 1910, Jatindra Nath Mukherjee or *Bagha Jatin* (Tiger Jatin) as he was popularly called emerged as the undisputed leader of the revolutionaries in western Bengal. His long term aim was to prepare for a countrywide revolutionary rising in which the Indian armed forces would play a crucial role. With this aim in mind, Jatindra Nath opened up channels of communication with the other revolutionary *samitis* including those in eastern Bengal. In eastern Bengal, the major revolutionary organization, the Dacca Anushilan Samiti, was outlawed in January 1909. Then followed the Dacca Conspiracy Case (1910–11), which resulted in a sentence of transportation of seven years for Pulin Das and his two principal associates. But the Dacca group too survived these losses and reorganized under a second generation of leaders. Like its counterpart in western Bengal, the Dacca group began to develop a widespread revolutionary network by first getting in touch with the revolutionary centre at Chandannagore and then, with the help of the renowned revolutionary Rash Bihari Bose, the revolutionary centers of northern India including the United Provinces, Punjab and the North-West Frontier Province. In both eastern and western Bengal, propaganda in the form of pamphlets continued as a main plank of revolutionary terrorist activity.

Revolutionary pamphlet propaganda soon became as much an object of governmental concern as seditious newspaper articles. The Press Act of 1910 that was passed by the government in February 1910 with the intention of providing better control of the press was directed towards both newspaper and pamphlet propaganda. But despite the best efforts of the British government, pamphlet propaganda proved almost impossible to control. Unlike newspapers, pamphlets were very difficult to trace to their sources. Published from the underground presses and distributed by elusive figures or mailed anonymously through the post, pamphlet propaganda always seemed to remain a step ahead of governmental intelligence and flourished during these years on the margins of the legal press. All through the years 1908–18, the government struggled ineffectually to stamp out the underground pamphlet press even as it marshaled all its resources to suppress the revolutionary movement. But seditious pamphlets continued to appear, seeming to mock all government efforts at detection and suppression.

Thus, almost immediately after the passage of the new Press Act in February 1910, a new 'highly seditious' pamphlet titled '*Om Bande Mataram*' appeared, presumably 'as a defiance of the New Press Act'[53] in both eastern and western Bengal. Copies of the leaflet were delivered through the post to almost all the important educational institutions in the town of Dacca and there were reports of its circulation in other provinces as well. The leaflets came in conspicuous pink envelopes. The leaflet evidently aspired to take the place of the *Jugantar* leaflets and its writing was reminiscent of the *Jugantar*. The 'style was remarkably good' and the religious and mythological allusions were worked in with great skill and in a manner 'likely to produce the profoundest impression on the Hindu mind.'[54] The government was seriously discomfited by the 'open and public manner' in which the distribution was made, which made it apparent that the dispatchers of the pamphlet had intended that many of the copies should fall into the hands of the authorities. It was thus an act of open defiance of the authorities and a test of the effectiveness of the measures undertaken by government to check the circulation of seditious propaganda. The coincidence between the timing of the dispatch and the passing of the Press Act 'was obviously meant to be striking and dramatic.'[55] The pamphlet circulated widely in the western parts of the province as well. Several copies were received by different schools in Hoogly, Cuttack, Midnapore, Chinsura, Berhampore, Birbhum etc. which all bore the Calcutta postmark of 16 February and were dispatched from the Bow Bazar post office. It was printed on both sides of a single sheet of foolscap paper and was perhaps more 'violent and inflammatory than even the old "Who is our King" and "Sonar Bangla", exhorting the Indians to rise in revolution against the oppression of the *Feringhees*'.[56] Though a reward was announced for the detection of persons responsible for the issue and distribution of this leaflet, not much headway could be made in this case.[57] More *Jugantar* leaflets followed in the same year and were promptly proscribed.[58]

Also in the month of February 1910, there appeared a leaflet entitled *Swadhin Bharat* (*Independent India*) in several parts of the province. Soon after, in March 1910, the police were able to track down the original manuscript copy of a leaflet entitled *Hatya Noi Jagna* (*Not Murder, Sacrifice*). Both were proscribed under the Press Act which meant that their production, distribution or storage were declared a criminal offence and liable to prosecution. Though intensive searches hampered the distribution of these pamphlets and prevented their appearance in the *mufassils*, the authors of these leaflets or their places of production could not be traced. In the following months, leaflets like *Mukti-Mantra*, (*The Mystic Formula of Liberation*) of which multiple issues were printed in consecutive months, *Mahasakti*, (*Great Power*) *Jugantar- Year 1317*, *Sandhya*, and *Krishaker Sarbanash* (*Destruction of the Cultivators*), which was a chapter of the proscribed book written by Sakharam Ganesh Deuskar entitled *Desher Katha*, appeared. The *Mukti Mantra* (which claimed to be the second issue), which was described as 'particularly well-written in stirring language', was lithographed or cyclostyled from manuscript and from the fact of it not being printed, it appeared that it was produced in some place where there was no Bengali press and then sent by post to Calcutta to be circulated. The leaflet was suspected to be the handiwork of Aurobindo in Pondicherry because of the frequent appearance of the word Maya or, Illusion, a word of which Aurobindo was particularly fond.[59] Another 'grossly seditious' leaflet entitled *Mahasakti*, which was cyclostyled on ordinary country-paper, was mailed to the Second Master of Ranaghat High School in Nadia in October. The *Sandhya*, that appeared in July 1910 was a small leaflet of about fifteen lines of open incitement to the murder of Europeans and so called traitors to the country. It declared that during the three years in which there had been bloodshed the harvests had been exceptionally good and was purportedly signed by the Brahman Raja Nanda Kumar and Nawab Siraj-ud-daula. It was of better workmanship than the *Jugantar* leaflet that appeared earlier that month but was badly printed on common paper. [60]

Most disturbing from the point of view of the authorities was the continued appearance of the new series of pamphlets titled *Swadhin Bharat*, which like the

Jugantar series contained open incitements to violence and assassinations. The police were discomfited both by their frequency and their reach. The *Swadhin* Bharat pamphlets first began to appear early in 1910 and eight editions of the pamphlet had been distributed by October 1911.[61] A police officer commented that 'the frequency with which these leaflets are now being issued is a bad sign and may reasonably be regarded as foreshadowing trouble of a more serious kind…'[62] The *Swadhin Bharat* pamphlets originated in Calcutta but were mailed widely to all parts of the province of Bengal as well as Eastern Bengal and Assam. In Dacca town, which was the most important centre of revolutionary activities in eastern Bengal, copies of the *Swadhin Bharat* pamphlet of February 1910 duly made an appearance. The consecutive editions of the pamphlet followed in the months to come. As each issue was published, copies were freely distributed in Dacca to various persons. They were also posted up in all the highways and by-lanes of the town. The students of the numerous schools and colleges of Dacca were specially targeted and received these pamphlets in large numbers. Copies of the *Swadhin Bharat* leaflets were also distributed widely in many other districts of eastern Bengal. Thus issues appeared in consecutive numbers in the districts of Dacca, Mymensingh, Tippera, Faridpur and Noakhali. Copies were smuggled out of Calcutta by hand and distributed in steamers and trains. It was suspected that one such leaflet was posted on the steamer running between Goalundo and Naraingunj on 28 April 1911 when the steamer made one of its two stops at Tarpasha and Behar. Others were circulated by hand through the districts and posted up in different localities, more particularly in the neighbourhood of schools. 'It is an audacious custom with the circulators of these leaflets to send copies to the principal police officials and newspaper Editors' commented a police report.[63] Careful enquiries revealed that all of the first seven leaflets had been printed either in a galley press or a hand press. The same compositor had put together the type for the several copies for exactly the same mistakes had been made in putting up the type in all the issues. The printing was probably done in a regular printing office as the copies obtained of all the issues had been 'Hot pressed' after printing, a process for causing the disappearance of the impressions of the type on the reverse side of the paper, and which was not likely to have been resorted to by any amateur. The writing style, as well as the common historical, mythological and religious allusions in the *Jugantar*, *Sandhya* and *Swadhin Bharat* pamphlets, appeared to indicate that the pamphlets emanated from the pens of the same groups of writers. Though strenuous attempts were made, all efforts to trace the origins and means of production of these pamphlets ended in failure. At least a dozen more new editions in print of the *Swadhin Bharat* would appear by 1917 and many more manuscript editions as well. [64]

The *Swadhin Bharat* pamphlets followed the *Jugantar* line of exhorting Bengalis to rise in violent revolution against the British. The idiom through which this message was conveyed was completely religious. Thus the revolution was often represented as a Hindu religious sacrifice (*Jagna*) for which the revolutionaries were asked to shed blood in order to propitiate a wounded mother goddess. The figure of the mother goddess was itself drawn from the Hindu pantheon and the imagery of devoted sons heroically sacrificing their lives to free their mother from the chains of servitude went a long way in establishing a strong emotive bond between the revolutionaries and the general public. One typical passage thus exhorted its readers,

> Come on all be united in this Demon destroying *Jagna* (a sacrificial ceremony) disregarding your petty individual interests – and then the Mother *Ranachandi* (goddess of war) would again appear in the midst of her children.[65]

Side by side with the *Swadhin Bharat* pamphlets, new editions of the *Jugantar* and *Sandhya* continued to appear. Particularly interesting was a leaflet in Bengali headed *Sandhya, Second Edition, Fourth Year* that appeared around July 1911 and heaped reproach on the youth of Bengal for forgetting the vows taken at the feet of Tilak, Aurobindo and Bipin Chandra Pal and allowing themselves to sink into slothful slumber. This pamphlet was one of the very few among the pamphlets, perhaps the only one, that called upon women to play an active role in the revolution to come.

> Just as a paralytic man cannot move around without the help of a stick, so the national life cannot be developed without the assistance of women..... Through the union of *Prakriti* (Nature) and *Purush* (Power) this world was created and is now working out its destiny. Come, ye brothers and sisters. Let us unitedly offer floral offerings at the feet of the Mother.[66]

This leaflet was suspected to be the work of a woman writer named Kumudini Mitter, relative of Aurobindo Ghose, who was also reputed to be the author of the first *Sandhya* pamphlet that appeared in June 1910.[67] This was followed in quick succession by a third *Sandhya* leaflet that appeared in September and was headed *Sandhya. Number Four, Fourth Year.* The leaflet warned that if the Partition of Bengal was not abrogated, violence and dissatisfaction would continue in Bengal and would turn into a rebellion as soon as an opportunity offered itself. The writer who signed off as 'A loyal Bengali' was again suspected to be Kumudini Mitter.[68]

Then, in 1912, there appeared a leaflet entitled *Bande Mataram Yugantar*, printed on one side of a sheet of ordinary printing paper that alluded to the recent events associated with revolutionary terrorism and encouraged its readers to rise in rebellion. Another entitled *Yugantar, Fifth Year* printed on both sides of a sheet of ordinary foolscap folio printing paper and signed 'Navinananda', appeared the same year. The last line of the pamphlet urged its readers to distribute the leaflet among all patriots after having read it themselves.[69]

The widespread dissemination of revolutionary leaflets .... indicates unmistakably that the forces of unrest are again manifesting themselves and assuming renewed vitality.' [70] By the end of 1912 official reports such as these, that tracked the dissemination of seditious pamphlets as well as revolutionary activity, noted that Chittagong, Noakhali, Tippera, the whole of the Dacca Division, Khulna and Calcutta had become honeycombed with the revolutionary movement and there were indications that the movement was spreading to North Bengal, specifically Dinajpur, Jalpaiguri and Rangpur.[71] But the situation, from the official point of view, was to go from bad to worse. For from 1912–13 Bengal had become part of a larger network of propaganda involving the United Provinces, the Punjab, Bihar, Orissa and Delhi Province whose intention was to prepare the Indian public for a revolutionary outburst that would involve the armed forces as well as workers and peasants. The revolutionaries also began to establish connections with foreign countries and with centres of revolutionary activity in foreign lands, notably with the Ghadr Party in San Francisco that had been established by Hardayal. From this time onwards, the leaflets began to dwell on the international situation, analysing the implications of the momentous occurrences and providing a public commentary on events for the enlightenment of the reading public. Thus a *Jugantar* pamphlet that appeared towards the later half of 1912 warned its readers of an impending conflagration on a worldwide scale and urged them to follow the example of nations like Egypt and China who were throwing off the yoke of western domination and asserting their sovereignty. The growing links with revolutionary centres that had been established overseas became evident with the appearance of a pamphlet in March 1913 titled *Jugantar Circular: The Delhi Bomb* and subscribed *Bande Mataram*. This pamphlet was the handiwork of the brilliant revolutionary from Punjab,

Lala Hardayal who had moved to San Francisco and made it his headquarters. He started a newspaper called Ghadr and named his press the *Jugantar Ashram.* The pamphlet that he composed made its way into India by way of Paris and was proscribed both in the Delhi Province and Bengal and its importation into India prohibited under the Sea Customs Act.[72] This pamphlet extolled the bomb attack on the Viceroy, Lord Hardinge, on 23 December 1912, in Delhi with these memorable words:

> Deep down in the human heart, like a diamond in a mine, lies hidden the yearning for justice, equality and brotherhood. We do not even know it ourselves, but it is there all the same. And that is why we instinctively honour those who make war on inequality and injustice by any means in their power – the pen, the tongue, the sword, the gun, the strike, and last but not the least, the Bomb.
>
> ...
>
> And whether it hits or misses, a bomb is a blessing on all such occasions. Where tyranny issues her proclamation, Freedom must also do the same. No bomb at an 'Imperial' or 'Royal' procession is inopportune. It breaks the spell, it is an antidote to the hypnotism of power, which paralyzes the people. It is the voice of millions speaking a tongue that all can understand. It is the Esperanto of Revolution.

This pamphlet, which announced the revival of revolutionary activity in India was followed by a new series of pamphlets titled *Liberty.* The *Liberty* pamphlets, written in English, circulated widely in Bengal, Punjab and the North-West Frontier Provinces in the course of the year 1913.[73] The first of the *Liberty* pamphlets appeared in May 1913. It was titled *Liberty* 4 May 1957 and subscribed with Vivekananda's famous slogan 'Awake, Arise and Stop Not Till the Goal is Reached.' This pamphlet was notable for the emphasis that it placed on Hindu-Muslim unity. It pointed out that the result of the Mutiny of 1857 was a state into which the Indian nation had to go in order to be reborn as a great Indian Nation: one that transcended petty Hindu or Islamic kingdoms. It was clear that revolutionary propaganda was now aiming to bring as many Indians as possible within its gambit. A second edition of the *Liberty* leaflet titled *Liberty,* 20 July 1913 and subscribed *Arise, Awake and Stop Not till the Goal is Reached* followed soon after.[74]

Towards the end of 1913 the true extent of the revolutionary network was revealed with the chance arrest in November 1913 of Amrita Lal Hazra, alias Shasanka Shekhar Roy in Calcutta. Amrita Lal Hazra was an inhabitant of Dogachi village of Dacca. An expert *lathi* (staff) player, he was a member both of the Dacca Anushilan Samiti and of Kartik Dutt's *Jugantar* gang and was suspected in a number of *dakaities* (robberies).[75] Early next month, one Kalipada Ghosh who was known to be a close associate of Shashanka was also brought within the police dragnet when he was arrested and found to be in possession of 10 copies of a *Liberty* pamphlet. In the course of the investigations that followed and which resulted in the institution of the Rajabazaar Bomb Case in 1913, the close association between Calcutta and Dacca and the North Bengal districts and the coalescing of the *Jugantar* and Dacca Anushilan Samiti became apparent. A report sent by the Inspector-General of Police, Bengal to the Government of Bengal claimed that in Calcutta 'we find the bomb factory, the printing press for the publication and dissemination of the most inflammatory and seditious literature, the counting-house and the magazines of the society.'[76] The startling disclosures in the course of the Delhi Conspiracy Case in 1914 made it evident that the revolutionary network had come to include Bengal, Assam, Bihar and Orissa, the United Provinces, Delhi and the Punjab, though the nerve centre was undoubtedly Bengal, and more specifically, Calcutta. Evidence produced in the course of the Delhi Conspiracy case showed that bombs used in Delhi and Lahore as well as in Bengal were manufactured in Bengal while at least the third and fourth editions of the *Liberty* pamphlets that had been circulated widely in Punjab and the United Provinces had been composed and printed in the Loke-Nath Yantra Press in Calcutta.[77] During this same period, new editions of the *Swadhin Bharat* and *Jugantar* leaflets, together with one-off manuscript leaflets, continued to appear alongside the *Liberty* leaflets. It was clear once again that the production of bombs and inflammable literature went hand in hand in furthering the ends of revolution.

The next year saw the outbreak of the First World War and Indian politics became caught up in the intricacies of this conflict. The pamphlet literature of the period gives us insights into the revolutionary interpretation of the international situation and of India's role in it. With the outbreak of war, revolutionaries in Punjab and Bengal began to strive afresh for a countrywide conflagration under the leadership of Rashbehari Bose with the help of imported German arms. The plan ended in failure in 1915 but the pamphlets of this period and its immediate aftermath gave voice to the increasingly ambitious aspirations of the revolutionaries. One overarching theme that connected the pamphlets of this period was the oft reiterated conviction that the First World War marked a watershed in world history. It signaled the end of the domination of the west and the rise to power of the east. India's position in the international scheme of things was especially sensitive because both the western and eastern countries had gone to war for possession of India which was the 'jewel in the crown of the British empire'. The pamphlets drew a stark contrast between what the pamphleteers perceived as the decadent materialism of the west and the life giving spiritualism of the east. Within the eastern block of nations, pride of place was accorded to the Indian nation which was depicted as singularly suited to lead the world because the Indians had inherited from antiquity deep reservoirs of knowledge, faith and the energy that had been bequeathed to them by the eternal *dharma* of India. It was of utmost importance that Indians constitute themselves into a nation because as the pamphlet pointed out,

> *Jagate bharoter vedanto protishthito dharmer aboshyok acche o ashonno shwet-pite juddhe shrashtar shrishtirokkhar janyo bharotkei madhyostho hoite hoibe, shutorang swadin hoite hoibe.*[78] (Translation: The *dharma* founded on the *Vedanta* is essential for the world and in the imminent war between the whites or westerners and yellow coloured or people of the east India has to act as the mediator in order to preserve the creator's creation; therefore India had to be free.)

The pamphleteers assigned to Bengal the task of bringing together all Indians within the umbrella of an 'Indian Nation'. It was of the utmost importance that Indians establish themselves as a nation before they could embark on any significant enterprise. The pamphlets therefore called on the young men of Bengal to seize the moment and throw themselves heart and soul into the task of freeing the motherland from the chains of servitude even if it meant sacrificing their lives in an apocalyptic blood-bath.

> *He deshbashi, he jubak mondoli, jahate ei mahendrakhson bohiya na jae, tahar jonye esho mahajogne jeebon moron utshorgo koriya uthiya darao! He tetrish koti bharotbashi, mayer jonyo ek lokkho santan boli dao dekhi – amra ar odhik chaina, amra bideshi eingrajke sagor pare pathaiya di. Iti –Bande Mataram.* (Translation: O countrymen! O youths, in order that this auspicious moment may not pass away unutilized, come on, and offering up life and death in a great sacrifice, stand up! O three hundred and thirty millions of Indians let us see you sacrificing a hundred thousand sons for the Mother's sake we do not want any more. Let us drive back the English foreigners back across the seas. End – Bande Mataram.)[79]

Meanwhile the *Liberty* pamphlets kept up their call for a country wide revolution. One such pamphlet rued the failure of the Revolution that had been planned for Northern India, giving details of the plans that had only been ruined because of the treachery of a wretched spy but concluded that,

> Things should be judged according to spirit and not by events. Spirit is the chief deciding factor in every undertaking. In spirit we have gained much as a result of our work of these few years, though in events we are seemingly losers. It has been amply demonstrated now that Hindus, Muhammedans, Sekhes (Sikhs), Bengalees, and Mahrattas can all conjointly work for a common cause.[80]

The evidence of a growing national consciousness among the revolutionaries caused serious discomfiture in government. Having reached the conclusion that the forces of law and order working through ordinary channels were inadequate to suppress revolutionary violence, the government took recourse to extraordinary laws. The *Defence of India Act* of 1915 made possible both preventive and punitive measures against the militant revolutionaries including summary arrest and internments and trial by special tribunals without appeal. The pamphleteers responded with fresh issues of new pamphlets. In 1916, pamphlets headed, *From the Office of the Director General Indian Revolution Vigilance Department, Bengal Branch* (addressed to) *the Public in General and members of our Camp; Indian National Defence Camp* (addressed) *to Our Patriotic Countrymen: Declaration of Our Policy;* and *Administration Report issued from the Indian Revolutionary Camp (Bengal Branch): Office of the Director General, Administration Department* made their appearance in Bengal. A report from the Khulna Office of the Intelligence Branch mentioned that the first two leaflets bore an imitation of the signature of Mr Clarke, the Police Commissioner of Calcutta.[81] In the course of searches carried out in Chandernagore the police also came across two brass seals that corresponded to the impressions made on the pamphlets and letters issued by the 'Revolutionary Camp'. It is apparent that the revolutionaries wanted to create the impression that they were a sovereign unit working independently of the colonial government.[82] Then, on 30 June 1916, the revolutionaries murdered Deputy Superintendent Basanta Chatterjee in Calcutta. Afraid that the revolutionaries had achieved their objective of demoralizing the police force the government cracked down with a draconian enforcement of the *Defence of India Act*. A wave of arrests, detainments and confessions followed that broke the back of the revolutionary movement in Bengal by the end of 1917, temporarily at least. Consequently, revolutionary propaganda also faded away the same year, though the pamphleteers vowed not to be diverted from their revolutionary endeavour by the 'demoniac oppression' unleashed by the government of Lord Carmichael. This oppression, claimed a pamphlet, would not be able to achieve its objective of driving 'the selfless and devoted workers, who have consecrated their everything (to their work) to renounce their duty, to lose their manhood and to accept service at the Englishmen's feet as their duty.'[83] Leaflets continued to appear sporadically in 1917 such as a *Swadhin Bharat* pamphlet, copies of which were found in Diamond Harbour and Hajipur in the South 24 Parganas in February 1917 or issues of an older edition of a *Swadhin Bharat* leaflet that were sent out in the guise of *Saraswati Puja* invitations in Tippera District in the same month. The last of the pamphlets to appear in Bengal during this period was published in December 1917 and was concerned with Mr Montagu's visit to India. It took the form of a proclamation: '*By order of the Executive, Indian Revolutionary Committee*' and made clear, said a government report, that an attitude of utter 'irreconcilability' had been maintained by the propagandists.[84] But these pamphlets were like the last flickering flames of a fire that was soon to be extinguished, at least temporarily.

By way of conclusion, it may be said that any study of the revolutionary nationalist movement is incomplete without a corresponding analysis of revolutionary propaganda. Revolutionary propaganda helped structure a mental universe, at least among a section of the Bengali educated public, within which the revolutionary nationalist movement found acceptance and understanding. The role of pamphlet propaganda in the revolutionary scheme of things was to stoke passions in such a way that public opinion was persuaded of the justice of their cause and thus moved to support the idea of a violent revolution. The pamphleteers proved themselves adept in the performance of this task.[85] The pamphleteers drew a simple but stark contrast between a homogenous national collectivity and its enemy. They helped foster a sense of national identity by pointing insistently to the figure of the other and around this 'other' they built up a virtual demonology, so much so that the destruction of the other appeared to the readers as just and honourable. Through their collective discourse they were able to evoke a highly emotive response to their cause and thus mobilize support for the revolutionary nationalist movement. Their success in this direction pointed to the effectiveness of their propaganda.

Endnotes

1 *Bandhab*, vol. 1, no. 1, Asadh, 1279 (1874), quoted by Tapti Ray 'Disciplining the Printed Text: Colonial and Nationalist Surveillance of Bengali Literature' in *Texts of Power. Emerging Disciplines in Colonial Bengal* (Samya, Calcutta, 1996), p. 56.

2 Sumit Sarkar, *The Swadeshi Movement in Bengal: 1903–08* (Permanent Black, Ranikhet, 2010, second edition).

3 Ibid., p. 215–85.

4 Nandogopal Sengupta '*Sambad Patra: Swadhinata o Sanskriti*' [*Newspapers: Independence and Culture*] in Rathin Chakrabarty ed. *Gano-Andolan o Sangbad Patro* (*Peoples' Movements and the Press*), (Lokmat Prakashani, Kolkata, 1984).

5 The Ilbert Bill that was promulgated during the Viceroyalty of Lord Ripon in 1883 sought to empower Indian judges to try cases involving Europeans in the mofussils. The Bill created uproar among Europeans and their distaste for the bill was expressed in the European press in terms most insulting to Indians. Indian newspapers, in turn, denounced the European response to the bill and the controversy over the bill caused a deep polarization between Europeans and Indians. According to the revolutionary, Hemchandra Qanungo, 'It was from around the time of the promulgation of the Ilbert Bill that dislike of the English grew stronger...... This dislike [of the English] ultimately came to be known as nationalism.' *Banglay Biplab Pracheshta* (*The Revolutionary Endeavour in Bengal*), (Chirayata Prokashan, Kolkata, 1928), p. 6.

6 J. H. Broomfield, *Elite Conflict in a Plural Society: Twentieth Century Bengal* (Bombay, Oxford University Press, 1968), p. 31.

7 Note prepared by A. H. L. Fraser, Lieutenant Governor of Bengal, dated 29 June 1907 on Press Legislation in Government of Bengal, Political Department, Political Branch, File No. 132 of 1908 in West Bengal State Archives, Writers' Building (hereafter WBSA-WB).

8 Benedict Anderson, *Imagined Communities: Reflections on the Origin and Spread of Nationalism* (Verso, London, 1983).

9 The *Bengalee* of 7 February 1906, *Report on Native Newspapers* in Bengal (January–March 1906). Unless otherwise mentioned all information about the content of newspapers have been taken from the newspaper accounts that were compiled in *Report on Native Newspapers* by the Bengal Government.

10 *Daily Hitavadi*, 19 March 1906; *Sanjivani*, 19 April 1906.

11 For the events surrounding the Bengal Provincial Conference of 1906, see the accounts that appeared in various newspapers and were compiled in the government *Report on Native Newspapers in Bengal* of April 1906.

12 *Sanjivani*, 19 April 1906, *Daily Hitavadi*, 21 April 1906.

13 Ibid.

14 *Bengalee*, 29 April 1906.

15 *Amrita Bazar Patrika*, 26 April 1906 and *Sandhya*, 19 April 1906.

16 *Annual Report on Native-owned Newspapers Published in Bengal during the Year 1907*

in Government of Bengal, Political Department (Confidential) Political, File Number (hereafter FN) 44/08.WBSA-WB.

17 *Report on Native Papers in Bengal, 1907.*

18 See, for example the *Basumati* of 6 April 1907, the *Amrita Bazar Patrika* of 3 April, the *Sanjivani* of 25 April, the *Sandhya* of 29 April and the *Daily Hitavadi* of 30 April 1907.

19 See chapter III.

20 *Annual Report on Native-owned Newspapers Published in Bengal during the Year 1907,* Government of Bengal, p. 4.

21 This secret society was born of the merger of a *samiti* or voluntary association that had earlier been set up by the barrister P. Mitter with an athletic society begun by Jatin Banerjee, who had been sent as an emissary to Bengal by Aurobindo Ghose. Subsequently, the society split into two and P. Mitter's organization came to be known as the Calcutta Anushilan Samiti while the other organization headed by Jatin Banerjee and Barin Ghose came to be later known as the *Jugantar* group from the name of the newspaper founded by Barin Ghose and his associates. Both these groups had branches all over Bengal that were only loosely affiliated to them. The most famous of these was the Dacca Anushilan Samiti that was set up as a branch of the Calcutta Anushilan Samiti but that functioned as an independent organization under the leadership of Pulin Das. According to government reports, these *samitis* outwardly functioned as volunteer organizations devoted to social service such as famine relief and to the physical training of young boys in gymnasia set up for the purpose, but also had extensive underground networks devoted to preparation for the impending revolution. See *Note on the Growth of the Revolutionary Movement in Bengal* by F. C. Daly, Deputy Inspector General of Police, S. D. dated 7 August 1911 reprinted in Amiya Samanta, ed., *Terrorism in Bengal: A Collection of documents on Terrorist Activities* (Government of West Bengal, Calcutta, 1995), Vol. I, p. 12–15. The term *anushilan* (cultivation of moral and physical faculties with the aim of reaching perfection in character) was taken from Bankimchandra's novel *Anandamath* and testified to the deep influence of the novelist's ideas on the revolutionaries.

22 This version of the *Jugantar's* origins is, in large part, based on the account of Abinashchandra Bhattacharya that appeared in the *Jugantar* of 15 August 1947, reproduced in Kamal Chaudhuri ed. *Bangabhanga o Samakalin Samaj* (Dey's Publishing, Kolkata, 2005), p. 593–97.

23 *Biplab Tattva* (*Theory of Revolution*) in Ashoke Kumar Mukhopadhyay ed. *Mukti Kon Pathe* (Punascha Publications, Kolkata), p. 143–45. *Mukti Kon Pathe* (*Which Way Lies Liberty*) a collection of seditious *Jugantar* articles, was originally published in 1908. See below.

24 See Chapter III for further details.

25 Sri Aurobindo, *Sri Aurobindo: Bankim – Tilak – Dayananda* (Aurobindo Ashram, Pondicherry, 2006, sixth edition), p. 10–11.

26 No less a person than Rabindranath Tagore had praised Upendranath Bandopadhyay's memoirs, *Nirbashiter Atmakatha* profusely and commented that it was an 'astonishing book.' See *Collected works of Syed Mustaba Ali* (Mitra and

Ghose Publishers, Kolkata, 1978 [BE1385]) vol.1, p. 317. I am grateful to Prof. Sanjib Sanyal for providing me with this reference.

27 For the idea of unity among people of diverse races, religions and castes living in India see article titled '*Bhut O Bhobishshyot* (*The Past and the Future*) in *Mukti Kon Pathe*, op.cit. , p. 146.

28 Hemchandra Das, *Banglay Biplab Pracheshta* (*The Revolutionary Endeavour in Bengal*), (Chirayata Prakashani, Kolkata, 1928), p. 25, 41.

29 *Annual Report on Native-owned Newspapers, 1907*, p. 4.

30 Jadugopal Mukhopadhyay *Biplabi Jibaner Smriti* (*Reminiscences of a Revolutionary Life*), (Academic Publishers, Kolkata, 1956), p. 189–90.

31 *Annual Report on Native-Owned Newspapers*, 1907, p. 3.

32 *Memorandum on the History of Terrorism in Bengal* (Calcutta, Bengal Government Press, 1933), p. 3.

33 *Note on the Growth of the Revolutionary Movement in Bengal, Eastern Bengal and Assam and United Bengal* drawn up by R. H. Sneyd-Hutchinson, Deputy Inspector General of Police, Intelligence Branch, dated 1 May 1914 in Samanta, *Terrorism in Bengal*, p. 247–48. Also see Daly's report, ibid., p. 16.

34 *Memorandum on the History of Terrorism in Bengal*, p. 22.

35 *Annual Report on Native-Owned Newspapers in Bengal, 1907*, p. 2–3; Government of Eastern Bengal and Assam, Political Branch (Confidential), File No. 165/1909, West Bengal State Archives, Writers' Building.

36 *Note on the 'Jugantar' Gang, Subsequent to the Search of Manicktola Garden*, report drawn up by G. C. Denham, dated 30 July 1909, reprinted in *Terrorism in Bengal*, Vol. II, p. 655–75.

37 In 1867 a *Press and Registration of Books Act* had come into existence to keep track of Indian publications. The government kept track of the nature of the publications by directing that extracts of political importance from vernacular journals be translated and sent to the viceroy's office. From material thus accumulated an annual report on the native press was drawn up. Government translators were appointed for each of the presidencies. In 1870, the Indian Penal Code was amended to make seditious writing punishable under the law. *The Vernacular Press Act* of 1878 authorized the magistrates of districts and commissioners of police in presidency towns with the previous sanction of the local governments to demand bail bonds from printers and publishers and either the deposit of a certain sum or the submission of proofs for inspection. See Uma Dasgupta, 'The Shackling of the Vernacular Press' in *Rise of an Indian Public: Impact of Official Policy, 1870–80* (Rddhi, Kolkata, 1977), p. 269–300.

38 *On the present political situation and lines on which the seditious movement is now being conducted* – Note sent by J. G. Cummings, Officiating Chief Secretary to the Government of Bengal to the Commissioners of the Presidency, Burdwan, Dacca, Chittagong and Rajshahi Divisions, dated Darjeeling, 20 May 1913, in West Bengal State Archives, Intelligence Branch, (hereafter WBSA-I.B.), Serial Number (hereafter S.N.) 9/1913, File Number (hereafter F.N.) 504/1913.

39 Daly's report in Samanta ed. *Terrorism in Bengal*, Vol. I, p. 7.

40 'Come with expanded chest', means to show courage.

41 A copy of the leaflet in the original Bengali and its English translation may be found in the *Smaraniya Bichar Sangraha,* Alipore Sessions Court, Kolkata.

42 From *Note on the Midnapore Revolutionary Conspiracy,* report drawn up by G. C. Denham, Special Assistant to the Deputy Inspector General of Police on 10 July 1909 in SN 3/1908, FN 699/1908 WBSA-IB.

43 Bhupendranath Dutt, *Bharater Dwitiya Swadhinata Sangram* (Nababharat Publishers, Calcutta, 1893), p. 33, 146. Three editions of the *Sonar Bangla* (two of them from English translations) have been reproduced in Sandip Bandopadhyay's *Nathipatre Swadeshi Andolan (The Swadeshi Movement in Documents)* (Grantha Mitra, Calcutta, 2004), p. 24–9.

44 Daly's report in Samanta ed. *Terrorism in Bengal,* p. 7.

45 *History of the Political Agitation and Bhadralok Crime in the City of Dacca from 1905 to 1913,* SN 52/1913, FN 119/1913 in WBSA- IB.

46 *Fortnightly Reports on the Agitation in Eastern Bengal and Assam,* reports of September and October, 1907 in National Archives of India.

47 *Political Branch Proceedings,* Government of India, Home Department, August 1909, No. 162 in National Archives of India.

48 *Jugantar* pamphlet titled *Jugantar, Volume III, No. 7, June 13, 1908.* From the official English translation in Samanta ed. *Terrorism in Bengal,* Vol. IV, p. 389. The authorship of this pamphlet was later traced to Kiran Mukherjee, a member of the *Jugantar* terrorist group and suspect in the Bighati dacoity case.

49 The four parts of *Mukti Kon Pathe* appear to have been published at various times by different printers. According to a report drawn up by the librarian of the Bengal Library, Manmatha Bhadra, *Mukti Kon Pathe,* (*Which Way Lies Liberty*) *Prathama Bhag* (First Part) had two editions and the second edition, printed by Abinash Chandra Bhattacharya was registered in the Bengal Catalogue of Books and was an exhibit in the Alipur Bomb Case of 1908. According to a police report in the same file, *Mukti Kon Pathe, Prathama Bhag,* of which the printer was Abinash Chandra Bhattacharya, consisted of reprints of *Jugantar* articles published in 1907–08. According to the same report, another edition of *Mukti Kon Pathe, Prathama Bhag,* published by Basanta Kumar Bhattacharya, also registered in the Bengal Catalogue of Books during the last quarter of 1908 comprised reprints from the *Jugantar* during 1906–07. It appears that the latter volume was probably the first edition, though registered in the same quarter as the second edition. All reports concerning *Mukti Kon Pathe* may be found in SN 36/1913, FN V/26 of 1913 in WBSA-IB.

50 Ibid, extract from the diary of Inspector P. N. Mukherjee, dated 20 July 1909.

51 *Sedition Committee Report,* 166.

52 The above account is based on the *Note on the Jugantar Gang, Subsequent to the Search of Manicktola Garden,* drawn up G. C. Denham, Special Assistant to the Deputy Inspector General of Police and dated the 30 July 1909. The Note has been reprinted in Samanta, *Terrorism in Bengal,* Vol. II, p. 658–59.

53 *Intelligence Branch, C.I.D. Bengal: Weekly Reports of 1910:* week ending 19 February 1910 in WBSA-IB.

54 Government of India, Home Department, Political Branch Proceedings, April 1910, Nos. 40–42 in National Archives of India.

55 Ibid.

56 *Feringhees*: A pejorative term for the English.

57 See Footnote 53.

58 SN 36/1910, FN V/94/1910 in *WBSA-IB*.

59 Note drawn up by the Special Branch, Police Department Calcutta on 27 May 1910 in SN 25/1910, FN V/105/1910, WBSA-IB.

60 From *Eastern Bengal and Assam Abstract* dated 30 July 1910 in SN 25/1910, FN V/105/1910 in *WBSA-IB*; *CID Weekly reports* of 1910 and 1911in WBSA-IB.

61 SN 17/1911, FN 38/1911 in WBSA-IB.

62 Letter from F. C. Daly to H. T. Cullis dated 3 May 1911 in SN 35/1910, FN 191/1910, *WBSA-IB*.

63 F. C. Daly dated 5/4/1911, SN 35/1910, FN 191/1910 in *WBSA-IB*.

64 *History of the Political Agitation and Bhadralok Crime in the city of Dacca from 1905 to 1913*; Note on the *Swadhin Bharat* leaflets drawn up by a printing expert, in *Eastern Bengal and Assam Abstract*, dated 25 March 1911, paragraph 1123 in SN 35/1910, FN 191/1910; Note drawn up by E. C. Ryland, Deputy Inspector-General in Charge of C.I.D., Railway and River Police, Eastern Bengal and Assam in SN 38/1910, FN 1318/1910 all in WBSA-IB.

65 From official English translation of *Swadhin Bharat* leaflet in SN 14/1910, FN 1318 A in WBSA-IB. Proscribed by Bengal government notification No. 1302. P.D. dated 2 June 1910.

66 From official English translation of the original in SN 14/1911, FN V/105A/11 in WBSA-IB.

67 Ibid. Letter dated 3 August 1911, sent from the Office of F. L. Halliday, Commissioner of Police to Stevenson Moore, Chief Secretary to the Government of Bengal. Kumudini Mitter had earlier published a seditious book called *Shikher Bolidan*.

68 Ibid.

69 SN 17/1913, FN 37/1913 in WBSA-IB.

70 From C. J. Stevenson Moore, Chief Secretary to the Government of Bengal to the Secretary to the Government of India, Home Department dated Calcutta, the 25 March 1913 in SN 9/1913, FN 504/13, WBSA-IB.

71 Ibid. Cummings' note *On the present political situation*, dated 20 May 1913; *Note on the Political situation*, dated 24 December 1913 prepared by Hughes Buller, Inspector General of Police, Bengal.

72 *Jugantar Circular: The Delhi Bomb*, SN 61/1913, FN 482/1913 in WBSA-IB.

73 According to Jadugopal Mukhopadhyay, the renowned revolutionary terrorist, the *Swadhin Bharat* pamphlets were the work of the Anushilan group while

the Liberty series was issued by Rash Behari Bose's group. See Jadugopal Mukhopadhyay, *Biplabi Jibaner Smriti* (*Memoirs of a Revolutionary Life*), (Kolkata,) p. 321.

74 SN 5/1913, FN 663/1913 in WBSA-IB

75 Extract from *Intelligence Branch C.I.D. Weekly Report*, dated 18 December 1913, S.N. 33/1913; F.N. 1273/1913 in WBSA-IB.

76 *Note on the political situation in Bengal*, dated 24 December 1913, drawn up by Mr R. Sneyd-Hutchinson, Deputy Inspector-General of Bengal, Intelligence Branch, CID and sent by R. B. Hughes Buller, Inspector General of Police, Bengal, to the Chief Secretary to the Government of Bengal, dated 6 January 1914, Calcutta, SN 65/1914, FN 258/1914 in WBSA-IB.

77 The trial of the accused in the Delhi Conspiracy Case was held at Delhi from 21 May 1914 to 1 September 1914. The Delhi Conspiracy case centred around a plan made in 1912 by the revolutionary terrorists to launch a revolutionary movement in Punjab and the United Provinces on the lines of Bengal under the leadership of Rash Behari Bose. In the Delhi Conspiracy case the prosecution laid 'great stress on the two-fold nature of the work for which the organization was formed, namely the preparation and distribution of inflammatory literature and the overt acts of violence such as the throwing of bombs' and it was accepted by the court that the two branches of the activities were inextricably bound up. The first four of the *Liberty* pamphlets were produced by the revolutionaries as part of this plan. For further details of the Delhi Conspiracy Case see SN 41/1914, FN 430/1914 in WBSA-IB.

78 From the *Jugantar* pamphlet, *Samay Hoiyacche ki* (*Has the moment arrived?*) in SN 115/1916, FN 2223/16, WBSA-IB. The other pamphlets issued during these years express the same sentiments.

79 The original *Swadhin Bharat* pamphlet beginning with the words, *Deputy Superintendent Basanta Chatterjee'r hotya loiya* (*The Murder of Deputy Superintendent*) may be found in the Police Museum Collection.

80 *Liberty: Arise, Awake and Stop Not Till the Goal Is Reached* in Samanta, ed. *Terrorism in Bengal*, Vol. II, p. 499.

81 SN 155/16, FN 579/16 in WBSA-IB. Report is dated 9 April 1916.

82 Uma Mukherjee, *Two Great Indian Revolutionaries: Rash Behari Bose and Jyotindra Nath Mukherjee* (Dey's Publishing: Calcutta, 2004), p. 228.

83 Translation of a *Swadhin Bharat* leaflet of 1917 reproduced in I.B. Police Abstract, dated 24-3-1917; also see report prepared by G. L. Dixon, Special Superintendent, IB in SN 7/19, FN 128/19, WBSA-IB.

84 For reports of such appearances, see SN 5/1917, FN 786/17 in WBSA-IB. *Sedition Committee Report*, p. 108–09.

85 See Chapter III.

2

The Signs of the Times
Constructing a Nation

The British had created the framework of a modern state in India. The carving out of a well defined territorial space with fixed boundaries, the establishment of British sovereignty and the proclamation of British responsibility for the well being of the people within this territory, the equality of all citizens before the law helped to bestow the trappings of a modern state on India.[1] But this state was not yet a nation. A nation could emerge from the state when a majority of its population came to share a sense of common belonging in a community or participate in the idea of a shared destiny. The transition from state to nation is not a foreordained process and does not take place in a straightforward teleological fashion. The crucial gap between the formation of the state and that of the nation may be overcome in various ways: but the final end is to foster the feeling of belonging to a collectivity. Language, territory, religion, race, ethnicity, shared history, culture and values: actors imbricated in the formation of identities have to be utilized and manipulated in order to fashion a homogenous identity from within which internal tensions are ironed out. The nationalist claim to sovereign nationhood can then be staked on the basis of this shared identity. In the case of India, before the colonial state could become a nation, the inhabitants had to be made aware that they were common members of a wider community: a community, moreover, whose interests were opposed to that of the rulers of the modern state. This would require a profound upheaval in the realm of consciousness.

This chapter explores one such attempt at fashioning a nationalist consciousness through the analysis of the propaganda pamphlets published by the revolutionary nationalists of Bengal in the early twentieth century. This essay will analyse this body of pamphlets as an example of the efforts being made to conceptualize a national community in a particular region, a process that was no doubt being replicated in other regions of India where the national movement was strong. Admittedly, this process was not begun by the pamphlet writers. It had already been set in motion over the past half century. Nationalist yearnings were expressed through a wide variety of forms. But a popular rhetorical device to propagate the nationalist message that was common to all these forms was to recount stories about the historical past of the nation. These stories would delve back into the mists of past times to recount histories of shared experiences with a view to generating emotions that would help foster a sense of belonging to a collectivity called a 'nation'. It is perhaps obvious that the process of constructing 'old histories for new nations'[2] would involve a selective appropriation of events from the past and their reworking into new narrative frames, for the process overtly involved the harnessing of the past to present concerns. In these narratives, 'history' was constituted as much of myths and memories as by actual events, and its role was to forge an intimate relationship between the past and the present of the nation. Through these stories, the storytellers articulated their visions of the nation that they sought to bring into existence. The shared histories that the narrators attributed to the people 'naturalized' the people's call for self-determination. They reveal the diverse ways through which the narrators sought to legitimize their versions of the ideal future nation through their distinctive interpretations or representations of the nation's past.

Coming back to the propaganda pamphlets of Bengal, we find that the revolutionary nationalists shared the national enthusiasm for recounting stories of the collective past of the Bengali, and by extension, of the Indian people. In this essay, these stories will serve as an entry point for an analysis of the revolutionaries' vision of the Indian nation. This essay argues that disentangling the meaning of these narratives from the vantage point of the present requires a special effort on the part of the historian because the logic behind the selection of these stories and the language in which the stories are narrated are embedded in contexts that are specific to a particular conjuncture in Indian history, a conjuncture that was witnessing a profound transition in the realm of consciousness. People who for centuries had been accustomed to think of themselves as members of traditional forms of communities that were shaped by long established religious, social and cultural mores were now preparing themselves for membership in a modern form of political community of which their awareness stemmed from relatively recent times. The language in which they expressed their new found awareness of collective belonging often revealed continuity with older terms and concepts, but the meaning of the latter was quite altered to suit the early twentieth century context. On the basis of this analysis of political language, this essay will argue that a more empathetic understanding of the political imagination of the revolutionary propagandists than that has been accorded them by a significant body of scholarly literature calls for a nuanced and more context-specific reading of revolutionary literature.

As pointed out in the last chapter, the anonymous pamphlet writers were erudite men with superb literary skills, and their beautifully crafted prose, breathing passion and fire, proved an able vehicle for the dissemination of their ideas.[3] They propagated their ideas through clever use of cultural symbols such as stories, images, figures and momentous events that found immediate resonance among an educated Bengali audience. Thus the revolution was often represented as a Hindu religious sacrifice (*Jagna*) for which the revolutionaries were asked to give blood in order to propitiate a wounded mother-goddess. The figure of the mother-goddess was itself drawn from the Hindu religious pantheon and the imagery of devoted sons heroically sacrificing their lives to free their mother from the chains of servitude went a long way in establishing a strong emotive bond between the revolutionaries and the general public. Because space was a constraint, the pamphlets limited themselves to allusions to historical, mythological and religious figures and events with which their targeted audience was intimately familiar. To a literate Bengali readership the logic behind the selection of such stories was immediately evident, as was their meaning and message. These stories thus functioned as cultural codes that enabled the transmission of ideas from the revolutionaries to their readers.[4] The symbols and metaphors as well as the idiom through and in which the pamphlets expressed their ideas and views had much in common with those used in the nationalist literature of the period. The political and cultural environment of Bengal in the late nineteenth and early twentieth century thus provided the matrix within which these symbols and codes were understood and interpreted.

Taken as a whole, the pamphlets tell a story. The ideas and images that went into the making of this narrative may be described as tools used to forge a national identity in the present based on a particular representation of the past. The story is a familiar one, though the conclusions that the pamphleteers draw from it are not. The story is woven around the idea of an ancient civilization which had religion at its sacred centre. It was religion that held this rich and complex civilization together. Thus, the pamphlets tell the tale of an ancient land, the *Aryabhumi*, that was the fount of a rich and flourishing civilization.

Then follows the sad tale of the decay and fall of this civilization and the ultimate humiliation of the land being conquered by foreigners. The pamphlets describe, in graphic detail, the inequities perpetrated on the land and its people by the foreign conquerors. The ultimate concern of the pamphleteers is to provide a remedy that will end the miserable state of affairs and restore the land to its ancient glory. The entire narrative is constructed around the myth of a nation that the pamphlets claimed had existed in the past and that should be resurrected in the future.[5]

Thus, the following lines from the opening paragraph of a pamphlet that was widely circulated in 1910 were fairly typical of the pamphlets.

> Awake, awake, the time has come. The faint light of India's independence has appeared in the Eastern horizon. The Mother's cradle of childhood used to swing in time with the Psalm songs of the great Saints of the Vedic period, who lived in the cool shade of hermitages, brightened by the rays of a rising sun, at the early dawn of human civilization.[6]

By seeking to channel collective memory towards a particular period in the nation's past, the pamphlet provides an insight into the type of nation that was being imagined. The pamphlet dates the beginning of human civilization from the Vedic period and elides any reference to the period that went before. The reference to the psalm songs of the Vedic period indicates the identification with the Aryans who had the *Vedas* as their holy scripture and who were held to be the founders of the Hindu religion and civilization. This identification becomes clearer as the story proceeds.

> *Hay hay, ei ki shei Aryabhumi! Ei ki shei Aryajati? He Bharatbashi! He Bharater unnotir asha bhorsha sthal jubak-brindo, ei ki tomader swadeshpriyota?* (Translation: Alas! Alas! Is this that land of the Aryans!! Is this that Aryan race! Ye inhabitants of *Bharata* (India).Ye youth of *Bharata* who constitute the hope for *Bharata's* progress, is this your brand of patriotism?)[7]

The pamphlet bemoans the fact that the nation *Bharat* that is described as the land of the Aryan race has fallen on hard times. The reasons for the decline are also clear.

> First in Philosophy, first in civilization, the home of martyrdom, the nursery of warriors, this my land, this my Mother, indeed was mighty

> – but what do I see now around me? Chains and shackles and night and chaos and dust! And, in that dust, beaten unconscious is rolling my Mother; while the Foreigner stands over her degradation as a sentinel of hell![8]

The personification of the land as mother or mother-goddess served an integrative function because it brought together the inhabitants of the land in a bond of fraternal kinship. But the deification of the land through the invocation of the figure of the mother-goddess again identified the nation as the land of the Hindus, for the mother-goddess was a Hindu religious icon. This identification is evident in the following pamphlet which, in an effort to persuade its readers to join the struggle for independence, rhetorically poses the question,

> *Tomra ki Bharatbashi... Tomra ki shei Hindu?* (Translation: Are you inhabitants of *Bharatavarsha*? ...Are you Hindus?)[9]

The pamphlet then goes on to warn its readers,

> *Paradhinotar anibarjyo phal Dharmahinota.*(Translation: The inevitable effect of the loss of independence is loss of *dharma.*)[10]

To uphold the *dharma* is portrayed in the pamphlets as the sacred duty of the Hindus:

> *Mlechhadhikare Hindu ke bash korite nai... Mlechho raja hoile Brahman hoite oti Antyojo shakol jati shamobeto hoiya tahar shanghar koribe. Iha-i Hindur param Dharma.* (Translation: Hindus are not supposed to live under the rule of foreigners. If a foreigner becomes king then all the castes from Brahmans to untouchables should unite to destroy him. This is the essential *dharma* of the Hindus.)[11]

In the course of establishing the precepts of *dharma,* the pamphlet lays emphasis on inter-caste unity. The Hindu revivalist discourse of the period with which the pamphleteers shared so many attributes, often overlooked the abuses of the caste system and instead attempted to establish the institution as a guarantor of social order and harmony. The pamphleteers utilized the integrative potential of the theme of intercaste unity as they went about their task of moulding a Hindu Nation.[12]

The political goal envisioned by the pamphlets is summed up in the following lines,

> *Je sanatan dharmer sreshtthotar janyo Bharat chirogorioshi, je dharma rakkhar jonyo Sri Krishna juge juge abotirno hoiben bolia amadigoke*

> *Gitar ashshash bani diyechhen, shei dharmer aj eto lanchhona. ... aj Bharater abal bridhho bonita hridoyer antosthale ei katha jalanto akhhare likhiya rakhook Bharater abhhuythyan Dharmarajya sthaponer janye.* (Translation: That eternal *dharma* on the excellence of which the glory of India rests, that *dharma* for the protection of which Srikrishna has assured us through the Gita that he will be born in every age, that *dharma* suffers such humiliation today. ... Let everyone in India from the old to the young write in burning letters in the innermost recesses of their hearts that the uprising in India is for the establishment of the *dharma-rajya*.)[13]

The religious sensibilities that suffused the political imagination of the revolutionary nationalists have come in for a fair share of criticism from some historians of Indian nationalist politics. They have detected a narrowness of political vision in the effort to make Hindu religion the cement that would hold together the heterogeneous and disparate collectivities that would come together to form the Indian nation. This homogenized and unitary view of the nation, they argue, marginalized the role of the non-Hindu communities within this cultural formation and was responsible for widening the mental gulf between the Hindus and Muslims. This festering animosity between the two communities led to the development of communalism with tragic consequences for the future of the nation. Amales Tripathi, the eminent historian of extremist politics, has taken to task the Extremists for their failure to 'understand the Muslim mind' and maintained that the 'Extremists were prisoners of their own interpretation of Hindu religion.'[14] He argues that Extremism in Indian politics was marked by a retreat into the past. Unable to grapple with the problems posed by western modernity, the extremists sought refuge in the 'protective womb' of ancient Hindu religion and spirituality. Extremism in Indian politics thus symbolized the conflict between the traditionalism of Hindu religion, ethics and values and the modernism of western values, laws and institutions.[15] As religion became an all-encompassing force with the extremists, it no longer remained merely a way to attain a political end. Rather, religious fervour and nationalism became one, that is, the means became the end in themselves. Sumit Sarkar, author of the canonical study, *The Swadeshi Movement in Bengal*, has drawn attention to the special value of religion to *swadeshi* politics because of its tremendous power to influence the imagination and thus mobilize popular support for the movement. But he has also expressed his unease at the leaders of the movement conflating religion with nationalism. Professor Sarkar shares Amales Tripathi's view that the religious revivalism of the *swadeshi* era signified a retreat from modernism to traditionalism and a shift from reason and humanism to a championing of outdated social mores coupled with a petty sectarianism that prefigured the ultimate descent into communalism. The politics of revolutionary terrorism was also not free of this defect. Sumit Sarkar lays emphasis on the idealism and heroism of the youthful terrorists but his analysis of the movement indicates that the religious fervour that shaped the politics of some of the proponents of revolutionary terrorism created disquiet among others and weakened the movement from within. [16]

In recent years, some historians have looked at the religiosity of *swadeshi* era politics from other, different perspectives. Dipesh Chakrabarty has argued in one of his essays that 'modernity' does not have natural qualities or a universal essence, but is in fact, culturally contingent in time and place. His view is that the sharp demarcation of the sphere of the religious from the secular, and that of the affective from the rational were distinctive features of European modernity ushered in by the eighteenth century Enlightenment. Yet 'European modernity' became valourized as the 'modular form' in the European colonies in course of the nineteenth century. One of the results of this assimilation of the European form of modernity to the colonial experience was that the discourse of the 'colonized intellectual' began to exhibit the European trait of making a hostile split between the secular and the religious and the affective and the rational.[17] To judge from the tenor of Chakrabarty's arguments, an alternative discourse held sway within the domain of *swadeshi* era nationalist thought. This discourse that operated within a sovereign space free from European thought control erased the divide, artificial in the Indian context, between the secular and the spiritual and was more in tune with the everyday thought processes of the average Indian. The problem with this formulation lies in the difficulty of verifying it empirically. Whether colonialism allowed a pristine space for sovereign thought to hold sway is a question that will be debated endlessly. What is more relevant to the purposes of this essay is the fact that Bankimchandra, Vivekananda and Aurobindo, thinkers who most influenced the political imagination of the militant nationalists, all grappled with the problem of colonial modernity in their agonizing search for intellectual truth and personal enlightenment.

Dipesh Chakrabarty's formulation also raises, but does not dwell, on another question that is equally relevant to a study of *swadeshi* era nationalist politics in Bengal, that is, the relationship between the traditional or archaic on the one hand and the religious on the other, in the context of early twentieth century extremist nationalist thought. It is widely acknowledged by historians today that the religious revivalism of early twentieth century Bengal cannot be fully explained in terms of a straightforward attempt to resurrect the ancient Indian past. The revivalist rhetoric can more fruitfully be understood as representations of the past which were in tune with contemporary and competing visions of the nation that was still in the making. The connecting link between these varied representations was the common effort to construct a national identity that was based on a shared Hindu religious identity that supposedly dated back to ancient times. But then, religion does not have a trans-historical essence that is immune to change and that can be resurrected at any historical moment with the same meaning attached to it by different groups divided by class, caste and outlook, irrespective of context. What was it in religion that the proponents of religion based nationalist politics appealed to and sought to mobilize for their political ends in the early-twentieth century? The answer is that different groups utilized the 'religious' in different ways depending on their perception and understanding of the role of religion in politics. This can be demonstrated in the case of the pamphlet writers as well.

As pointed out earlier, the pamphlets drew their meaning from within a specific political-cultural conjuncture in the history of Bengal and they cannot be discussed or understood in isolation from this context. There is a large body of scholarly literature which deals with Bengali thought and culture in the late nineteenth and early twentieth centuries. Drawing on this literature, this essay will explore the ideas of three representative thinkers of this period: Bankimchandra Chattopadhyay (1838–94), Swami Vivekananda (1863–1902) and Aurobindo Ghose (1872–1950), who exercised a profound influence on the thought of the revolutionary nationalists and then go on to explore the connections between the thought of the pamphleteers and the mental universe of which they were a part.

That the lack of nationhood was an immense tragedy in the life of the people who were suffering in the chains of servitude was a familiar theme in late nineteenth and early twentieth century nationalist writings. Because the present was unhappy, there was a tendency to return to a past which, in its representations, bore the marks of the peoples' engagement with the present. In the words of Sudipta Kaviraj 'The past was an image created in the interest of the present. History was in major respects, the myth of a people, its construction of its self'.[18] Thus, the past was deemed glorious because the inhabitants of the land had then been free and the architects of a civilization that had been the envy of all. These ancient inhabitants were described as the *Aryas* (Aryans) a term that received racial connotations in this period. Because the Indo-Aryans were believed to be racially allied with their European counterparts, this identification was a source of great pride for the Bengalis as it allowed them to claim kinship with their conquerors. Nationalism became inextricably bound up with history – writing. People turned towards the past because it provided evidence of the achievements that the Indians were capable of and helped in understanding the causes of present day degradation. Moreover the past had to be learned about because it had to be resurrected in the future – the future was the time when the nation would throw off its chains and reclaim its rightful place as a leader in the council of nations.

The intense desire for independence that coursed through the writings of the pamphleteers echoed the longings of many Bengalis who yearned for political freedom. Earlier on, in the nineteenth century, Bankimchandra Chattopadhyay, whose writings exercised a deep influence on the pamphlet writers, expressed this longing in his historical essays and tracts. Thus in his essay, *Bharat Kalanka (India's Shame),* Bankim rued the lack of the love for independence among Indians. In his words 'That we must be ruled by members of our own country or race, and not by foreigners, was not a thought that entered the minds of Indians. That the rule of fellow nationals was a matter of welfare or happiness while that of foreigners was oppressive or humiliating was not an instinctive feeling among them.'[19] While taking care to acknowledge that the Indians had learnt much from the English and had been introduced to the ideas of independence, nationality and the nation by them, he indicated his frustration with the contemporary political situation by writing about the possible emergence of an Indian Nation. Bankim mentioned the empire of the Marathas under Shivaji and the Punjabi kingdom under Ranjit Singh as examples of instances in the recent past when the Hindus[20] had witnessed the birth of a nation. If the love for nationhood in a particular region could bring about so much change, then what could not be achieved, he wistfully wondered, if all Indians came together to form a nation?[21]

Like so many other Bengali intellectuals of the period, Bankimchandra Chattopadhyay believed that the recovery of the nation's glorious past through the writing of history would be a way of instilling pride and self confidence among Bengalis. His lament that the Bengalis had no history[22] was more rhetoric than fact. All through the nineteenth century nationalist thinkers like Bhudev Mukhopadhyay, Rajendralal Mitra, Haraprasad Sastri, Akshyay Kumar Maitreya, Rajanikanta Gupta and others attempted to restore the importance of the study of the past through their historical works, tracts and essays. Moreover periodicals like Akshyaykumar Dutta's *Tattvabodhini Patrika,* Rajendralal Mitra's *Vividartha Samgraha,* Akshyay Kumar Maitreya's *Aitihasik Chitra* and Bankimchandra's own periodical the *Bangadarshan* also published historical pieces.[23] As with so much other writing of the period, Bankim's call for history was meant to serve an express purpose, which was to contribute to the construction of the nation. Bankim declared that the study of the past would reveal that the Hindus had not always been so disunited. The Aryans had conquered a large swathe of the country and established a nation, but as they spread into diverse regions, the nation fell apart. Over the course of time, various races with diverse homelands, languages, genealogies and religions tore India apart. Only when the Hindus reunited, Bankim maintained, would a nation be reestablished.[24]

In Bankim's conceptualization of the nation as made up of the Hindus, the ties of race and religion played an important role. Moreover he was also influenced by the three part schema introduced as the framework for the writing of Indian history by the colonial historians. In this scheme, a glorious Indian ancient past had been followed by a period of medieval decline, which was followed by a dawn in modern times. The ancient, medieval and ancient periods, corresponded to the Hindu, Muslim and British periods. Bankim's sometimes derogatory references to Muslim rule together with his valourization of the ancient Hindu Nation, was indicative of a cast of mind that was not isolated in its time. Other thinkers might write of a nation that included both Hindus and Muslims as its inhabitants but the core of the nation they imagined was made up of the Hindus. Bhudev Mukhopadhyay thus wrote paeans of praise to the greatness of the Hindus, as did Rajnarayan Basu, although the nation they wrote about would include both Hindus and Muslims. In his *Imagined History of India,* Bhudev wrote that India was truly the motherland of the Hindus who alone were born from the womb, though Muslims had also been reared by her as her foster children. Rajnarayan Basu wrote about the 'Superiority of Hinduism' and called for the establishment of a 'Great Hindu Association' even though its representatives in the Congress would 'work jointly with our Muslim brothers'.[25]

The definition of the nation as Hindu served to invest Indian nationalism with deep religious roots. Bankimchandra Chattopadhyay thus declared that apart from the love of God, love for the country was the highest form of religion.[26] But Bankimchandra's understanding of religion did not involve pontificating on finer points of abstract doctrine or quibbling over rituals. Instead, religion had an eminently social and practical end which was to serve as the instrument of regeneration of the Bengali Hindu race, (a term which Bankim used interchangeably with the Indian Hindu). *Dharma,* (rightful conduct or the proper way of life) for Bankimchandra, involved the cultivation (*anushilan*) of one's physical and mental faculties with the aim of reaching perfection. This was best exemplified by the figure of the god Sri Krishna as he was depicted by Bankim in his treatise *Krishnacharitra.*[27] In this treatise, Sri Krishna, divested of his supernatural qualities, was more the epitome of human perfection rather than the incarnation of the Godhead, whom Bankim personally believed him to be. Sri Krishna, in Bankim's writings, was not the romantic God of the *Gaudiya Vaishnava* sect or the *Bhagvata Purana,*[28] companion to Radha and playmate to the *gopis* or mikmaids. Instead, he was a historical figure, the serious philosopher of the *Gita,*[29] thinker, warrior and political leader, in short a figure moulded by the sensibilities of the author who had been greatly influenced by the Western Enlightenment principles of rationalism and humanism. The exemplary figure of Sri Krishna, as shaped by Bankim, emerged as the perfect political role model who could lead India on the path to strength and glory just as he had led the Pandavas[30] to victory in the great battle of *Kurukshetra.* The *Gita,* which Bankim foregrounded in his study of Krishna, was to become the central text of the revolutionary nationalists with its message of selfless action in the service of humanity.

The concept of the *dharmayuddha* in the *Gita,* that is war that was waged for the right cause and without any self interest attached, carried a special message for the revolutionaries.[31]

Bankimchandra's special contribution to Indian nationalism was to provide nationalists certain symbols, figures, texts and slogans around which national identity could be constructed. Bankim's ideas were spelt out in detail in the novel *Anandamath* which was published in 1882. *Anandamath* was deeply imbued with Hindu nationalist sentiment. Not only did the story revolve around a band of Hindus who were determined to put an end to Muslim rule but the symbolism and imagery used in the novel was also unabashedly Hindu. Bankimchandra's novel became a seminal text for Hindu nationalists and especially the revolutionary nationalists of Bengal. The example of the *santans,* who lived and worked together in brotherhood, shorn of internal divisions of wealth, status and caste and willing to sacrifice their lives in the service of the motherland, was one that the revolutionary nationalists sought to emulate. The song *Vande Mataram* or Hymn to the Mother that was composed earlier, but first appeared in the novel, exercised a tremendous influence on the nationalist movement. The chant of *Vande Mataram,* (Hail Mother!) the war-cry of the *santans,* became a 'slogan for power,' 'a rallying cry and a vow of fealty to the nationalist cause'.[32] But above all it was the personification of the land as mother that captured the nationalist imagination and provided a symbol around which nationalist sentiment could rally. Aurobindo Ghose, the charismatic leader of the revolutionary nationalists, said that in this song:

> ... The Motherland reveals herself to the eye of the mind as something more than a stretch of earth or a mass of individuals,.... as a great Divine and Maternal power in a form of beauty that can dominate the mind and seize the heart. ... A great nation which has had this vision can never again bend its neck in subjection to the yoke of the conqueror.[33]

Another figure to exercise a profound influence on the revolutionaries was the patriot cum prophet, Vivekananda. Vivekananda, himself a disciple of Thakur Ramakrishna, the Bengali saint from Dakshineswar, carried the message of Hinduism to the western world and in the process made a profound impression on his compatriots. Vivekananda mentioned repeatedly in his speeches and writings that each nation appeared to have a particular ideal that defined its very essence. 'Not politics nor military power, not commercial supremacy nor mechanical genius furnishes India with that backbone, but religion; and religion alone is all that we have and mean to have. Spirituality has been always in India.'[34] It was this ideal that would define how the nation should be conceived and shaped. In Vivekananda's view the nation would have to be differently conceived in the east than in the west. Vivekananda thus wrote, 'The one common ground we have is our sacred traditions, our religion. That is the only common ground and upon that we shall have to build. In Europe political ideas form the national unity. In Asia religious ideas form the national unity.'[35]

Vivekananda had well defined ideas about the role that religion should play within the newly emerging polity. Religion and patriotism were inextricably linked within this vision. His religious message was grounded in the *Vedanta philosophy,* which he intended to serve as the basis of a universalistic faith. The assertion of India's spiritual heritage and the confidence with which it was proclaimed was a sign of Vivekananda's intense patriotism. Patriotism for Vivekananda called for a whole programme of national regeneration. Within India, Vivekananda's programme of national regeneration called for the raising of a band of young monks and nuns who would work selflessly for the upliftment of the poor and helpless. The similarity between this order and that of the protagonists of Bankimchandra's *Anandamath* was marked, for both involved men who had renounced the world to devote themselves to the service of the motherland.[36] By emphasizing a common code of conduct based on collective activism, Vivekananda, like Bankimchandra, moved beyond doctrinal hair splitting and ritual rigidity and instead provided a practical, this-worldly slant to religion at the core of which was a heartfelt love for humanity. The revolutionary pamphlets bear witness to the depth of the influence of this brand of activist religiosity though the service to which the revolutionaries dedicated themselves was of a different order.

Just as much as Bankimchandra's, Vivekananda's religious worldview was a Hindu one. He envisioned a Hindu nation within which Muslims constituted a caste among several others while Indo-Muslim rule marked an episode in the long life of the nation. As Amiya Sen points out, such a view in Vivekananda's case stemmed not from prejudice or hostility, but from a political quest for a self-conscious nation. [37] The last three decades of the nineteenth century in Bengal witnessed a neo-Hindu revival among sections of the Hindu intelligentsia. This revivalism was partly a reaction to the condescension and contempt exhibited towards India's culture by the foreign rulers and partly born of a keen sense to escape to a past where they had been free. This past could be remoulded in imagination and memory to suit the needs of the present. This revivalism could sometimes take the form of an ultra-defensive stance where tradition was regarded as unchallengeable and immutable. But for sections of the intelligentsia, it also involved sincere introspection and rethinking in the light of rational and critical readings of Hindu texts. In the latter case, the tenets of Hindu tradition could be used to push forward a modern agenda. Bankimchandra's critical reconstruction of Hindu religious personalities, texts and images into nation building tools has already been referred to above. Vivekananda, in his turn, introduced a note of activism into the quietist faith of the Vedanta. Vivekananda emphasized that religion was not simply a question of individual salvation but involved selfless service towards one's fellow countrymen. When viewed from this perspective, religion served to promote unity with one's compatriots and could thus serve as the binding cement that would hold together a nation so incredibly and intractably diverse. Vivekananda's self-confident assertion in the universalism and superiority of the Hindu religion also strengthened its claim to be regarded as a valid foundation for the construction of a nation. However, for Vivekananda himself, religion was of much greater importance than politics. Only after the process of religious renewal was complete could India think of political freedom, social reform and economic renewal.[38]

But the revolutionary admirers of Vivekananda thought otherwise. Aurobindo Ghose declared that 'Political freedom is the life-breath of a nation; to attempt social reform, educational reform, industrial expansion, the moral improvement of the race without aiming first and foremost at political freedom is the very height of ignorance and futility.' [39]

Their immediate goals might have been different, but Aurobindo's view of the Indian nation was strikingly similar to that of Vivekananda. Speaking on the composite culture of modern India, Aurobindo remarked that

> The Hindu culture, however, on account of its age and its superior numerical strength, will always form the ground work of this composite Indian culture and civilization. The dominant note of Hindu culture, its sense of the spiritual and universal will, therefore be the peculiar feature of this composite Indian nationality.[40]

Aurobindo's was a mystical concept of the nation whose essence he defined as being constituted out of the union of the life force of each of its inhabitants. The nation he envisioned was also to be Hindu — Aryan in character, a sacred land — the *Aryabhumi*, whose inhabitants were the descendants of their glorious ancestors, the *Aryas*. Aurobindo thus declared that the new nationalism that was sweeping over the country 'was an attempt to create a new nation in India, by reviving in spirit and action ancient Indian character, the strong, great and lofty spirit of old Aryavarta, and setting it to use and mould the methods and materials of modernity for the freedom, greatness and well-being of a historic and immortal people.'[41]

Once again, the emphasis is on the crafting of 'materials of modernity' out of the reservoir of ancient religious wisdom. Here, it may be pointed out that his vision was also a gendered one, for like Bankimchandra, the brotherhood of renunciates whom he depicted as being dedicated to the service of the nation was not complemented by any matching sisterhood. The religious and masculine character of this vision was faithfully reproduced by Aurobindo in his pamphlet *Bhawani Mandir*, which was published in 1905. Along the lines laid down by Bankimchandra, Aurobindo wrote of a hermitage or *math* where men who had renounced their all, would work for the Mother. They would form a nucleus who 'having the fire of Bhawani in their hearts and brains, will go forth and carry the flame to every nook and cranny of the land'. The end result would be the creation of a nation, the consolidation of an age and the Aryanization of the world.

But the end also called for great sacrifice.

> A sacrifice of which the mightiest *Yajña* of old can only be a feeble type and far-off shadow, has to be instituted and the victims of the sacrifice are ourselves, our lives, our property, our hopes our ambitions, all that is personal and not of God, all that is devoted to our own service and taken from the service of the country. The greatest must fall as victims before the God of the sacrifice is satisfied.[42]

This idea of an apocalypse, a thorough cleansing of the nation embodied in the form of the mother with the blood of her patriot-sons formed an integral part of the metaphoric imagination of the revolutionary nationalists.

It is evident that the national community which the political thinkers referred to above sought to construct was modeled on the image of a religious community. Benedict Anderson has traced the emergence of the modern nation-states to the breakdown of older forms of communal self-identification.[43] In the Indian case, the religious community was the most powerful form of communal self-identification prior to the rise of the nation-state.[44] Many among the nationalist thinkers sought to harness the loyalties that the idea of the religious community evoked to the cause of a new form of community – the nation state. If a new polity based on a participatory model was to be constructed, then religion that had provided the bases of social and cultural cohesion could be utilized as a force for forging a nationalist identity. Aurobindo was intensely conscious of the power of religion in unleashing the energies and loyalties of the Indian faithful. As he wrote in the *Bhawani Mandir,*

> All great awakenings in India, all her periods of mightiest and most varied vigor have drawn their vitality from the fountain-heads of some deep religious awakening. Wherever the religious awakening has been complete and grand, the national energy it has created has been gigantic and puissant; wherever the religious movement has been narrow or incomplete, the national movement has been broken, imperfect or temporary.[45]

Moreover, it was religion that would give the Indian nation its distinctive identity, marking it off from the secular nations of the west. All the three thinkers referred to above spoke out against the blind imitativeness of the west and repeatedly called upon their compatriots to draw upon India's main strength, her spirituality, while undertaking their task of national regeneration.

Liah Greenfield, the theorist of nationalism has pointed out that nationalism is not a uniform phenomenon and it changes nature as the idea of the nation is transferred from one society to another. In her own words:

> The original meaning of the 'nation' - the definition of the people as sovereign and fundamentally homogenous – was retained in every nationalism. ...At the same time, the imported idea was everywhere modified in accordance with the local circumstances and reinterpreted in terms of indigenous traditions where they existed. The new society which emerged on the ruins of the old one, therefore, was everywhere different from others.[46]

The nation that Aurobindo and the revolutionaries set out to build was oriented around the consciousness of a shared religion. Their primary concern in this undertaking was not to promote a particular brand of religious ideology but to foreground certain ethical values that were peculiarly appropriate to the construction of the polity that they had imagined. For Aurobindo, spiritual faith was the first condition of success in every heroic undertaking. In his own words

> Faith is the one predominating characteristic of all great souls. ...In the region of politics faith is the result of imagination working in the light of history; it takes its stand on reason and experience and aspires into the future from the firm ground of the past.

In an insightful essay on the connections between religion and nationalism in Aurobindo's thought, Sugata Bose has rightly pointed out that the former envisioned the future nation-state as an ethical polity which would exalt the performance of *sanatan* (eternal) *dharma* (ethical obligations) towards humanity as a primary reason for its existence.[47] Social responsibility, a mystical adoration for everything associated with the motherland and a spirit of sacrifice which encompassed a desire to serve one's compatriots were the foundations on which this ethical polity would be built. Thus, certain universal spiritual values rather than religious dogma would structure the envisioned polity and provide the lineaments of the nation-state which was to be constructed in supposed continuity with the primordial Hindu nation that was imagined to have existed in the mythologized version of the past.

The writings of these three thinkers exercised a deep influence on the revolutionaries as they did on a sizeable section of the Hindu *bhadralok* class of the late nineteenth and early twentieth century. The ideas expressed in the pamphlets and the language and idiom used, show that they were very much the cultural products of the times. The pamphleteers dwelt on certain ideas then prevalent in the public political realm and wove them into a tapestry to get their message across to their audience. Despite the commonality in themes with other texts of the period, the revolutionary pamphlets did not simply reproduce any one variety of political ideology of the time. The political message that the pamphleteers wished to transmit to their intended audience was more radical in certain critical respects than the general current of public opinion of the period. But by using familiar ideas, emblems and language as part of the frame of reference the pamphleteers established common ground with their readers. The unfamiliar part of the political message could then be inserted within this frame as logical corollaries to the ideas that were integral to the nationalist discourses of the period. Thus we find that in an effort to get across their message to their readers, the pamphleteers valourized certain aspects of their religion that had not been emphasized in Hinduism as it was conventionally understood in the early twentieth century. The pamphleteers foregrounded the collectivist, militant and activist side to what had been traditionally perceived as an individualistic and quietist faith. In this respect, the influence on the pamphleteers of thinkers like Bankimchandra, Vivekananda and Aurobindo who had all emphasized social service over personal salvation, was clear. Bankimchandra's band of *sannyasis* or ascetics who had renounced the world to devote themselves to the service of their nation, Vivekananda's 'practical Vedanta' that placed service to humanity at the core of religious doctrine and Aurobindo's 'political Vedanta' that brought together the practice of politics and religion had all made communitarian service to the nation an integral part of religious practice. Understandably, an interpretation that marked activism and service as signifying practices of religion held great appeal for the revolutionary nationalists. The pamphleteers were at pains to point out that religious practice involved not philosophical speculation alone but activism as well. As a *Swadhin Bharat* pamphlet proclaimed

> In our country along with *Smriti, Samhitas, Darsanas* and *Upanishads,* the thunderbolt of *Basav,* the fetters of *Varuna* and the *Sudarshan* (discus) of *Vasudev* were associated. Behind the wise intelligence of *Atri-Angira, Janak, Yajnavalkya, Vyas Vasistha* an unconquerable warrior force was always awake.[48]

The religious rhetoric in which the propaganda of the pamphleteers was couched served a definite political purpose. For the revolutionaries, religion was the medium for propaganda and mobilization and religious categories and terms were given a new flavour and meaning to accord with political ends. This is most in evidence in the resurrection of the archetype of the mother-goddess. This figure had been revered by the Hindus since ancient times but was now given new political overtones within a changed context. As Sabyasachi Bhattacharya has pointed out '...it was not merely an act of rediscovery of something that belonged to the past. It was also a revelation of something that was new, an old object of worship now reinvented as the motherland'.[49] Following the example of Bankimchandra in *Anandmath,* Aurobindo in his pamphlet *Bhawani Mandir,* called for the consecration of a temple to the mother goddess Bhawani whom he identified as a source of Infinite Energy. This energy could assume different forms and various aspects according to the needs of the age. *Since the need of the present hour was strength,* the mother-goddess in her present incarnation would manifest herself as *Shakti* or force. Aurobindo identified this *Shakti* with the nation. 'The *Shakti* we call India, Bhawani Bharati, is the living unity of the *Shaktis* of three hundred million people …' This *Shakti* was lying inactive but could be released if the sons roused themselves from torpor and engaged in action or Karma. The highly emotive response that the figure of the motherland evoked no doubt had much to do with its religious associations.

A common theme that runs through almost all of pamphlet literature is the state of decadence and sloth into which the nation had sunk. Thus the pamphlets repeatedly bemoan the absence of *dharma* (ethical duty) in the nation's life and culture, a state which is described as *dharmahinata* and exhort the audience to participate in a religious war or *dharmayuddha* that would lead to the extirpation of the demons and the reestablishment of a *dharmarashtra* (a state ruled by dharma). Here again, the religious idiom serves as a rhetorical mechanism. The pamphlets make clear that *dharmahinata* is the absence of independence and the establishment of the *dharmarashtra* is only possible when independence has been won.[50] The articles in the *Jugantar* newspaper, of which several pamphlets were condensed versions, had frequently dealt with this question of *dharma* in public life and politics. In an article titled *Dharma aar Swadhinata (Dharma* and Independence), the writer said,

> India rose to greatness through *dharma* and not through politics – this statement means nothing. We have confused *dharma* with the English word religion. Many among the old and new school of thinkers use *dharma* to mean the religion of the Brahmans or asceticism. Therefore we have deviated from the *dharma* of the

> householder. ...We have forgotten that service to one's society and nation is as important as service to one's parents. The whole of *dharma* in all its aspects is no longer visible to us.We have cleared the way for catastrophe by forgetting that self-defence for upholding *dharma* and violence for self-defense are also necessary.[51]

Elsewhere *dharma* is defined as right conduct and humanity is defined as the *dharma* of all human beings, be they Hindu, Muslim or Christian.[52] The same idea was expressed in a Liberty pamphlet that declared:

> Our Movement rests on the firm foundation of our National Dharma, which we are pledged to glorify. We know no distinction of caste and creed, we recognize no differences of so called religion (really only ceremonies); but we believe in the strength of the three hundred million of gods of our Motherland, we have the fullest faith in the great destiny that awaits this LAND of the RISHIS in the near future, and which the will of God is working to bring about in ways inconceivable by the Human Mind. [53]

The pamphlets do not have much to say about the nature of the state that would emerge after independence had been wrested from the colonial government, but make clear that *dharma* would be the foundation of the new nation – the *jati* – a term that evolved in the late nineteenth century to mean the modern nation in place of its earlier usage as religious community. The *Jugantar* writers had used the term *swadeshdharma* to mean nationalism and had emphasized that *swadeshdharma* alone could help to overcome the divisions of caste and religion and lead to the establishment of the nation-state.[54] The emphasis on the observance of *dharma* and its definition in the pamphlets demonstrates that the pamphlet writers were envisioning a nation-state that was to be established on non-sectarian foundations. The impression that emerges from the reading of the pamphlets is that the pamphleteers mobilized certain terms and concepts that had wide reach and resonance in the traditional Hindu community and proceeded to invest them with universal meaning so as to serve as nation-building tools.

Such examples may be multiplied. The importance of the *Gita* as a preparatory text for the mental training of the young revolutionaries has been referred to above. The pamphlets repeatedly proclaim that *Gita* had enjoined all to perform one's *dharma* (moral duty) fearlessly without the thought of personal gain. Bhupendra Kishore Rakshit-Ray, a well known revolutionary, has written with rare insight on the role of the *Gita* as a source of inspiration for the young revolutionaries. 'Just as one cannot enter the temple of language without reading the alphabet, so one could not, in those days, enter the realm of the revolutionaries without reading the *Gita*' wrote Rakshit Ray. He then explicated at length on the revolutionary interpretation of the verses of the *Gita*. According to Rakshit-Ray, the verses of the *Gita* held special meaning for the revolutionaries, for it helped them to overcome fear and hesitation in the face of danger by instilling in them a deep conviction about the rightfulness and sacredness of their undertaking. The message that the young revolutionaries took away from the *Gita* was that

> The soul has no body. Therefore weapons cannot pierce it, fire cannot incinerate it, water cannot damp it nor can the air dry it… ….. The soul is eternal… [55]

The role of the *Gita*, it appears, was to legitimize revolutionary violence and inculcate in the revolutionaries the outlook and attitude indispensable to their revolutionary mission.

It was not as if the pamphleteers' interpretation of the nation's past through the Hindu prism never betrayed cultural insensitivity. The pamphlet-writers sometimes expressed the view that the age of colonization in India had effectively begun with the Muslim incursions. Thus the pamphlets evoked memories of warriors like Shivaji, Pratapaditya and Rana Pratap as true patriots who had fought to protect the Hindu nation from the Muslim invaders. The pamphleteers then proceeded to compare the exploits of the Hindu heroes with those of Lakshmibai and Tantia Tope who had fought against the British in 1857.[56] The implication of such a comparison is made clear in the following pamphlet which expresses its opposition to rule by a 'foreign race' and includes Muslim rule in this category.

> *Boliya rakhi amader kono jati biddesh nai. Ingraj na hoiya pharashi kimba musalman raja hoile, amra shukhe thakitam – e kotha boli na. Tobe iha ashonkoche bolibo, ingrajer kapot kaushal, jaha jatike pranhin koriyachhe, onahare maritechhe, tahar chaite gnoyar saral musalmaner prokashyo otyachar je sohosro gune bhalo chhilo.* (Translation: Let us make it clear that we have no race hatred. We would have been better off had the French or the Muslims been our king instead of the English – we do not say this. But this we shall say plainly, a thousand times better than the devious stratagems of the English, that have left

> the race without life, in a state of starvation, was the open oppression of the headstrong, uncomplicated Muslims.)[57]

Despite its opposition to the idea of Muslim rule, the pamphlet favourably compares Muslim rule to that of the British. A distinction is thus made between varieties of foreign rule. Amiya Sen has made the point that the Hindu revivalists of nineteenth century Bengal were battling the Christians and Brahmos and not so much the Muslims.[58] The same argument may be made for the pamphlets as well. A careful reading of the pamphlets shows that in the discourse of the pamphleteers, the celebration of the ancient Hindu nation is not accompanied with proclamations of hostility towards the Muslims. The pamphlet writers are not guilty of communalism, as the term has come to be understood by scholars. In fact, Muslim rulers who fought against the English are eulogized in the pamphlets. Siraj-ud-daulah, is remembered as a patriot and martyr to the cause of Bengal's independence. While Mir Zafar is denounced for his treachery and deceit, Mir Qasim is celebrated for his bravery and leadership.

> *1757 khrishtabde Palashi prangone Bharater param sarbonashkari jaliat Clive desho-drohi Mir Zafar er bishwasghatokatae ebong amader'er i swadeshbashi 2,100 jan bharotiyo sipahir bahubale banger shesh swadhin nabab hotobhagyo Siraj-ud-daulah er sarbonash shadhan koriya tahake singhashonchuto kare. Ihar por 1764 khrishtabde Buxar'er juddhoshektre swadhin chitto o swajitibatshal Mir-Qasim er Rajya kariya loiya nijerai banglar masnade judiya bashe.*[59] (Translation: In the year 1757, on the field of Palashi, the great destroyer of Bengali fortunes, the forger Clive, with the help of the treachery of Mir-Zafar and the strength of 2,100 of our fellow countrymen ruined the last independent nawab of Bengal, the hapless Siraj-ud-daulah and deposed him from his throne. After this in 1764, on the battlefield of Buxar, they wrested the kingdom from Mir-Qasim who was independent-minded and benevolent to his compatriots and proceeded to install themselves on the throne of Bengal.)

In this section, the pamphleteers foreground the Bengali identity over the religious one. The rulers perceived as patriotic are described in glowing terms and as being in communion with their subjects, despite the differences in religion, because of their common stance against the invader English. Here is clearly an example of nationalist sentiments overriding social and cultural barriers. Feelings of antagonism towards the Muslims do not figure as a constant in the pamphlets, though social tensions between the two communities as during the communal riots in Mymensingh and Comilla in 1907 do find expression in the texts. Here too, it should be pointed out that the ultimate responsibility for the riots are placed at the door of the British who are accused of adopting a policy of divide and rule in order to further their evil designs.

Scholars have made a distinction between the ideology of Hindu nationalism that lays claim to the formation of a nation-state on the basis of a homogenized Hindu identity from which internal differences of caste, class and gender have been ironed out and that of communalism. To quote Sumit Sarkar, 'The crucial differentia of communalism is not a developed sense of religious community or identity, not even its 'politicisation', but a further assumption of conflict with a similarly imagined communal Other as both inevitable, and overriding…'.[60] The 'other' in the pamphlets are the *feringhees,* a pejorative term for the British and the grounds for opposition to the 'other' is political, not religious. In the pamphlet propaganda of this period, the myth of the Hindu nation was intended as an integrative device, a way of drawing together the intended readers of such propaganda into fraternal communion. The intention of pamphlet propaganda was not to divide but to unite. But it cannot be denied that this message of unity was directed towards a limited audience. As mentioned earlier, the pamphlet writers came from educated, upper caste, Hindu male backgrounds and their propaganda was directed towards a similar kind of audience. This audience did not include the popular classes. Some pamphlets openly called for young and educated supporters to join them.[61] The pamphleteers were resoundingly silent on the question of women joining the movement.[62] Similarly the indifference towards Muslim participation in the movement had more to do with the cultural insularity of the pamphleteers than with any deep-seated racial animosity or ideological bigotry. Part of the explanation may also lie in the social background of the pamphleteers. The revolutionary nationalists from whom the pamphleteers were drawn had strong connections with the rural gentry and their acquaintance with Muslims could have been limited to their peasant subjects which made it all the more difficult for them to conduct a dialogue with Muslims on equal terms.[63] Sometimes, the pamphleteers could be patronizing and condescending towards the Muslims. Thus one pamphlet clearly stated that the British had been able to oppress the Hindus by turning against the latter 'their illiterate Moslem brethren.'[64] Added to this cultural insularity was the political environment in early twentieth century Bengal in which far fewer numbers of Muslims than Hindus were active participants in the nationalist movement, making it easier to disregard them as a political force whose support had to be mobilized in order to make a political impact. All of these factors intertwined to limit the political vision of the first generation of revolutionaries.[65] A similar kind of elitism is noticeable in the pamphlet rhetoric directed towards the lower classes. Though the pamphleteers repeatedly call for all the Hindu castes to unite in a war against the British, the Sanskritized language and erudite allusions of the pamphlets appear incongruous in view of the fact that a majority of the population could not relate to them and so made it difficult to take the exhortations seriously. But this elitism cannot be equated with a deliberate goal to exclude certain sections of the population. A few of the pamphleteers were able to cross cultural and social barriers and reach out to the Muslims. For instance, some of the *Jugantar* pamphleteers, despite their heavy reliance on Hindu religious imagery, consciously conceived of the struggle for independence as a war to be waged in a united way by the Hindus and the Muslims against the British.[66] The *Liberty* pamphlets made it clear that the ideological basis of the nation should not conceived of in terms circumscribed by religion. Thus one pamphlet proclaimed that the upheaval of 1857 was followed by a period of quiescence during which time the Indian Nation had to learn to transform itself from Hindu and Islamic kingdoms into a great United Nation. The conscious effort at drawing in Muslims into the movement became more noticeable as the movement began to assume pan-Indian dimensions and the necessity of drawing in more groups into a pan-Indian community became clear.[67] In the wake of the collapse of the Lahore Conspiracy, a *Swadhin Bharat* pamphlet had this to say,

> *Ingrajer baro bharsha chhilo je bharotbarsho bibhinno jatir bashbhumi shutorang jati boliya edeshe kichhui gojaiya utthite pare na. Aj Lahorer mukoddomay ingraj bujjhibe desher shakal santan-i ek joge kaj korite pare – Marathi, Panjabi, Bangali, Hindu-Musulman shokole-i ek-i patakar nimne mayer mukh chahiya samabeto hoite pare. Ek-i uddeshye buker rakto akatore pat korite kicchhute- i kuntthito noy.* (Translation: The English placed great store on the fact that since India is peopled by many different races, a united nation is unlikely to arise. The English will come to know now from the Lahore case that the sons of the country can work together; that looking at the face of the Mother, the Mahratta, the Punjabi, the Bengali, the Hindu and the Muslim can work together under one banner and that they do not hesitate to shed their hearts' blood freely for the common cause.)[68]

Sensitive readings of the pamphlets indicate that the language of the pamphleteers may be best understood as inflected by the signs of a political culture that was undergirded by deep religious sensibilities. The nation, as it was imagined within such a culture, assumed the form of a composite religious (rather than a secular or non religious) entity, the constituent elements of which coexisted, sometimes in tension and at other times in cooperation. The political imaginary mirrored the social situation on the ground where co-operation and conflict had co-existed for centuries and was regarded as part of the everyday order of things.[69] But the political culture of the time was also constantly evolving, for changing political needs often demanded a recasting of the political imaginary. Thus, in the earlier editions of the pamphlets, the Hindu component played an overbearing role based on the assumption (itself imagined) that since the Hindus were the oldest of the groups that had made India their home, they must necessarily be the most important. The exigencies of nation building brought about a change in sensibilities and tone with strident claims to Hindu predominance being replaced with the idea of a multicultural polity based on the cooperation of all its various component elements.

As the early revolutionaries were increasingly exposed to a cosmopolitan world and as they gathered greater experience of different cultures, there was a parallel move away from religionized politics to more secular sensibilities. Hemchandra Qanungo who met and worked with European revolutionaries in Paris was among the first of the revolutionaries to write against conceiving of politics as the practice of religion.[70] It may also be pointed out in passing that many among the first generation of revolutionary nationalists developed leftist sympathies and in later years drifted into the socialist fold, a trajectory that was hardly logical for those with proto-'Hindutva' tendencies.[71]

Some conclusions follow from the arguments presented above. A religious discourse with a political objective is not inherently communal or sectarian. Nor is it always backward looking or archaic. The real import of a religious discourse and its impact on events can only be gauged when it is understood as part of a larger picture. It is not enough to accept a discourse at face value. One must also look at the purpose of using a particular language and how this language is received and interpreted in different situations. The same language may serve different functions in different periods and also be interpreted differently in changed contexts. In early twentieth century Bengal, given the political atmosphere and the *mentalités* of targeted audiences, a political language couched in a Hindu religious idiom might have appeared a viable and legitimate form of political mobilization even to those Hindu political groups whose intention was not to not to create or increase religious and political divisions but rather to rally the larger population behind the nationalist cause. It may also be pointed out that Muslims did not respond as a homogenous unity to the use of Hindu religious images, icons and discourses in nationalist politics. The *swadeshi* movement provoked much opposition among Muslims for a number of reasons,[72] but there were others who passionately supported the movement without being greatly concerned about its religious overtones. The same point may be made about the Brahmos, who, according to Bhupendrananth Dutt, joined the revolutionary nationalist movement in significant numbers, despite its Hindu religious idiom.[73] More important than the religious idiom which framed *swadeshi* and revolutionary politics was the interweaving of the social, political, economic and cultural factors which went to make up the context within which the political language was received and interpreted. This situation would change radically in the following decades. In course of the twentieth century the political and mental climate gradually began to change in ways that the use of religion in the public political sphere began to emerge as an increasingly controversial and divisive phenomenon. In such a situation 'religionized' political languages began to be tendentiously deployed in directions that made it well nigh impossible to interpret them as anything other than deliberately and perversely communal. Within this changed context, rhetoric and reaction combined in new and explosive ways to influence the course of subsequent events in Bengal.

Endnotes

1 See Peter Robb, 'The Colonial State and Constructions of Indian Identity. An Example on the Northeast Frontier in the 1880s' in *Liberalism, Modernity and the Nation* (Oxford University Press, New Delhi, 2007), p. 127–62. The construction of a modern state in India may have bestowed on the Indians the identity of colonial subjects but certainly not that of citizens of a nation-state.

2 I borrow this term from Ronald Grigor Suny's article 'Constructing Primordialism: Old Histories for New Nations' *The Journal of Modern History* Vol. 73, (4) (Dec., 2001): p. 862–896.

3 The pamphleteers were deeply influenced by the prose and writing style of the writers of the *Jugantar* newspaper like Bhupendranath Dutt, Debabrata Basu, Upendrananth Bandopadhyay and Aurobindo Ghose. Since the pamphlets were anonymous, it is difficult to trace their authorship, but names that crop up in the police records like Kartik Dutt, Kiran Mukherjee, Runkini Ray and Panna Lal Chatterji were all associated with the *Jugantar* group. The famous Sanskrit

scholar and revolutionary, Pandit Mokkhoda Samadhyayi, who allegedly helped Kartik Dutt with the composition of the *Jugantar* leaflets had been involved in the publication of the *Sandhya* newspaper.

4 For more on the rhetorical techniques employed by the pamphlet writers, see Chapter III.

5 Historians have pointed out that the concept of a monolithic Hindu religious community is a relatively modern construction. For pre-Islamic India, it is more appropriate to speak of a range of sects, castes and doctrines rather than of a united religious community. It was only in the fifteenth century that some people began to refer to themselves as Hindus and as the 'other' of the Muslims. In colonial India, Orientalist scholars, whose understanding of Hinduism was influenced by Christianity, also looked upon 'Hinduism' as a monolithic religion with a common body of doctrine and rituals subscribed to by all Hindus. Emergent national consciousness in the nineteenth century appropriated this definition of Hinduism. Many nineteenth century nationalists subscribed to the theory of a Hindu religion and civilization that had been founded by the Aryans in ancient times. The Aryans were described as a race that had conquered the non-Aryan indigenous people. The Aryans were identified with the upper castes while the lower castes were seen as non-Aryan and indigenous to the land. Such a theory furthered a sense of superiority among the upper castes who took great pride in claiming a common origin with the European Aryans. For more on this theme, see Romila Thapar, 'Imagined Religious Communities' in *History and Beyond* (Oxford University Press, New Delhi, 2000), p. 60–88.

6 From the official English translation of *Swadhin Bharat* (*Independent India*) pamphlet of February 1910 in National Archives of India, Home Department Political (Confidential), Part A, April 1910, p. 40–42.

7 From the pamphlet titled *Yugantar- Chaturtha Barsho- 1317 – sankhya 1* (*Yugantar, 4th Year 1317, No. 1*) in National Archives of India, Home Department Political, Part B, January 1910, p. 34–51.

8 From the official English translation of the pamphlet *Jugantar – Praphulla* reproduced in Amiya Samanta ed. *Terrorism in Bengal* (Government of West Bengal, Kolkata, 1995), Vol. IV, p. 384.

9 From the pamphlet *Swadhin Bharat* beginning with the words *Dekhe, dekhe hoilam stobdhopara* (*I am silenced by the sight*) SN 56/1913, FN 1340/13, WBSA – IB.

10 Ibid.

11 From the pamphlet *Swadhin Bharat* beginning with the words *Tomar desh, tomar swadhinata* (*Your country, your independence*), SN 56/1913, FN 1340/13 in WBSA - IB.

12 For pamphlets that deal with this theme, see SN 35/1910, FN 191/1910, WBSA - IB

13 *Jugantar* leaflet in SN 17/1913, FN 37/1913, WBSA –IB.

14 Amales Tripathi, *The Extremist Challenge: India between 1890 and 1910* (Orient Longmans, New Delhi, 1967), p. xiii.

15 Ibid., p. 1– 2.

16 Sumit Sarkar, *The Swadeshi Movement in Bengal* (Permanent Black, Ranikhet, second edition), 29, p. 410–14.

17 Dipesh Chakrabarty, 'Subaltern Histories and Post-enlightenment Rationalism' in *Habitations of Modernity*, (Permanent Black, Delhi, 2002).

18 Sudipta Kaviraj, *The Unhappy Consciousness: Bankimchandra Chattopadhyay and the Formation of Nationalist Discourse in India* (Oxford University Press, New Delhi, 1995), p. 108.

19 Essay entitled *Bharat Kalanka*, (*India's Shame*) in *Bibidha Prabandha* (*Various Essays*) reproduced in *Bankim Rachanabali* (*Collected Works of Bankimchandra*, hereafter BR) Vol. II (Kolkata, *Sahitya Samsad* [Bengali Era 1361], 1955), p. 234–41.

20 For the use of the term 'Hindus' in place of 'Indians' see below.

21 For more such examples of a desire for nationhood see Sekhar Bandopadhyay, 'From Subjects to Citizens: Reactions to Colonial Rule and the Changing Political Culture of Calcutta in the Mid-Nineteenth Century' in Mabel Lee, Michael Welding eds., *History, Literature and Society: Essays in Honour of S.N. Mukherjee* (Sydney Association for Studies in Society and Culture and Manohar Publishers: Sydney and New Delhi, 1997), p. 9–31.

22 *Bangalar Itihas* (*Bengal's History*), BR, Vol. II, p. 330.

23 S. P. Sen (ed.) *History in Modern Indian Literature* (Institute of Historical Studies, Kolkata, 1975).

24 BR, Vol. II, p. 239–40.

25 Tapan Raychaudhuri, *Europe Reconsidered: Perceptions of the West in Nineteenth Century Bengal* (Oxford University Press, New Delhi, 1988), p. 34, 41.

26 *Swadeshpriti* (*Patriotism*), BR II, p. 660–61.

27 *Krishnacharitra*, BR, II, p. 407–583.

28 *Bhagavata Purana*: One of the eighteen *Puranas*. The *Puranas* form part of the body of ancient Indian philosophical literature.

29 The *Gita* was a philosophical tract that was a part of the Indian historical epic, the *Mahabharata*.

30 The Pandavas: One of the two warring groups of cousins who were the participants in the great battle of Kurukshetra, which forms the subject matter of the Indian epic, the *Mahabharata*.

31 See below and Chapter III.

32 For the influence exercised by the song *Vande Mataram* (alternatively *Bande Mataram*) on the nationalist movement see Sabyasachi Bhattacharya, *Vande Mataram: The Biography of a Song* (Penguin India, New Delhi, 2003).

33 Sri Aurobindo, *Bankim-Tilak-Dayananda* (Sri Aurobindo Ashram Trust, Pondicherry, [1940] 2006), p. 14.

34 Swami Vivekananda, 'Reply to the address of welcome at Pamban' in *Lectures from Colombo to Almora* (Advaita Ashrama, Kolkata, 1992), p. 37.

35 Quoted in Amales Tripathi, *The Extremist Challenge*, p. 61.

36 Tapan Raychaudhuri, *Europe Reconsidered*, p. 248–59.

37 Amiya P. Sen, *Hindu Revivalism in Bengal, 1872–1905: Some Essays in Interpretation* (Oxford University Press, New Delhi, 1993), p. 343.

38 Amales Tripathi *The Extremist Challenge,* p. 27.

39 'The Doctrine of Passive Resistance' in the journal *Vande Mataram* of 11 April 1907, reprinted in *Sri Aurobindo, Bande Mataram, Early Political Writings* (Sri Aurobindo Ashram, Pondicherry, 1997), p. 86.

40 Sri Aurobindo 'The Bed-Rock of Indian Nationalism – II' (Vande-Mataram of 14 June 1908), quoted in Julius Lipner trans. *Anandamath,* p. 77.

41 From Aurobindo's, 'The Heart of Nationalism' reprinted in *Sri Aurobindo - On Nationalism: Selected Writings and Speeches* (Sri Aurobindo Ashram, Pondicherry, 1996), p. 355.

42 'New Conditions' in the *Vande Mataram* of 29 April 1908, reprinted in *Sri Aurobindo : Bande Mmataram,* p. 890.

43 Benedict Anderson, *Imagined Communities: Reflections on the Origin and Spread of Nationalism* (Verso, London, 1983), p. 20–8.

44 For a perceptive account of the role of religion in shaping the communal lives of Bengalis in the pre-colonial period see Tapan Ray-Chaudhuri, '*Adhunik Bangalir Manobhongi*' (*The mentalités of modern Bengalis*) in *Prabandha Sangraha* (*Collection of Essays*) (Ananda, Kolkata, 2009), p. 182–86.

45 From *Bhawani Mandir* reprinted in *Sri Aurobindo: On Nationalism,* p. 72.

46 Liah Greenfield, 'Nationalism and Modernity' in *Nationalism and the Mind* (One World Publications, Oxford, 2007), p. 76.

47 Sugata Bose, 'The Spirit And Form of An Ethical Polity: A Meditation on Aurobindo's Thought' in *Modern Intellectual History,* 4 (2007): p. 129–44; see also Andrew Sartori, 'The Transfiguration of Duty in Aurobindo's *Essays On The Gita*' in *Modern Intellectual History,* 7 (2010): p. 319–34.

48 Basav, Varuna, Vasudev: warrior heroes of the Hindu pantheon. Atri-Angira, Janak, Yajnavalkya, Vyas, Vasistha – Sages of ancient India.

From the official English translation of the *Swadhin Bharat* leaflet headed 'About Myself', in SN 38/1910, FN 13/8/1910 in WBSA-IB. See also, SN 14/1910, FN 1318 A in WBSA-IB where the pamphleteers state 'Our object is to raise the *Khatra* (the warrior caste) power in India and to place India to her proper position by driving out the foreign obstacles, and her dependence by means of that *Khatra* power, and to clear off the path for universal good. This is our aim and to fulfill this aim, we are prepared to sacrifice everything we have, and so should all Indians be ready for sacrifice'.

49 Sabyasachi Bhattacharya, *Vande Mataram,* p. 91–3.

50 *Jugantar* pamphlets, SN 56/1913, FN 1340/1913; SN 17/1913, FN 37/1913 in WBSA – IB.

51 '*Dharma aar Swadhinata*' (*Dharma and Independence*) in Uma Mukherji and Haridas Mukherji, *Bharater Swadhinata Andoloney Jugantar Patrikar Dan* (*The Contribution of the newspaper Jugantar to the Indian struggle for Independence*) (Firma KLM, Kolkata, 1996, second edition), p. 168–71.

52 '*Yoga-Khyapar Chithhi*' (Yoga-Khyapa's letter); '*Dharma-Rajya o Maharaja Shivaji*' (*Dharma-Rajya and Maharaja Shivaji*), ibid., p. 136–39; 182–88.

53 Pamphlet titled *Liberty, 20th July 1913* in SN 5/1913, SN 663/1913 in WBSA-IB.

54 For example, the *Jugantar* article *Bhut o Bhabishyat* (*The Past and the Future*) reprinted in Ashoke Kumar Mukhopadhyay ed. *Mukti Kon Pathe* (*Which Way Lies Freedom*, a collection of articles published in the weekly *Jugantar*), (Punoscho, Kolkata, 2006), p. 145–48.

55 Bhupendrakishore Rakshit-Ray, '*Banglay Biplab-bad o Gita*' (*The Gita and Revolutionary Ideology in Bengal*) in *Agniyug* (*Age of Fire*) (Purna Prakashan, Kolkata, 1978), Part II, p. 14–34.

56 *Jugantar*, '*4th Year - 1317, No.1*'.

57 *Swadhin Bharat* pamphlet, SN 45/1913, FN 380/1913, WBSA - IB.

58 Amiya Sen, *Hindu Revivalism in Bengal*, p. 234–35.

59 From *Swadhin Bharat* pamphlet beginning with the words, *Na Jani Janani* (*We do not know, O Mother*) in P.T.S. Collection, 18-A-15, Police Museum, Kolkata.

60 Sumit Sarkar, 'Hindutva and History' in *Beyond Nationalist Frames: Relocating Postmodernism, Hindutva and History* (Permanent Black; Delhi, 2004), p. 246.

61 *Swadhin Bharat* pamphlet, SN 15/1910, FN 1318B/1910, WBSA - IB.

62 There were a few notable exceptions. For example, in the pamphlet entitled *Sandhya: Second Issue, Fourth Year*, the woman writer Kumudini Mitter emphasized the importance of women in assisting their husbands in the freedom struggle. See, SN 14/1911, FN, V/105 A/1911 in WBSA-IB.

63 Rajat Kanta Ray, 'Land, Religion and Political Culture: The Militant Hindu Gentry of East Bengal, 1905–17,' paper presented at the Bicentenary Evaluation Seminar on the Permanent Settlement organized by the Bangladesh Itihas Samiti in November 1993.

64 From the pamphlet beginning with the words '*Deputy Superintendent Basanta Chattopadhyayer hotya*' dated 16 September 1916 from the Calcutta Police Museum Collection.

65 Barbara Southard, in an article titled 'The Political Strategy of Aurobindo Ghosh: The Utilization of Hindu Religious Symbolism and the Problem of Political Mobilization in Bengal' in *Modern Asian Studies*, Vol. 14, No. 3 (1980), p. 353–376, has made the point that the use of *shakta* religious symbolism by the upper caste extremist and revolutionary nationalist leaders like Bipin Chandra Pal and Aurobindo indicated their indifference to and indeed their ambivalence towards mass mobilization. The rural upper castes who were followers of the *shakta* cult of Kali worship could identify with the religious imagery and linguistic idiom of the extremist leaders but not the lower castes who were followers of the *vaishnava* cult. This view is based on certain unfounded assumptions and betrays unfamiliarity with the social and economic fabric of Bengal. First of all, the *shaktas* and *vaishnavas* of Bengal are better understood as parts of a mosaic of Hindu sects with plenty of mutual give and take in beliefs and practices rather than as exclusive and discrete religious groups. S Jasodhara Bagchi has pointed out, the cult of mother worship in Bengal is itself a blend of the Vaishnava sentiment

of bhakti with the worship of Shakti. See Jasodhara Bagchi, 'Representing Nationalism: Ideology of Motherhood in Colonial Bengal', *Economic and Political Weekly*, October 20–27, 1990, p. 65–71. Moreover, the evidence provided by the author makes clear that the religio-cultural divide also corresponded to a deep economic chasm with the interests of the upper caste landowning Hindus being clearly ranged against those of the cultivating lower castes, making it difficult for the latter to support the economic goals of the *swadeshi* movement.

66 For example, the *Jugantar* pamphlets headed '*Jugantar: The Creed of Independence*' and '*Om Vande Mataram, Yugantar, Yugantar, Yugantar*' in Amiya Samanta ed. *Terrorism in Bengal: A Collection of Documents* (Government of West Bengal, Kolkata, 1995), Vol. IV, p. 390–93; 405–08.

67 Pamphlet titled *Liberty 4th May 1857*, SN 5/1913, FN 663/1913 in WBSA-IB. Swarupa Gupta, in tracing the Bengali middle class quest for a national identity in the nineteenth century points out that the nationalist discourse of the Bengali literati which was framed in an Aryan-Hindu rhetoric was inflected by the high caste, Hindu origins of the writers. This made it difficult to integrate the voices of the 'lower orders' or of the Muslims within this discourse. But the author argues that linking the concept of nationhood to the idea of *samaj* or social collectivity that was rooted in *dharma* (righteous conduct) *atmiyata* (social relationships) and cultural Aryanism left room for the incorporation of 'others' into the national collectivity for presumably all those who conformed to certain rules of social conduct could, hypothetically, be a part of the nation. See Swarupa Gupta, 'Notions of Nationhood in Bengal: Perspectives on Samaj, 1867-1905' *Modern Asian Studies*, 40, 2 (2006): p. 273–302.

68 Police Museum, PTS Collection, 19-10-16. Accession No. 31-08-06.

69 Tapan Raychaudhuri, '*British Bharat-e Hindu-Musulman Samparko*' (Relations between Hindus and Muslims in British India) *Desh*, September 17, 2011, p. 23–31.

70 Hemchandra Qanungo, *Banglay Biplab Pracheshta* (Chirayata Prokashan, 1928), p. 37–44.

71 Notably Bhupendrananth Dutt, brother of Swami Vivekananda.

72 See Sarkar, *Swadeshi Movement*, Chapter 8.

73 Bhupendrananth Dutt, *Bharater Dwitiya Rajnaitik Sangram* (Nabobharat Publishers, Kolkata, 1983), p. 7. He went on to add that the national movement and the demand for independence had emerged as strong forces in those regions of the country where movements like Brahmo Samaj, Prarthana Samaj and Arya Samaj had posed a challenge to traditional religions and social systems and ushered in new streams of thought. Members of the Brahmo Samaj, who shared the elitist socio-cultural background of the revolutionaries, were obviously not deterred from joining the revolutionary nationalist movement despite its 'Hindu' overtones.

3

Legitimizing Violence

At the core of the propaganda campaigns of the revolutionary pamphleteers lay the problematic category of violence. The idea of violence occupies a peculiarly ambiguous place within any political culture. Violence is typically defined as the illegitimate use of force or coercion to make others submit to one's will. Violence is a universal phenomenon, yet an understanding of what constitutes violence or an illegitimate or unfair use of force is a matter of subjective perception. As has been pointed out, acts of violence usually involve three parties, the perpetrators, the victims and the witnesses, yet violence is 'very much a word of those who witness, or who are victims of certain acts, rather than of those who perform them.'[1] While victims protest the violence, the perpetrators, on the other hand, are convinced of the legitimacy of their cause and seek to persuade public opinion (witnesses) of the acceptability of their acts. They do so by appealing to certain cultural norms and values that provide their acts with meaning and supposedly justify their cause. Victims and perpetrators can both appeal to cultural values and social norms to justify their conflicting opinions of situations and actions and argue that rightness and justice lie with their respective interpretations. To the extent that they are able to persuade public opinion to side with their perspective on the situation, they may claim victory for their cause. The efficacy of violence rests on the fact that despite different perspectives on the rightness or justice of violent acts, all the parties involved are able to decipher the messages and meanings latent in particular acts of violence.

As the targets and perpetrators of revolutionary violence, the colonial government and the revolutionary nationalists understood the acts of violence committed by the revolutionaries differently. The colonial government portrayed these acts of violence as illegal attempts to subvert the state while to the revolutionaries these were acts of martyrdom or heroism that aimed at the undoing of a terrible wrong and the establishment of a just political order.

The idea of terrorist violence was a fundamentally new concept in Bengal nationalist politics nurtured, as it had been, on a restricted diet of council debates and boardroom intrigues. The revolutionary nationalists were aware of the fact that the success of their movement and their capacity to make new recruits to the cause depended on the extent to which the ideology and practices of revolutionary nationalism could be propagated among and made acceptable to the general population. Public opinion had to be persuaded of the rightness of the revolutionary cause. In other words, violence had to be legitimized. Violence has an ambiguous place within any political culture. We can cite the example of the Mahabharata in which even Lord Krishna has to justify bloodshed and war to a hesitant Arjuna. The activities of the revolutionary terrorists also came in for a fair share of criticism and condemnation from contemporary thinkers and politicians for both pragmatic and ideological reasons. A survey of reactions to terrorist activities during the earlier phase indicates that though Bengalis might secretly or otherwise admire individual acts of terror, they were hesitant to come out in full support of the revolutionary movement as a whole. Bipin Chandra Pal, the extremist leader wrote in an editorial in the newpaper *Vande Mataram* that 'Bombs and assassinations had.... absolutely no place in our propaganda. Both our instinct and our wisdom equally rebel against these outlandish methods of political warfare.' In the wake of the bomb throwing incident at Muzaffarpur in 1908, the *Amrita Bazar Patrika* described the revolutionaries as 'hare-brained and half-witted'. Rabindranath Tagore's deep aversion to revolutionary violence is well known and his writings on this subject have been carefully dissected by scholars and historians.[2]

Right from the very beginning, therefore, the terrorists concentrated as much on propaganda as they did on terrorist action. The character of this propaganda was necessarily polemical – its purpose was not the rectification or redress of an unjust state of affairs. Rather it was to persuade its targeted audience that the prevalent state of affairs was so unacceptable and so irremediable that the only available course of action was to put an end to it through revolution.

As mentioned in the first chapter, the earliest vehicles of this propaganda were newspaper articles, which expounded on the idea of violent revolution. The revolutionary newspaper par excellence was the *Jugantar*, which was founded in March 1906 by Barindra Kumar Ghose, Abinash Bhattacharya and Bhupendranath Dutt as a political weekly in the Bengali language.[3] The *Jugantar* newspaper served as the propaganda vehicle for a loose congregation of revolutionaries led by individuals like Jatin Banerjee and Barin Ghose who drew inspiration from the charismatic personality of Aurobindo Ghose.[4] When the *Jugantar patrika* (newspaper) was founded in 1906, there were other radical Bengali language newspapers already in existence, like Bipin Chandra Pal's *Swadhin Bharat,* and Brahmabandhab Upadhyaya's *Sandhya,* which through their columns, openly challenged the right of the British to rule India. But it was the *Jugantar,* which most consistently propagated the revolutionary ideology and became the standard by which to measure the seditious nature of other publications.[5]

From the outset, the *Jugantar* aspired to be more than a straightforward political newspaper. Its primary purpose was not the dissemination of political news. Rather, by presenting news selectively through its columns and providing it with a distinctive interpretative slant, the *Jugantar* sought to convince its readers of the legitimacy of its political position and mobilize popular support for the revolutionary cause. The political essays that the *Jugantar* writers like Debabrata Basu, Upendranth Bandopadhyay, Barindra Kumar Ghose, and more rarely Aurobindo Ghose, published through the newspaper's columns, also aimed to unite educated Bengali opinion around a particular ideology and movement. The *Jugantar*'s ideological position was that the only path to national regeneration – moral, social and cultural – was through the attainment of political independence. Striving for independence was the sole political goal that could inspire an entire nation.

> *Durbal anichchhasatwe, shudhu chabuker bhayei shabaler haste swadhon arpon kare. Shei chabuk ultadike chalaite parilei tahar bojhadander day katiya jay. Ei chabuk porichalonay shoktir darkar. Ei shokti-i swadhinata. Swadhinatai shudhu desher dhanman bajay rakhite pare.*
>
> *... Bishke dur korite hoile tibro-bish proyog korite hoy. Ei bishi–i biplab.*
>
> (Translation: Despite their unwillingness the meek hand over their wealth to the strong because of their fear of the whip. If the whip could be wielded in the opposite direction, the burden of suffering disappears. It requires strength to wield this whip. This strength is independence. Independence alone can guarantee prosperity and dignity.

> ...To get rid of poison, a stronger dose of poison is required. This poison is Revolution.)[6]

Past political experience had shown that the British would not willingly share power with Indians, let alone grant independence to India. The *Jugantar* had nothing but contempt for the politicians of the Congress party whose uninvited attempts to help Englishmen rule India had been overtly repulsed.[7] The only consequence of such politics had been to send up 'the price of paper in the market by using up quires and quires of paper for submitting petitions couched in the most correct and elegant language. But as a result of all this we have been fortunate enough to get nothing but thrusts of *lathis* (clubs) and the partitioned Bengal remains partitioned.'[8] Instead of 'political mendicancy' (*rajnaitik bhikkhabritti*), the *Jugantar* advocated self-reliance and use of strength. The *Jugantar* line was that just as the sovereign power relied on brute strength to repress its subjects, so the subjects had to fight back through strength alone.

> *Je deshe rajshakti poshubalke shahay koriya projake utpirhan kare, she deshe naitik baler shahajye biplab ba raj-paribarton anayan kara ashambhab. Shekhane projakeo poshubalke shahay korite hay.*
>
> (Translation: In a country where the ruling power relies on brute force to oppress its subjects, it is impossible to bring about Revolution or a change in rulers through moral strength. In such a situation, subjects too must rely on brute force.)[9]

The *Jugantar* writings marked a paradigmatic shift in Bengali political outlook by inverting the traditional assumptions concerning the relationship of a colonized people and their colonial masters. The paper consistently mocked the so-called might of the British Raj. The British had conquered India, the *Jugantar* argued, not through might, as had the Muslims, but through political chicanery and intrigue. The British continued to rule India not because they were strong but because the Indians, lacking in self-confidence and unity let them stay on in India. Despite outward appearances, the foundations of the Empire were actually very weak. The day Indians decided to rise, the Empire would collapse like a house of cards.[10] In another article, *Sedition O Bideshi Raja* (Sedition and the Foreign King) the *Jugantar* challenged the legitimacy of British rule by using the very language of law and right that served as the props of British sovereignty.[11] Since the British had conquered India through treachery, the *Jugantar* argued, their rule lacked ethical and legal basis. As such, the Indians owed them no loyalty. So if the Indians as a nation rejected the rule of the foreign king, they could not be charged with sedition. The *Jugantar* thus challenged both the coercive and legal sovereignty of British rule in India by questioning its might and its legal basis. In short, the *Jugantar* aimed to bring about a transition in the mental world of Bengalis by portraying the British not as colonial masters who commanded respect and loyalty, but as treacherous and hated intruders. It called upon its readers to overcome fear and fight for independence. Independence could only be won and the nation restored to health through a revolutionary uprising.

The *Jugantar* position thus amounted to a fundamental *critique* of the British government. By challenging the legitimacy of British rule in India and mocking its supposed might, the *Jugantar* threatened to undermine its very foundations.

The *Jugantar* message caught the imagination of a population that had already been persuaded by recent events that Bengal needed to chart a new political course if meaningful political change was to be effected in the future. *Jugantar* propaganda was so effective because the ideas that it propagated corresponded to the desires of a sizeable section of Bengalis who were growing increasingly impatient of 'conventional' politics and becoming convinced that political change could only be brought about by radical means.[12] The strong prose and penetrating analyses of the political situation provided a spark to the tinder of raw Bengali emotions. The soaring sales of the newspaper were a testimony to its escalating popularity. By 1907 the paper was selling 7000 copies, a figure that went up to 20,000 soon after.[13] The *Jugantar* ideology was basically addressed to an elite audience that was young, literate and politically radicalized. Implicit in the *Jugantar* writings was the conviction that the need of the hour was for a group of revolutionary leaders who, through its actions would set an example of sacrifice and heroism that, in turn, would inspire the rest of the nation. The *Jugantar*'s role would be to instill self-confidence and love for independence among such a group of potential leaders, recruit them for the cause, and inspire them to commit the ultimate sacrifice for the motherland.[14]

The British administration soon reacted to the danger posed by a vernacular newspaper that was trying to convince its readers of the practicability of overthrowing the government by violent means. After issuing a warning to the paper on 7 June 1907 for publishing articles that used language, which was 'a direct incitement to violence' the government decided to move against the paper by invoking laws designed to combat sedition. Bhupendranath Dutt, the editor and proprietor of the *Jugantar* was arrested in July 1907 and charged under section 124 A of the Indian Penal Code with attempting 'to excite disaffection towards the government of India' for articles published in its issue of 16 June 1907. In response, Bhupendranath Dutt issued a statement claiming sole responsibility for all the articles in question and declaring that 'I have done what I have considered in good faith to be my duty by my country.'[15] Bhupendranath was sentenced to a year's rigorous imprisonment.

The Jugantar's stance was typically defiant. Aurobindo wrote an article entitled *Mithyar Puja* in the *Jugantar* after the arrest of Bhupendranath Dutt in which he declared,

> *Jugantar to Jatiyo bhabshomoshti matro. Loker praner bhitor diya je bhabshrote chhutiyacche tahar ek ekta konamatro Jugantore ashiya dhakka lage. Shampadoke to tahar obhibyaktir jantro matro. Jantroke dhorle jantri to dhora porhe na: jontri je ashariri. Oi je pale pale unmad baloker dal "bande-mataram" mantre mugdho hoiya ajana lokkher dike chhutiyachhe, oi jahara nrimundomalinir kharpar tole atmobolidan dia amaratyer jonyo utshuk – taharai deshe Jugantar anibe; taharai Jugantarer shampadok.*
>
> (Translation: *Jugantor* is the collective emotion of the nation. Each infinite particle of the emotions that race through the arteries of the people touch the *Jugantar.* The editor is merely the organ of its expression. You can catch the organ but not the organ player: the organ player is intangible. Those groups of young lads who, inspired by the mantra of Vande-Mataram, race towards an unknown end, all those who are intent on achieving martyrdom through self-sacrifice at the feet of the Goddess Kali – they will bring about a new age in the country; They are the editors of the *Jugantar.*)[16]

The *Jugantar* trial merely served to strengthen the determination of the *Jugantar* group to spread its message and the paper did nothing to tone down the rhetoric in its future editions. The *Jugantar* best summed up its own position in an article published in April 1908,

> *Ingrej bharatbashir raja nahe.*
> *...Amar desh, amar jati, tahadigake mon khuliya duiti katha bolibo, tumi majhkhane porhiya amar adhikar bhango koribe, manusher nitite eirup ain utthapito hoite pare na.*
>
> (Translation: The English are not the rulers of the Indians. ... [this is] my country, my property, my race, if I speak plainly to them you

> interfere and take away my rights, human ethics cannot mandate such laws.)[17]

This attitude cost the paper dearly. It suffered five more prosecutions that, by July 1908, brought about its financial ruin. *The Newspapers (Incitement to Offenses) Act* of 8 June 1908 also made the position of the paper more vulnerable and ultimately forced it to close down. But persecution served to further precisely those objectives that the government had sought to prevent and that is to arouse in the minds of the readers 'feelings of hostility to the government or a disposition to disobey, resist or subvert its lawful authority.'[18] The trials brought the paper a great deal of publicity and helped greatly in the dissemination of the revolutionary ideology. The letters written by ordinary readers to the *Jugantar* editors bear testimony to the fanatical loyalty that the paper inspired in its readers and the deep impression that the *Jugantar* writings made on them.[19] The *Jugantar*'s achievement was to create a consensus among a significant section of Bengalis on the course of future political action in Bengal. This is not to say that a majority of Bengalis became terrorists, only that revolutionary terrorism as an ideology began to win if not overt, then at least the tacit, support of Bengalis. The British government stepped in once again to tackle a dangerous situation.[20]

Delivering his judgment in the Bhupendranath Dutt Case, the presiding judge, D.H. Kingsford declared 'it is intolerable that ill-advised persons should be permitted to disseminate excitements to violence amongst a class which is only to ready to accept as truthful and authoritative whatever it sees in print.'[21]

The 'class' that Kingsford had in mind was not, in his own words, 'the highly educated classes alone, but also the lower orders and the more ignorant masses of the population.' Whether the *Jugantar* was really aimed at the popular classes is debatable, but the important point here is that the government was aware of the tremendous subversive potential of the printed word in the Bengali language. Kingsford's words, in fact, echoed the traditional sensitivity of the ruling classes towards the vernacular press.[22] The vernacular press alone had the capacity to take politics to the people and this made it a more venerable enemy than the English language press could ever hope to be. The government cracked down on seditious newspaper articles through the *Criminal Law Amendment Act* of June 1908. But the result of government policy was that the seditious press simply went underground. Seditious newspaper articles were simply substituted by seditious pamphlets whose publication the government found impossible to suppress or control. The *Jugantar* pamphlet referred to above was the first of a series from 1908 through 1911 that came to be known as the *Jugantar* pamphlets as they all began with the header *Om Jugantar*. Stray editions continued to appear from 1912 through 1916. From 1910 there began to appear another series of pamphlets that were identified as the *Swadhin Bharat* pamphlets since they all began with the header *Swadhin Bharat*. Both the *Jugantar* and *Swadhin Bharat* series circulated in Calcutta and East Bengal districts. Then, from May 1913 there began to appear a third series, the *Liberty* leaflets, which were published in English.[23] In addition, there appeared and circulated numerous single edition printed, as well as, manuscript pamphlets which were the carriers of subversive propaganda. These pamphlets were sent through the post to schools and colleges, to government officials and pleaders of Bar Libraries and also put up in public places.

Revolutionary pamphlets were deeply influenced by the *Jugantar* example both in the way that they conceptualized politics and in the rhetorical techniques that they employed. Their intention was to propagate the idea of a violent revolution. It was this emphasis on violence that distinguished the revolutionary press from the established press and drew forth a near hysterical response from the British government. This violence had a functional purpose and a symbolic meaning, both of which were deeply disruptive of the continuance of hegemonic British rule in India. The functional or instrumental purpose of political violence was transparent. It was to bring about a change in the political arena. The revolutionary terrorists argued that violence was the only effective means of achieving independence for India. For Aurobindo Ghose, the inspirational leader of the movement, revolutionary terrorism had only a limited role to play in his larger scheme of bringing about an open armed uprising in India. According to him,

> Revolutionary terrorism was only a subordinate movement. It could have been important when the armed revolution would have come ...This terroristic movement was to prepare the young men to have some sort of a military training, to kill and get killed.[24]

Barin Ghose in his confessions before a police official expressed roughly similar views. Thus Barin claimed that he did not believe that political murders would bring about the desired regeneration of the motherland. They were means to educate the people for facing death and doing anything for the country's sake.[25] But the violence of revolutionary terrorism had a symbolic or expressive purpose as well. Scholars have pointed out that the expressive function of acts and images of violence draws potency from the probability that all those involved – the perpetrators, the recipients and the witnesses – however different their cultural backgrounds, are able to draw at least some common meaning from the acts and images involved. This fact, together with the visibility of violence, makes it an excellent communicative tool.[26]

From this perspective it may be said that the violence of revolutionary terrorism was also being used to communicate a political message. This message concerned the distribution of power and authority in society. Implicit in violence is the idea that the perpetrator of violence wields power over the recipient. Absolute violence as exemplified by assassinations or killings is thus symbolic of the absolute power that the perpetrator seeks to exercise over the recipient. Violence wreaked by colonized subjects on the colonial masters was symbolic of a negation of (inversion) existing power relations. In the colonial dispensation, the exercise of power by the colonial masters meant, in practice, the maintenance of order and discipline, obsequious acceptance of colonial authority and unquestioned obedience to colonial laws. Acts of revolutionary terrorism inverted this very order of things and was indicative of the will to exercise political sovereignty. The identity of the British as the rulers and of the Bengali as ruled, was sought to be erased and a new set of identities put in place. Political revolutionary terrorism thus involved an exercise of the will to power.

This symbolic understanding of power, so evident in the *Jugantar* writings that have been sampled above, was also central to pamphlet literature. It was this will to political sovereignty, communicated through the violence that was being propagandized, that formed the matrix of meaning within which the corpus of pamphlet literature took shape.

But in order to propagandize violence, it was necessary first to legitimize it. It is a truism to point out that there is a deep ambivalence about violence in every culture. Indian culture was no exception. Ancient Indian philosophical texts, even while they expounded on the sacredness of life, nevertheless accepted violence as an inevitable feature of Hindu existence which they sought to normalize and justify. As Bhikhu Parekh points out

> The two Hindu epics freely acknowledged not only the necessity, but also the desirability of political and military violence, and their heroes, who are both incarnations of God, engage in and justify massive acts of violence. In the Gita, which is a part of Mahabharata, the Lord himself makes out a formidable philosophical case for the use of violence to combat injustice.[27]

The need to legitimize or justify violence clearly stems from the ambivalence about violence that is common to most cultures.[28] It was a problem that the revolutionary terrorists also had to contend with. Politically too, the terrorists had to contend with other political groups, notably the moderates and the extremists, both of whom opposed violence in political life. In order to counter the influence of the latter the terrorist revolutionaries first had to make violence acceptable as a political method to public opinion. The pamphlets adopted a variety of rhetorical mechanisms through which they sought to build up a community of consensus around the idea of violence.

To put across their ideas as simply and clearly as possible within the constraints of space imposed by the pamphlets, as well as to underline the legitimacy of their political position, the pamphleteers relied on the technique of contrasting dual sets of opposed images. One set of images was represented as everything that was good and virtuous, and then contrasted with the second set that was its mirror opposite. In other words, the nationalist self-image as conceived of by the pamphlet writers, was constructed by contrasting it with its Other. In the Manichean view of reality presented through these images, the reader had no trouble distinguishing between the good and the bad, the legitimate and the illegitimate. The struggle for independence was represented as a 'conflict ... between virtue in its full glory, armed with the Might of Justice and Freedom, and vice with a drooping body.'[29] The bearers of this virtue were the patriotic *santans* (sons) who had taken a vow to sacrifice their lives for the motherland and the *brahmagyanees* or the army of saints who had acquired valuable insights into cosmic consciousness. The representatives of vice were the white *rakshashas* (demons) or the debauched and demoniac *firinghis*.[30] The demons were the products of a materialistic and decadent civilization that had made use of their unlimited reservoirs of cunning and stratagem to destroy a spiritual people with an ancient and glorious philosophical tradition. But while the former were dissipating their strengths in the enjoyment of worldly pleasures, the latter were emerging from the stupor and slavery of centuries and with their resurgence the ancient land would soon regain her status as the spiritual leader or Guru of the world. The future belonged to the east, and particularly to India.[31]

> *Ekta bishal shoktiprobaho shakoler agyatoshare abanato jatishomuhoke unnoto korite pashchatyo hoite prachyabhimukhe aashitechhe ebong bodh hoy taha bharote protighato hoiya karmogyan o bhaktir bidyutjhaloke bishwe bichchhurito hoiya prachyo hoite prashchatye kolyan o shantir bani niya chhutibe.*

> (Translation: Unnoticed by all, an immense wave of energy is flowing from the west to the east to raise up the degraded races, and it appears that dashing against India, it will radiate in the glory of knowledge and spirituality all over the world, and carry the message of peace and beneficence from the east to the west.)[32]

Especially striking are the spatial and temporal contrasts that were embedded in these images. The West was associated with all that was superficial and decadent while the East was celebrated as the abode of spirituality and wisdom.[33] Time was also represented not as a smoothly flowing secular movement but broken up into sharply delineated periods of past, present and future, which were then sharply juxtaposed against each other. Thus was India's glorious past when 'she was first in philosophy and first in civilization' distinguished from the shameful present when the country was likened to a cremation ground. The present was however described as an interlude for the 'land of the rishis (sages)' was destined for greatness in the future.[34]

The idiom of expression in a majority of pamphlets was purely religious. Time was depicted as the unfolding of the will of Providence and all events that occurred within this framework were divinely ordained.

> *Kaler bherir protikulacharan kono din kritokarjo hoite pare nai, paribeo na. Janio jagater jabotiyo ghatona ekta naishorgik niyame shadhito hoy ebang shamosto jamniyomshashon ekjon mongolmoi bidhata ekjon sharboshaktiman niyamoker icchadhin.*
>
> (Translation: Resistance to the knell sounded by time has never proved successful. Know that all the events of this world are guided by a natural law, and all punishments and rules are subject to the wishes of a beneficent Providence, an all-powerful ruler.)[35]

The religious idiom used for the expression of ideas helped to harness primal emotions to the idea of independence and served a useful integrative function by helping to transcend divisions of caste and class.[36] It was also a skilful rhetorical device. If a struggle for independence against the British was divinely foreordained, then human will was powerless to prevent it. One could go further and argue that it was a religious duty to act as an instrument of God's will and participate in such a struggle. The readers could identify with, and legitimately be a part of what was represented as a righteous war (*dharmayuddha*) between heathens and true devotees and where, moreover, it was divinely ordained that the righteous would triumph.

> When the destructive sword of Providence is raised against the head of the oppressor, can it be in the power of anybody to check its fall?[37]

To build a consensus around the idea that the struggle for independence was justified was the less difficult part of the process of mobilizing public support for the revolutionary terrorist movement. To large sections of the Bengali public the position was not even debatable. Here the pamphlets simply reiterated the *Jugantar* line:

> *Amra chai bharoter swatontro; bharotbashir sharirik, manoshik, adhyattkik, shorbangyin swadhinata. Amra chai shotodhabichhinno bibhinno shamprodaye bibhokto bharotbashir eikyo bandhan. Ar? Ar chai abaidho upaye protishthito bideshiyo odhikarer ucchhed-shadhon o engraj borjito Bharatborshe swarajyo sthapon.*
>
> (Translation: We want independence: the physical, mental, spiritual, total independence of Indians. We want the unity of Indians who are disunited and divided into diverse communities. And? And we want the uprooting of the illegally enforced rights of the foreigner and the establishment of self rule in India freed from the English.)[38]

Far more controversial were the means that the terrorists advocated in achieving independence. Having declared the political goal, namely, the acquisition of independence, the pamphlets next went on to delineate the method of acquiring independence.

> *...[J]atodin na shay (Bharatborsho) prochur shoktishali hoiya balapurbak ingrajer hasto hoite apnar shashon dwando kariya laye tato din ingraj bharotborsho ke shwayottwoshashoner anodhikari –i janibe.*
>
> (Translation: ...[T]he English will not acknowledge Indians as entitled to self-government till India becomes abundantly powerful and snatches away her own scepter of government from their hands by force.)[39]

And here lay the crux of the problem. The pamphleteers had to contend with their political opponents who were opposed to the use of violence to achieve political ends. As a *Swadhin Bharat* leaflet put it,

> *Amra chai swadhinata. Kobi, shahitwik, ukil, daktar, kerani, byabshadar – emon ki gupto police porjyonto e kothar protibad korte parena. Gol hoitechhe upae loiya.*

> (Translation: We want independence. The poet, litterateur, lawyer, clerk, and businessman – even the secret police cannot protest against this. The debate is over the method.)[40]

Several pamphlets made the point that it was but natural that the British should regard the true patriots as their enemies but it was unfortunate that sections of their own countrymen should denounce those who were prepared to sacrifice their lives for the country as murderers, sinners and deviants. It was the latter who needed to be educated about the true state of affairs in the country. Therefore, one of the primary objectives of the revolutionary terrorist pamphlets was to legitimize the use of violence as a way of achieving political ends.

In the process of framing public meaning for the politics they sought to propagandize, the pamphlet writers cleverly made use of cultural symbols to serve as political tools. The pamphlets made repeated use of certain arguments, images, stories, figures and messages that had deep resonance in Indian society as they were drawn from the rich reservoir of Indian mythology, philosophy, religion, history and contemporary politics, to convey their thoughts, ideas and emotions to their readers. These symbols and leitmotifs may be regarded as cultural codes that were repositories of meanings and associations, which were easily recognizable to the readers of propaganda. The pamphlet writers made use of these meanings and associations, which they simplified, clarified, reproduced, manipulated, legitimated and interpreted to get across their political message. Through the use of these themes the pamphlet writers deftly built bridges of communication with their readers. Political ideas could be simply and effectively conveyed through the use of metaphors, analogies and imagery because these rhetorical devices made it easier to influence emotions and mobilize the imagination, without which it would not have been possible to gain popular support for revolutionary terrorism. The common logic, which held together these different arguments and multiform images in a single system, was the need to legitimize violence.

Many pamphlets reiterated the *Jugantar* argument that the only path to national regeneration lay in the attainment of independence. Loss of independence had led to a state of *dharmahinata* i.e., a state of apathy and torpor in which irreligion thrived and evil ruled. The British were not ruling India as a favour to the Indians. Rather the oppressiveness and rapacity of British rule were draining the country of its lifeblood and reducing it to a mere skeleton of its ancient glorious self. Moreover, the British had not shown the slightest inclination to heed the 'prayers and petitions' of patriotic Indians. On the contrary, when the Indians had sought to protest the oppressive and unjust acts of the British government, notably the Partition of Bengal, the British had reacted with violence.[41] The revolutionary nationalist perception of British policy was ably summarized as follows:

> *Bhuliya jao deshbashi je ingrej tomader swayottoshashon dibar jonyo rajdando skandhe bahan koritechhe. Bhuliya jao tomader dhan sampad gyanbidyay bibhushito koribar jonyo ingraj broto grohon koriyachhe, she oti swarthopor she oti chotur, chirojuger deboshatru mahadaitya. Tahar binash tomay koritei hoibe, debobhumi bharoter she dashrupe niyojito hoibe.*
>
> (Translation: Do not delude yourselves, my compatriots, that the British are bearing the heavy burden of administration (*rajdondo*) to ultimately give you independence. Do not delude yourself that the British are sworn to flood this land with riches and knowledge. They are extremely selfish, extremely manipulative, the eternal enemy of the gods, the great demon. You must destroy them, they will be reduced to slavery in this land of the gods - Bharat.)[42]

The pamphlets further argued that leaders who denounced revolutionary nationalism did so not because they were repulsed by violence or inspired by the ideal of universal love, but because they were cowards and sycophants. One pamphlet thus commented ironically that those Indians who lamented the murder of one human being had only to look at those whose views they repeated and then keep silent. The real murderers were those, whose oppressive policies had reduced *lakhs* [43]of men and women to starvation and led the country along the path of ruin.[44]

Many of the pamphlets made the point that since the British had conquered India through deceit and treachery, the claim of the colonial rulers that the revolutionaries were trying to subvert a legally established government did not hold water. One pamphlet woefully recounted the story of the sad reversal of fortunes whereby the English, who had set foot in this land as petty traders, had gradually established their suzerainty over its three hundred million inhabitants. It alluded to the Battle of Plassey of 1857 when the treacherous Clive had come together with the treasonous Mir Zafar to depose Siraj-ud-daulah from his throne. The Battle of Buxar, where Mir Kasim had been defeated by the English, had completed the process whereby Bengal came under the control of the British.

The pamphlet then referred to the misdeeds of Hastings, who brought about the ruination of many Indian rulers through his machinations. The Brahmin King Nanda Kumar, the pamphlet pointed out, had also fallen victim to the ire of the former because he had tried to defend the hapless weavers of the country from the rapacity of the English traders. Finally the robber Dalhousie, had completed the process of spoliation of the Indian rulers through his 'Doctrine of Lapse'. And these were the examples of English ethics and bravery, the pamphlet rhetorically proclaimed. These were the legal methods by which the English had established their empire in India! The message that the pamphlet conveyed was that since the British Empire rested on foundations of chicanery and force, the British could not expect or demand loyalty from their Indian subjects.[45]

The pamphlets also claimed that it had been amply demonstrated time and again that petitioning the British for reform or even passive resistance would serve no purpose. As one pamphlet pointed out,

> *Bangalar koti koti niriho proja jakhon bangobhanger birudhdhhe ain shangoto protibad koriachhilo takhon ki ingrajraj mado-garbo bhare she protibad upekkhha pradorshon koriya gurutoro aporadh koren nai?*
>
> ...
>
> *Ardhhoshatobarsho jaboth ain shangato andolon koriya desher abhab obhijog ingrajer karnogochar kara hoitechhe; kintu desher mongolshadhone ingrajke kakhono udyogi dekhiyachho ki?*
>
> (Translation: Did not the English commit a heinous crime in arrogantly dismissing the constitutional agitation of the millions of Bengalis against the Partition of Bengal?
>
> ...
>
> The English are being apprised of the woes of the country through constitutional agitation for fifty years; but have you ever seen the English take any initiative for the welfare of the country?)[46]

Since constitutional agitation had failed, the pamphleteers maintained that what was needed was active resistance or the use of force. To use force for the cause of independence was not anarchism. The loss of independence had dehumanized the country. Once independence was achieved, the country would be restored to dignity and prosperity. As for the contention that revolutionary terrorism was a cowardly way of trying to win independence, and that open warfare would be more befitting, the pamphlets had this to say,

> *Je bhiru kapurush mlechchho barbar jati bharotbashir astro-shastro durer katha dughdhoposhyo baloker hater lathikhana porjonto karhiya niyachhe emon murkho ke achhe je tahader kaman banduker guligolar kachhe prokashyo juddhe pran dan korite jaibe?*
>
> (Translation: When a fear-stricken, cowardly, unclean and barbarous race has deprived all Indians of their weapons, indeed snatched away even the *lathis* (sticks) of very young boys, who is that fool who will go to die in open warfare against their cannons, guns and bullets?)[47]

The summary of these various arguments was that it was British policy that had left right thinking Indians with no option other than to use violence as the sole way of achieving independence.

> Amra bahubar boliachhi abar boli ingrajer karjokalapei bangalir prane rakto-pipasha jagiachhe.
>
> (Translation: We have said it numerous times, we say this again, the activities of the English have made the Bengalis hungry for blood.)[48]

The pamphleteers sought to back up their political arguments by seeking sanction for their activities from the teachings of Indian philosophy. Thus, the pamphlets reiterated the widely held philosophical conviction that preservation and destruction were both inevitable and unavoidable in existence and sometimes an act of destruction could also be desirable.

> Preservation on the one side and destruction on the other, cherishing on the one side and killing on the other, draining away on the one side and nourishing on the other – this is the law of nature. So we have a right to commit murders given us by Providence. We must destroy those whose fortunes have been built up on our ruin, ... whose riches consist in our poverty......A nation which has a separate country, religion and society must for ever do battle in order to keep its own individuality unimpaired.[49]

Immanent in virtually all of the pamphlets was the philosophy propounded in the *Gita,* which may be described as the philosophical guide book of the terrorists. The figure of the all knowing and all powerful Sri Krishna, who helped the Pandavas destroy the Kauravas so as to bring about the establishment of a *dharmarajya,* or righteous world, became the iconic hero of the terrorists. Many of the *Jugantar* pamphlets begin with the famous verse of the *Gita* where the Lord Sri Krishna informs Arjuna,

> Whenever virtue declines and iniquity flourishes, O Bharat, I incarnate myself. For the deliverance of the virtuous and the destruction of the wicked and the maintenance of virtue, I come into being in every age.[50]

The *Jugantar* pamphlets repeatedly referred to the incident on the battle site of Kurukshetra when Arjuna was initially reluctant to slaughter his relatives in battle but awoke to a sense of his true duty following the Lord Sri Krishna's words of advice to him.[51] Sri Krishna had persuaded Arjuna to carry out his duties as a *khatriya* (warrior) by pointing out that true *dharma* consisted in upholding the cause of truth, virtue and justice without being swayed by one's personal feelings or motivated by expectations of personal gain. So also, true patriots – who were the *khatriyas* or warriors of the hour – had to do their duty by their motherland. If the nation's sons did not rush to the defence of their mother, then who would protect her?

Imagining and representing the nation as mother carried with it tremendous emotional potency which the pamphlets ably exploited. This image of the mother-nation as mother was not, of course, a creation of the revolutionary pamphlets. This image of *Bangamata* had gradually taken shape in the works of poets, artists and literary writers from the late nineteenth century, notable among whom were Bankimchandra Chattopadhyay, Rabindranath Tagore and Abanindranath Tagore. This figure captured the nationalist imagination and it became perhaps the most widely used cultural symbol in the nationalist movement in Bengal. This gendered image has also attracted the interest of historians who have tried to unravel the many intertwined meanings latent in this image and have sought to understand their implications for determining the shape of Bengali political culture from the late nineteenth century.[52] This image, in which the Bengalis had invested so much emotional energy, obviously had tremendous propaganda value and the pamphlets sought to extract maximum political leverage from their use of this figure.

It might be recalled here that Bankimchandra Chattopadhyay's novel *Anandamath*[53], another work of seminal importance for the revolutionary terrorists and indeed the whole of the nationalist movement, and itself a brilliant work of literary propaganda, had presented three contrasted images of the mother-nation. The first figure was that of the mother in the past, an extraordinary figure of luminous beauty, limitless prosperity and incredible strength – mother in her Jagathdhatri (nurturer of the world) image. This image was contrasted with the terrifying icon of mother in the present, mother in her image of Kali, clad only in a necklace of skulls, brooding, shrouded in darkness and trampling underfoot the figure of Shiva – her husband and wielding the club (*khetak*) and human skull (*kharpar*). This image is then transcended by that of the ten-handed warrior-goddess Durga,[54] wielding the weapons of war, with her enemy at her feet, riding the lion, yet radiant, serene and domesticated because she is accompanied by her children – the image of the mother as she will be in the glorious future.

It is immediately apparent that in Bankimchandra's work, the nation is imagined not through the body of an earthly mother but through the more polysemic figure of the mother-goddess. This form allows the existence of several apparently disparate meanings within a single image. When imagined as a mother, this figure is the embodiment of womanly virtues, nurturing, comforting, domesticated and deserving of protection, while as goddess she is the repository of primordial energy or *Shakti*. In her latter form, she transcends the weakness that is traditionally associated with the figure of woman and instead becomes all powerful, capable not only of nurture but also of destruction, and demanding of the devotion of her sons. The figure of the mother-goddess was an integral part of the chain of imagination that went into the making of the nationalist narrative. In this narrative, the nation was conceptualized as a fraternal compact, a league among sons.[55] Bengali cultural mores lay a premium on the sons' duty to protect the mother and also to give her unquestioned obedience. It followed therefore, that in the nationalist narrative, the task of freeing the mother-nation from foreign bondage fell on the sons who were also responsible for carrying out her will.

The pamphlets, which were very much a part of this framework of political imagination, utilized the plural meanings that inhered in the figure of the mother-goddess to spread their message. In the earlier *Jugantar* pamphlets, the nation is most often imagined as goddess and is invariably represented in her more terror-inspiring forms, as Kalika, Ranochandi, Rudrani, Chondika, Karali, – the wreaker of revenge and the destroyer of evil. Reeling under the twin blows of the Maniktala garden raids[56] and the closure of the *Jugantar* press, the terrorists hit back in anger with the early *Jugantar* pamphlets of 1908–10. The dominant theme of the latter is blood-curling threats of revenge. The mother-goddess was represented as thirsting for blood, a thirst that could only be quenched by drinking the blood of the white invaders. It was the duty of the sons to provide the mother with this blood. Agency, or the will to power was wielded by the mother figure while the sons were represented as merely carrying out her will. The legitimacy of violence stemmed from the single fact of the mother-goddess commanding such violence.

By contrast, the *Swadhin Bharat* and the other (including the later *Jugantar*) pamphlets that followed after, manipulated the meanings associated with the figure of the mother-goddess in multiple ways. The dual images intertwined in this figure were separated and then made to convey meanings that legitimized the idea of violence in very different ways. In many of these pamphlets the nation was imagined through the figure of a real, earth-bound mother. This mother was invariably portrayed as a desolate figure – humiliated, insulted, exploited, and what was worse, betrayed by her sons, who stood by, while their mother suffered untold abuse at the hands of the white devils. The pamphlets rued this state of affairs, and in tones that were variously exhortatory, pleading or contemptuous, called upon the sons to put an end to the suffering of the mother.

> *Tomar desh, tomar swadhinata, tomar dhan, tomar jan, tomar jiban parjanto apaharan koriya je shwetango doshyu tomar janonir bakkhosthale bhishon tandab nrityo koritechhe tomra tetrish koti bharotbashi, arya-rishi santan, Bhimarjuner bangshodhar idrisho bhishan atyachar ar katokal shajhyo koribe?*
>
> (Translation: Those white robbers who dance on the breast of your mother after having snatched away your country, your independence, your wealth, your relatives, your lives even, you 33 *koti*[57]Indians, sons of Arya Rishis, descendants of Bhima and Arjuna, how much longer are you going to tolerate this inhuman torture?)[58]

Other female figures, which appeared prominently within this gendered framework, were that of sisters, wives and daughters. The pamphlets frequently referred to the constant threat that the colonial invasion posed to the preservation of the chastity and dignity of Bengali women.[59] These female figures, though lower down in the hierarchy of obedience and devotion within the traditional Hindu joint family, were nevertheless culturally privileged concepts.[60] Traditional notions of familial responsibility enjoined that since sisters, daughters and wives were as dependent on the male members of the family as the mother was, it was the duty of any male with an iota of self-respect, to protect them from dishonour. In their use of familial metaphors, the pamphlets drew upon deeply held cultural notions of familial duty to legitimize the use of violence in the cause of independence.

In the cases cited above, violence was being legitimized through its representation as familial duty, a sentiment which most middle class Bengali men, reared in the traditional cultural mores of devotion and responsibility to family, could readily identify with. But, as pointed out earlier, the mother-nation could also be represented as a figure with greater agency, capable of bending her sons to her will. Thus, the figure of the mother was frequently invoked in the pamphlets in her incarnation of mother-goddess, a figure shown as demanding that her sons carry out the reversal of the great wrong that had earlier been committed, when the mother-nation had been placed in bondage. For example, as in the following pamphlet

> *Tomapekhha shrishtisthiti prolaykarini mahashakti mahakali bishesh jane – kebol tumi tnahar karmer shahay hao – phalapholer bhar shab tnahar – tumi kebal apnake matrijogye utsargo koriya nishchinto hao.*
>
> (Translation: The creator, preserver and destroyer, the wielder of great strength, Mahakali knows better than you do – Your role is to help in her work–the results are up to her – rest easy in sacrificing yourself at the altar of your mother's sacrificial ceremony.)[61]

In some of these pamphlets again, agency cannot be attributed to any one figure, for the figures of the mother and the *santans* are collapsed into one, as are the figures of Lord Krishna and the mother goddess. For example,

> *nagonya ingraj – swadhinata prarthi santan-charone chirapronato Shib tumi.*
>
> (Translation: You insignificant English! You are but the eternally prostate Shiva lying at the feet of the *santans* who are aspiring towards independence.)[62]
>
> Or
>
> *Eibar ranochandir ranoranga. He santan. Prostut hao, shahoshe hriday drirho karo, aj parthosarothi swayam ashwer balga dhoriya jayer pathe rath chhutaiyachhen, tumi nishchinto mone tahar netritwe kebol tomar kartavya koriya jao.*

> (Translation: Now is the time for the war-dance of Ranochandi. *Santans*! Be prepared, strengthen your hearts with courage, today Parthosarothi himself has harnessed his horse and raced his chariot on the path of victory, just perform your duties with confidence under his leadership.)[63]

What is striking, however, is that violence was not sought to be legitimized in these later pamphlets as an act of revenge alone – to be inflicted by the true sons of the motherland on the invaders. The pamphleteers were obviously constrained by the possibility that the idea of revenge might not go down too well with an audience hitherto unfamiliar with political violence. In an exceedingly adept move, the pamphlets instead sought to represent the act of violence as an act of self-sacrifice committed by sons in the service of the motherland. Within this representation, the targets of violence were no longer its victims. Instead, victimhood was displaced on to the perpetrators of violence. Through an expert manipulation of images and meanings the revolutionaries were represented as the victims of providence, for divine fate decreed that they had to give up their lives for the mother.

> *Tai boli, de buker rakto de – mar mongol ichchha phiraiya an – jukti nai, tarko nai, bichar nai, achar nai, pap nai, punya nai – ke achho matribhakto tuchchho jibon diye mar mongol icchha phiraiya ano.*
>
> (Translation: So I say, give your heart's blood – bring back the desire for your mother's welfare - (there is no room for) logic, debate, deliberation, rites, sin, piety- all those who are devotees of the mother, bring back the desire for your mother's welfare with (the sacrifice of) your insignificant lives.)[64]

Anthropologists like René Girard[65] have pointed out that the act of sacrifice was designed to restore or preserve consensus in a community that was or threatened to be, fractured by violence between conflicting groups. In the pamphlets, the act of sacrifice was conceived as a way of preserving consensus in a community divided by political revolutionary terrorism. Thus, through the representation of revolutionary terrorists as willing victims of sacrifice, one moreover that was divinely decreed, the pamphleteers sought to tone down the more aggressive portrayals of the revolutionaries. Instead, they put in place stereotypes that were less controversial, and hence more acceptable to the general population. The motive was to build up bridges of empathy between the political terrorists and the audience they so sought to impress.

History could also be harnessed to the ideological project of wresting independence through violence. History, as recorded by the pamphlet writers, served one function of overwhelming importance–it revealed the inevitability of the present. The present, in turn, cleared the path to the future, a future that had already been decreed by providence. The dynamic that propelled all history was divine will.

This point of view, for instance, was clearly evident in the English-language *Liberty* pamphlet titled *Liberty*: 4 May 1857.[66] The pamphlet began by saying that the Indian War of Independence (Revolt of 1857) was apparently a failure because it could not bring about any material changes in the body politic of the Indian Nation. But then it noted that 'strange are the ways of Providence, and in His evolution, things seldom happen according to man's tastes and desires.' The pamphlet continued that a nation that had to play a prominent part in the history of the world had first to undergo penances and sufferings for only then could nations become fit instruments to carry out His Will. The consequences of the rising of 1857 were thus a burden that the Indian Nation had to bear in order to be reborn as a Great United Nation—not merely as Hindu and Islamic Kingdoms. The pamphlet went on to say that those who had made a clear study of the present day history of India were not only optimistic in foreseeing an independent India, but positively believed in a free Indian Empire having already been built over the ruins of British India. In this view of the relationship between the past, the present and the future, there was little room for the operation of contingency or the exercise of free will, for all was foreordained. As summarized by one propagandist, 'the present is a reaction to the past and a witness to the future.'[67]

The implication of this argument was that it was foolish, because it was impossible to resist the flow of events that had been set in motion by the Omniscient Being. Rather, all true patriots should look towards history to try and divine the lessons that history could provide them with. According to the above mentioned pamphlet again, Indians had learnt well the lessons of the immediate past.

> Ever since the saintly, nay the angelic action of Lord Curzon, i.e., the Partition of Bengal, India has been progressing by leaps and bounds. The Nation does not now believe in representations, and has no faith in the promises of the alien government, and realizes fully well that the liberty of the Indian people is to be achieved by the efforts and sacrifices of India's own sons. We believe in the teachings of the Lord

> Himself – that the Kshatriyas must slay the foes of their Motherland as their duty and they do it without sin.

Nothing was left to chance, for as the pamphlet pointed out 'Revolution has never been the work of men. It is always God's will that has worked through instruments.' Once revolutionary terrorism was represented as the implementation of God's Will and thus imbued with religious sanction, revolutionary terrorists were freed from the responsibility of having to explain their acts of violence to public opinion.

The past had other lessons to yield as well. The British, as the pamphleteers repeatedly pointed out, had conquered Bengal not through courage and physical strength, but through stratagem and cunning. Disgracefully, the Bengalis were also implicated in this sordid story. In their greed for wealth and power, traitors like Mir Zafar had sold out their country to the British. The pamphlets then went on to observe that the time for expatiation of past sins had arrived. The land that the Bengalis had handed over to the enemies had to be wrested back by any means necessary – through violence if need be. History was replete with examples of heroes who had fought and died to defend and protect their land from foreign invaders. The names that figured prominently in the list were those of much loved popular heroes like Shivaji, Guru Gobind, Rana Pratap, Pratapaditya, all of whom had fought against rulers of mighty empires. The political lesson that the pamphlets sought to impart was that if the former could have triumphed over impossible odds, so could the revolutionary terrorists.[68] The pamphlets also made compulsory obeisance to the memory of dead martyrs like Khudiram Bose and Prafulla Chaki. They reminded their readers that there were many other patriots suffering in British jails, or pining for home, as they languished in exile in distant lands. While some pamphlets argued that the martyrs had to be avenged, others lamented that if the work of these martyrs was not completed and the fight for independence was abandoned midway, all their sacrifices would have been in vain.[69]

Meaning and messages could also be conveyed through the telling and retelling of stories. A favoured technique of propagandists was to make allusions to mythological tales and figures. Mythological heroes personified values that were held sacrosanct by the community. In the telling of these stories, this meaning could be evoked to get across political messages. The pamphleteers chose their stories well, and through their adept use of analogies they left little room for disagreement as to the justness of their mission. By pointing to the similarities in dynamics that propelled events as well as the similarity of motives that guided the actions of heroes, both in the mythological past and in the present, the pamphlets attempted to justify the violence of political revolutionary terrorism.

Thus the pamphlets were liberally interspersed with references to incidents from the *Mahabharata* and the *Ramayana* to make the point that violence was sometimes inevitable to uphold the cause of truth and justice. One pamphlet referred to the Kaurava king Duryodhan's refusal to hand over to the Pandavas even the little land that could be accommodated on the point of a needle, thus forcing the Pandavas to wage war in order to regain their birthright. The implication clearly was that since all the efforts of the Indians to secure independence from the British through peaceful means had proved to be fruitless, the former were perfectly justified in resorting to violent means to reclaim what was rightfully theirs.[70]

The example of the great hero Ramchandra from the Ramayana was also used to sanctify the act of violence. Thus one pamphlet pointed out that Ramchandra, despite being a god, endowed with supernatural wisdom and strength and despite being armed, had secretly assassinated Bali, King of the Monkeys. The point was to show, the pamphlet argued, that humans while fighting beasts and *Khatriyas*[71] while fighting non-*Khatriyas* could resort to assassinations without causing any outrage to religion. Referring to the dictates of Manu, the ancient Hindu lawgiver, the pamphlet further argued that only a duly anointed *Khatriya* could be regarded as God's representative on earth. If the king was a *mlecchha* (barbarian) all *jatis* (castes), from the Brahman to the untouchable, had the right to assassinate him. That was the highest *dharma* for all Hindus.[72]

Another leitmotif in the pamphlets was the wars that had been waged in the mythological past to repulse evil and uphold the cause of truth. Inevitably truth and goodness had won. The pamphlets are replete with references to stories from Puranic mythology like the victory of the boy Prahlada over the demon Hiranyakashyipu, the battle waged by the gods against the demon brothers Shundo-Upashundo, the destruction of Illal and Batapi by the great sage Agastya, the defeat of the evil Kauravas at the hands of the good Pandavas in the great war of Kurukshetra, and the destruction of the demon king Ravana by Ramchandra. All of these stories went to bolster the central contention that violence that was intended to restore the right order of things was not only acceptable but also desirable. Many pamphlets expressed the conviction that with the blood of such heroes coursing through their veins, the Indians would not hesitate to rise against the demons-incarnate that is, the English, thus proving all over again that they were the worthy descendants of their great ancestors.[73]

The revolutionary pamphlets, as pointed out earlier, had the immediate aim of trying to persuade their readers of the legitimacy of violence as a political strategy. Violence, or to be more precise, tactics with which to strike terror into the minds of opponents of superior strength were not unknown in Indian history. Terror tactics have been part of the repertoire of violent practices that most cultures have at their disposal. But the violence of revolutionary terrorism preached by the pamphleteers had to be integrated into the discourse of early twentieth century Bengali nationalism from which it was noticeably absent. Hence, the importance of cultural narratives that had carried forth the memories and meanings of violence over the ages and that helped to make political violence familiar and more acceptable to public opinion. But these narratives had also to be adapted to meet the needs of the political moment. The refashioning of religious symbols and icons is a case in point.

Scholars have repeatedly drawn our attention to the fact that violence occupies a central place in religion. While violence in religion can have a symbolic dimension, it is equally true that religion can serve to legitimate real violence for a worldly cause like seizure of political power.[74] Herein lies the political power of religion. The pamphleteers exploited this resource skillfully to advance their aims. The pamphleteers derived sanction for the violence they advocated from age-old religious symbols and icons. But at the same time they manipulated the meanings of these symbols to make them more effective in the contemporary sociopolitical context. Thus if the figure of the mother-goddess symbolized the concept of *adhya-shakti* or primordial power, which was a dominant theme in ancient Indian religious texts, the recurrent images of a humiliated and suffering mother in the revolutionary texts appeared to be more in harmony with contemporary notions of womanly behaviour and were an apt representation of the position that the nation-as-mother occupied in the nationalist imagination. Again, by emphasizing the element of sacrifice in the actions of the revolutionary heroes, the pamphlets attempted to sanitize the violence of terrorist action by portraying it as a metaphor for a religious ritual. This textual mechanism was intended to make revolutionary terrorism more acceptable to public opinion.

The issue of integrating violence as a legitimate technique into the political discourse of early twentieth century Bengal is connected with a larger question that has been the subject of speculation among scholars, namely, whether revolutionary terrorism, as a technique and ideology was a foreign import that was grafted onto the body of Indian political ideologies. Ashis Nandy, following Rabindranath Tagore, has argued that revolutionary terrorism formed part of a process of cultural cooptation typical of colonial societies, whereby the colonized sought to become more like the colonizers by mimicking western colonial ideas of hyper-masculinity that was alien to their own culture. Stung by colonial aspersions of effeminacy and cowardliness, they sought to redeem their manliness by adopting colonial stereotypes that identified masculinity with 'violent power play and tough politics'. Harking back to the past, the revolutionaries recovered the supposedly ancient Indian ideal of Kshatriyahood or 'martial Indianness' which was used to justify this form of violent protest against colonialism.[75] If one were to accept the thesis of Ashis Nandy that the very idea of violent protest as embodied in revolutionary terrorism was the result of internalization of certain western cultural stereotypes, it follows that the immediate influences on the revolutionaries must have been those of western political theorists who advocated the idea of violence. Historians have written about the influence of Young Italy, particularly of Mazzini, the Irish nationalists and the European anarchists on the revolutionary nationalists.[76] Other historians like Peter Heehs have however maintained that revolutionary terrorism 'was a natural and indigenous response to British imperial domination' and that the revolutionaries were influenced by foreign examples only in a very superficial way. The revolutionaries were not part of an international group of conspirators and they would have developed their doctrines and organization in much the same way even if they had never made contacts with foreign revolutionaries. He quotes Upendrananth Banerjee, member of the Jugantar group of revolutionaries who had written in his memoirs that '[T]he same forces that had brought about revolutions in Italy, Poland and Ireland and other countries were operating in India as well and drove some people into daring and violent paths.'[77]

The propaganda pamphlets are of great value in helping us to gauge the kind of influences that inspired and energized the revolutionaries. Books recovered from libraries of the secret *samities* or found in the private possession of revolutionaries in the course of police raids give us an idea of the kind of political indoctrination that the revolutionaries underwent in the course of their training. A large number of books were found at the search of the Anushilan Samiti headquarters in Dacca in November 1908. A complete catalogue of the Anushilan Library was also found, together with a Library issue book which gave an idea of the kind of literature that was popular with the members of the

Samiti. 'Seditious and revolutionary' books were greatly requested. Thus books like *Jaliat Clive* (Clive the forger), a reference to the treacherous methods by which the British won Bengal, *Pratap Singh*, *Sikher Balidan* (the martyrdom of the Sikhs) and *Chatrapati Shivaji*, historical novels that glorified the exploits of the Rajputs, the Sikhs and the Marathas against the Mughals were in great demand. *Mukti Kon Pathe* (*Which Way Lies Liberty*) which was a collection of *Jugantar* articles and *Bartaman Rananiti* (*The Modern Art of War*) which spoke of the necessity of war and revolution in order to combat oppression were also read by a large number of members. Bankimchandra Chattopadhyay's *Anandamath* and *Debi Chaudhurani*, Vivekananda's works and of course, the *Gita*, were also widely read. The revolutionaries also read accounts of the Russo-Japanese and Boer Wars, as well as the revolutions in France, Ireland and Russia.[78] Other evidence also indicates that the writings cited above were representative of widely read revolutionary literature. Suresh Deb, a member of the Dacca Anushilan Samiti, was questioned in connection with the circulation of *Swadhin Bharat* leaflets in Gaibandha in 1917. In his confession Suresh talked about his indoctrination and activities and mentioned that he had been asked to read the *Gita* and *Sannyasi Giti* (*The Songs of Sages*), Vivekananda's *Patrabali*, *Brahmacharyar Palan* (*Practicing Celibacy*), *Desher Katha* (*The Story of our Country*) by Sakharam Ganesh Deuskar, Brahma Sutra etc.[79] The *Sedition Committee Report* also mentions certain textbooks like the *Bhagavad Gita*, the writings of Vivekananda, the lives of Mazzini and Garibaldi, the *Bhawani Mandir*, *Mukti Kon Pathe* and *Bartaman Rananiti* that all initiates into the revolutionary enterprise had to read.[80]

Particularly poignant was the find of some revolutionary literature in the home of Mohendra Das, accused in the murder of his Headmaster, Nabin Babu, of the Maldah Zilla School at Mukdumpur in 1916. Among the articles recovered from Mohendra's home were a book called *Bharat Bani* (*Message of India*) written by Hari Narain Bhattacharya and Swami Vivekananda's *Bartaman Bharat* (*Present Day India*) as well as a tiny note book of Mohendra's containing extracts as well as ideas of his own. That Mohendra had read both *Bharat Bani* and *Bartaman Bharat* closely was evidenced by the fact, that extracts from the book were marked and underlined by Mohendra, who had also made notes in the margins. Thus on page 18 of *Bharat Bani* where the author had written that 'political freedom was but a part of freedom and did not constitute its entirety', Mohendra had written in the margins 'political freedom is the first step to perfection.' In his own note book he had copied out Vivekananda's famous saying 'Arise, awake and stop not till the goal is reached.' Vivekananda had paraphrased this saying from the Upanishads and it figured as the heading in many of the revolutionary pamphlets.[81]

From the evidence cited above it appears that the revolutionary ideology was shaped by multiple cultural influences. Since nationalism was a western import into nineteenth century India, as was the revolutionary variant, the revolutionaries were undoubtedly familiar with and influenced by western political ideas and institutions. Politicians of all hues in Bengal read much the same kind of literature. French and British literature of the Enlightenment and French Revolutionary literature constituted statutory reading for the nationalists. The writings of Tom Payne were especially popular. Similarly, most nationalists were familiar with the revolutionary activities of Young Italy, the Irish Nationalists and the Russian Nihilists. Surendranath Banerjee, the moderate leader lectured extensively on Mazzini to youthful enthusiasts in the course of his meetings in the 1870s. Yogendra Nath Vidyabhushan's lives of Garibaldi and Mazzini were also widely read. Even social reformers and religious minded scholars like Raj Narayan Bose and Sivanath Sastri were acquainted with revolutionary terrorist activities in Europe.[82] Some of the pamphlets referred in glowing terms to the achievements of Mazzini, the French philosophers Rousseau and Voltaire and the American freedom fighters, Franklin and Washington.[83] But as Hiren Chakrabarti has pointed out, the revolutionary terrorists, despite their familiarity with European revolutionary literature, did not adopt the ideas of the Italian republicans or the Russian nihilists[84] and they gave to revolutionary nationalism a distinctly indigenous twist. This was because of the overwhelmingly religious spirit in which they embarked on their mission. In the political imagination of the terrorists, the struggle with the colonial authorities was not conceived in terms of a secular struggle between two powers with diametrically opposed interests. Instead the struggle was framed in terms of a battle between good and evil. On one side were ranged the white demons (*asuras*), who were collectively depicted as the epitome of evil and who had to be stricken down by the *santans*, who represented goodness, if justice and peace were to be reestablished on earth. The triumph of good over evil was seen as a kind of deliverance or salvation. This deliverance would only come about with divine help and it would be achieved through an apocalyptic battle, the results of which were to be interpreted as the writ of providence. The revolutionaries saw themselves as the instruments of this divine will and their duty was to implement the divine will by devoting their lives to the cause.

As mentioned in an earlier chapter, this intense religiosity was bequeathed on the revolutionaries by thinkers like Bankimchandra and Vivekananda who had the greatest influence on the revolutionaries. The example of the *santan-dal* in *Anandamath* provided the revolutionaries with an ideology of nationhood, an organizational model characterized by an austere and celibate life style and the tactics of guerilla warfare. Bankimchandra included the song *Bande Mataram* in his novel and the wondrous beauty of the motherland that he described cast its spell on the revolutionaries for whom the motherland became 'the symbol of the nation-idea ... ... the Divine Idea, the Logos ....'[85]

Several among the first generation of revolutionaries have dwelled on the impact of the *Anandamath* in helping to shape their lives as revolutionaries.[86] Vivekananda's profound influence on the revolutionaries is evident from the fact that many sentences in the pamphlets are directly inspired by his quotes and aphorisms. Vivekananda was not a political theorist and his primary concern was the transformation of Indian society which he found inert, oppressive and an obstacle to India's progress. But there was much in Vivekananda's thought that the revolutionaries found directly relevant to their political concerns. Vivekananda was as deeply a nationalist as the revolutionaries though his love for the country found expression through his intense concern for his fellow Indians, specifically the poor and the oppressed who represented the vast majority of the Indian population. Vivekananda lay emphasis on an organized social movement rather than individual acts of charity as the means of eradicating poverty and social ills and called upon educated young men to sacrifice their lives to the cause of alleviating the suffering of the motherland. Aware of the immensity of the task that lay ahead, Vivekananda sent out a clarion call of 'abhi' or to be fearless and to 'stop not till the goal was reached', words that made an abiding impression on the young revolutionaries as evident in the following excerpt from a pamphlet that combined slogans coined by Vivekananda and Bankimchandra:

> *Vedanter sarbosreshtho shabdo 'abhi' arthat bhoyeshunyo hoyo! Bhoye Mrityu, bhoye abanati, bhoye sharboprokar hinotar mool! Ato eb bhoye porityagpurbok shomoshhore bolo Bande Mataram!*[87]
>
> (Translation: The greatest word in the Vedanta is *abhi* or be fearless! From fear comes death, from fear comes decline, fear is the source of all kinds of degeneracy. Therefore, having conquered fear, raise all your voices to say Bande Mataram.)

Vivekananda's social activism was extended to the political sphere by his admirers who sought to give a political inflection to his sayings. Thus, the voluntary associations that were set up in the *swadeshi* days not only engaged in political work but also played a sterling role in organizing aid campaigns during natural calamities like floods. Aurobindo grafted the ideas of these two thinkers into his particular brand of political activism. It may be argued that the ideal that these thinkers championed was that of the *karmayogi*, the wise man of Indian tradition whose spirituality and religiosity does not constitute a hindrance to activism in the social and political spheres. The revolutionary ideal was not *Kshatriyahood*, alone, or the superficial mimicking of western sexual stereotypes as Ashis Nandy would have us believe, but a more composite ideal that combined the qualities of *rajas* (courage, activism) and *sattva* (goodness), and gave a distinctive stamp to the revolutionary enterprise. The same inspiration lay behind the revolutionary veneration for the *Gita*, a veneration that led Bankimchandra to write a commentary on the *Gita* and Vivekananda to take the initiative to have a Bengali version of the *Gita* published. Drawing inspiration from the Gita, Aurobindo declared:

> The sword of the warrior is as necessary to the fulfillment of justice and righteousness as the holiness of the saint. ... To maintain justice and prevent the strong from despoiling and the weak from being oppressed is the function for which the Kshatriya was created. Therefore, says Srikrishna in the Mahabharat, God created battle and armour, the sword, the bow and the dagger.[88]

The emphasis on a distinctive group identity which is defined in contrast to other groups constitutes a core feature of nationalism. This emphasis is evident throughout the text of a *Swadhin Bharat* leaflet issued in 1910. The leaflet emphasizes that 'the nation that has a separate country, religion and society must for ever do battle in order to keep its own individuality unimpaired.' Under the heading of 'Our Ideal' the leaflet then goes on to say:

> The Russian Nihilist is not our ideal, we do not imitate the French Communist either. Nor do we hold the views of the Italian Carbonari. Our work is not pre-eminently *Tamas* (the quality of ignorance and darkness) like that of the Irish and Scot secret societies. We are following in the footsteps of our ancestors. ... Again shall we restore to the Brahmin his knowledge of the *Sattwa* (the quality of goodness) and the strength of his arm to the Kshatriya. Not only this. This time India shall not uplift herself to be great herself alone. We shall seat

> India on the seat of the preceptor of the world. The all devouring hunger of the western world that is rushing like a madman on the path of worldliness and is thoroughly permeated by the poison of unrest arising out of the vortex of enjoyment and luxury will be stayed by the new India by her spiritual restraint and education. Restless and ferocious human beasts will be turned into gods; the earth will be like heaven. This is our vow; this is what we aim at; this is what we struggle for. [89]

The manuscript pamphlet that police discovered in the house of Mohendra Das, a revolutionary, accused in the murder of the Headmaster of Malda also laid stress on a revolutionary enterprise that was totally indigenous.

> Thou impart devotion into our hearts and give strength to our arms – we will then be able to worship thee with our own blood – No longer shall we try to offer you flowers from the gardens which are foreign – but we will worship thee with flowers plucked up from the garden of our own hearts... [90]

Thus, if the revolutionary texts are treated as cultural products and the cultural influences that went to shape them are taken into account, it does appear that revolutionary terrorism, both in concept and in practice, was not entirely a foreign import but deeply rooted in indigenous traditions as well. Like Indian nationalism, of which it was a part, revolutionary nationalism was constituted of foreign as well as of inherited and local elements that went to give it its distinctive character. But the more relevant point here is that it was in the context of certain norms, values, memories and experiences that they shared with their audience that the revolutionary terrorists were able to ascribe particular meaning to their acts of violence, a meaning that their audience understood and more importantly, a meaning that helped to legitimize their acts of violence as necessary, desirable and heroic. On the other side of the divide, the colonial government may have understood the meaning latent in these acts of violence but definitely did not interpret it as legitimate. The colonial government interpreted revolutionary violence as constituted of acts of cultural perversion. It is to this interpretation that we shall now turn.

Endnotes

1 David Riches, 'The Phenomenon of Violence' in David Riches ed. *The Anthropology of Violence* (Blackwell, Oxford, 1996), p. 3.

2 Sandip Bandopadhyaya, *Nathipatre Swadeshi Andolan* (*The Swadeshi Movement in Documents,* Progressive Publishers, Kolkata, 2004), p. 55.

3 The name *Jugantar* (*New Age*) was inspired by Shivnath Sastri's novel of the same name that called for a social revolution.

4 For the early history of revolutionary terrorism in Bengal see, Hiren Chakrabarti, *Political Protest in Bengal: Boycott and Revolutionary terrorism, 1905–1918* (Papyrus Kolkata, 1992); Peter Heehs, *The Bomb in Bengal: The Rise of Revolutionary Revolutionary Terrorism in India, 1900–1910* (Oxford University Press, Oxford, 1993).

5 A collection of *Jugantar* articles has been edited by Anshuman Bandopadhyaya and published as *Agnijuger Agnikatha – Jugantar* (Sri Aurobindo Ashram Publications Dept., Pondicherry, 2001). Unfortunately some important articles are missing from this collection. This compilation may be supplemented by another valuable collection of articles (unfortunately, mostly undated) to be found in Uma Mukherji and Haridas Mukherji, *Bharater Swadhinata Andolane 'Jugantar' Patrikar Dan* (Firma KLM, Calcutta, 1996). Those *Jugantar* articles that were declared seditious by the government of India may be found in the *Jugantar* trial records, which have been preserved in the *Smaraniya Bichar Sangrahalaya,* (Museum of Memorable Trials, hereafter *SBS*) (Alipur Sessions Court, Kolkata).

6 *Naba-Tantro,* (*New System*) dated 18 April 1908, in *Agnijuger Agnikatha.*

7 *Amader Rajnaitik Adorsho* (*Our Political Ideology*), *Rajnaitik Bhikkhabritti* (*Political Mendicancy*) in *Bharater Swadhinata Andolaney Jugantar Patrikar Dan.*

8 Official English translation from *Lathyaushodhi* (*The Club as a Remedy*), to be found among the *Jugantar* trial records, *SBS.* collection.

9 *Biplab-Tattvo* (*Theory of Revolution*) in *Bharater Swadhinata Andolaney Jugantar Patrikar Dan.* All translations from the *Jugantar,* unless otherwise indicated, are mine.

10 *Bhay Bhanga* (*Overcoming Fear*) *Mithya Bhay* (*False Fear*), *Mithyar Puja* (*Worship of Falsehood*), all in the *SBS* collection.

11 *SBS* collection.

12 Jacques Ellul has made the important point that propaganda is, in large, self-inflected in that its success depends less on sinister manipulation by propagandists than on the desire on the part of the masses to have the world make sense. See Jacques Ellul, *Propaganda: The Formation of Men's Attitudes* (Vintage Books, New York, 1965), p. 118–19.

13 *Bharater Swadhinata Andolaney Jugantar Patrikar Dan,* 15

14 '*Deshe ekata koi*' (*Where is the unity in the country?*), '*Deshe lok koi*' (*Where are the people in this country?*), '*Ruchi-bikar*' (*Perversion of taste*) all in *Bharater Swadhinata Andolaney Jugantar Patrikar Dan.*

15 From the records of case No. 2913 of 1907, Emperor vs. Bhupendra Nath Dutt, preserved in the *SBS*.

16 From *Mithyar Puja* (*The Worship of Falsehood*) dated 5 August 1907 in *Agnijuger Agnikatha*.

17 *Jugantarer Abhibadon* (*Greetings from the Jugantar*), dated 18 April 1908, in *Agnijuger Agnikatha*.

18 From the statement made by the Chief Presidency Magistrate, D. H. Kingsford, presiding judge in the Bhupendranath Nath Dutt Case on 24 August 1907, preserved in the *SBS*.

19 These letters may be found in the *SBS* collection.

20 The reports drawn up by British government officials repeatedly pointed out that the limited success of the British in bringing the revolutionaries to justice was due to the lack of cooperation from the general public whose minds had been vitiated by revolutionary propaganda. See Chapter IV.

21 Judgment delivered by D. H. Kingsford in the Bhupendranath Dutt case. Trial records are preserved in the *SBS* collection.

22 Uma Dasgupta, 'The Shackling of the Vernacular Press'. *Rise of an Indian Public: Impact of Official Policy: 1870–1880* (Riddhi, Calcutta, 1977), p. 269–300.

23 Reports drawn up by R. H. Sneyd-Hutchison, Deputy Inspector General of Police, Intelligence Branch, dated 7 August 1911 and 1 May 1914 in SN 65/1914, FN 258/1914 in WBSA-IB.

24 Quoted in Peter Heehs, 'Aurobindo Ghose and Revolutionary Terrorism'. *Nationalism, Revolutionary Terrorism, Communalism. Essays in Modern Indian History* (Oxford University Press, Delhi, 1998), p. 46.

25 SN 14/1908, F. N. 449/1908 in WBSA-IB.

26 David Riches, 'The Phenomenon of Violence', in idem. ed. *The Anthropology of Violence*, p. 9–11.

27 Bhikhu Parekh, 'Gandhi's Theory of Non-violence: His Reply to the Terrorists', in Noel O'Sullivan ed. *Revolutionary Terrorism, Ideology and Revolution: The Origins of Modern Political Violence* (Wheatsheaf Books, Sussex, 1986), p. 178–202.

28 In an important article Veena Das and Ashis Nandy have postulated that Indian society has sought to legitimize and contain violence through a number of discourses which they label the discourses of sacrifice, feud and vivisection. In these discourses, violence is understood and communicated as part of a structure of ideas. In each of these structures, that violence is represented as justified in which the perpetrator and the victim share an understanding and appreciation of the code of values that is sought to be perpetuated through the act. Legitimate violence may be counterpoised to illegitimate violence where the victim loses all subjectivity and is merely reduced to a thing. See Veena Das and Ashis Nandy, 'Violence, Victimhood and the Language of Silence' in Veena Das ed. *The Word and the World: Fantasy, Symbol and Record*(Sage, New Delhi, 1986), p. 179–194. Their argument does not really explain whether, in any situation of conflict, all the participants – the perpetrators, recipients and witnesses, even while they shared a basic understanding of the significance of the act, would ever agree as to its justifiability and legitimacy.

29 *Liberty* pamphlet headed *4 May 1857* in SN 5/1913, FN 663/1913, WBSA-IB.

30 See, for example the *Swadhin Bharat* pamphlets in SN 56/1913, FN 1340/1913; SN14/1910, FN 1318/A/1910; SN 15/1910, FN 1318/B/1910, all in WBSA-IB.

Firinghis: A pejorative term for people of mixed race or Europeans.

31 *Jugantar* pamphlets headed *Amader Asha* (Our Hope) and *Samay hoiyachhe ki* (*Is it Time Yet?*) in WBSA-IB, SN 115/16, FN 2223/1916. *Swadhin Bharat* pamphlet in WBSA- IB, SN 38/1910, FN 1318/1910.

32 *Jugantar* pamphlet headed *Amader Asha* (*Our Hope*) in SN115/16, FN 2223/16 in WBSA- IB All translations from pamphlets, unless otherwise indicated, are mine.

33 IBID.

34 *Jugantar* pamphlet headed *Prafulla*, in Samanta ed. *Terrorism in Bengal*, Vol. 4, 384; *Swadhin Bharat* pamphlet in SN 38/1910, FN 13/8/1910, WBSA-IB; *Liberty* pamphlet headed 20 July 1913 in Samanta ed. *Terrorism in Bengal*, Vol. 4, p. 471–474.

35 *Jugantar pamphlet, Amader Aasha (Our Hope*) in WBSA. IB, SN 115/1916, FN 2223/1916.

36 The idiom was not merely religious, it was Hindu to boot. The terrorists were mainly young men from the Hindu upper castes and their writings bore the impress of this identity.

37 Official English translation of *Swadhin Bharat* pamphlet in WBSA- IB, SN 38/1910. FN 13/8/1910.

38 *Swadhin Bharat* leaflet beginning with the words, *Utshaho Udyom biheen (Devoid of enthusiasm and initiative*) in Calcutta Police Museum PTS Collection, 18 A -15.

39 Leaflet beginning with the words *Ingrajer shashone thakiya* (*Living under the rule of the English*) in SN 56/1913, FN 1340/13, WBSA- IB

40 From the *Swadhin Bharat* pamphlet *Bharoter Mongol Uddeshye* (*For the sake of India's welfare*) in WBSA- IB, SN 16/1915, FN 347/1915.

41 *Swadhin Bharat* pamphlet in WBSA-IB, SN 102/1916, FN 1465/1916.

42 *Swadhin Bharat* pamphlet beginning with words *Ingrajer shashone thakiya (living under English rule)* WBSA-IB, SN 56/1913, FN 1340/1913.

43 *Lakh:* Hundred thousand.

44 *Swadhin Bharat* pamphlet beginning with words *Bharatbarsher mongol uddeshye* (*For the welfare of Bharatvarsha)* WBSA-IB, SN 16/1915, F 347/1915.

45 *Swadhin Bharat* pamphlet beginning with the words, *Na jani janani* (*We do not know, O Mother*) in P.T.S. Collection, 18-A-15, Calcutta Police Museum.

46 From the pamphlet beginning with the words '*Deputy Superintendent Basanta Chattopadhyay-er hotya*' dated 16 September 1916 in Calcutta Police Museum Collection.

47 *Swadhin Bharat* pamphlet beginning with words *Tomar desh, tomar swadhinata (Your country, your independence*), SN 56/1913, FN 1340/1913 in WBSA- IB.

48 See footnote 46.

49 From the official English translation of a *Swadhin Bharat* pamphlet beginning with words (*I have awakened on the great cremation ground*), WBSA-IB, SN 38/1910, FN 13/8/1910.

50 English translation from the original Sanskrit.

51 The scene of the *Gita* is the battlefield of Kurukshetra where the Pandavas are ranged in battle against their cousins, the Kauravas. The Pandava hero Arjuna's bewilderment at the idea that his *dharma* (the range of duties that need to be fulfilled in order to lead a righteous life) required him to slaughter his own relations at the battle site of Kurukshetra constitutes the starting point of the *Gita*.

52 For example, Sugata Bose, 'Nation as Mother, Representations and Contestations of 'India' in Bengali Literature and Culture,' in Sugata Bose and Ayesha Jalal eds. *Nationalism, Democracy and Development. State and Politics in India* (Oxford University Press, Delhi, 1997), p. 50–75; Tanika Sarkar, 'Nationalist Iconography: Image of Women in 19th Century Bengali Literature,' *Economic and Political Weekly*, (November 21, 1987), p. 2011–2015; Jasodhara Bagchi, 'Representing Nationalism: Ideology of Motherhood in Colonial Bengal,' *Economic and Political Weekly*, (October 20–27, 1990), p. 65–71.

53 *Anandamath* was published in 1880. The brand of aggressive Hindu nationalism preached through the novel fired the imagination of the revolutionary terrorists and deeply influenced their movement.

54 Jagadhatri, Kali *and* Durga are varied representations of the mother-goddess in Bengali Hindu pantheon.

55 Dipesh Chakrabarty, *Provincializing Europe: Post Colonial Thought and Historical Difference* (Oxford University Press, Oxford, 2001), p. 228–32.

56 One of the main centres of revolutionary terrorist conspiracy was a garden house at Maniktala, in Calcutta. A police raid on the house in May 1908 led to the arrest of the members of the Maniktala group.

57 *Koti:* 10 million.

58 Pamphlet titled *Om Swadhin Bharat* beginning with words *Tomar desh tomar swadhinata* (*Your country, your independence*) in WBSA-IB, SN56/1913. FN 1340/1913.

59 Ibid. See also pamphlet headed *Om Bande Mataram Sadhana* in WBSA-IB, SN 37/1913, FN 512/1913.

60 Ibid. Dipesh Chakrabarty has pointed out that the joint family, a much-celebrated ideal within the renascent Bengali cultural nationalism of the late nineteenth and early twentieth centuries, was itself a much used political metaphor in the nationalist narrative. See *Provincializing Europe*, p. 228–232.

61 *Swadhin Bharat* pamphlet (1916) beginning with words *Amra Swadhin Bharater goto samkhyai* (*We, in the last edition of Swadhin Bharat*) WBSA-IB, SN72/1916, FN 133/1916.

62 *Jugantar* pamphlet, WBSA-IB, SN 115/1916, FN 2223/1916. In Hindu religious imagery, the goddess Kali is portrayed with her consort, the god Shiva, lying prostrate at her feet.

63 Ibid.

64 *Swadhin Bharat* pamphlet beginning with words *Amra Swadhin Bharater gato samkhyai* (*We, in the last edition of Swadhin Bharat,*), WBSA-IB, S. N.72/1916, FN 133/1916.

65 René Girard, *Violence and the Sacred* trans. Patrick Gregory (John Hopkins University Press, Baltimore, 1977).

66 SN 5/1913, FN 663/1913, WBSA-IB.

67 *Swadhin Bharat* pamphlet, SN 38/1910, FN 13/8/1910 in WBSA-IB.

68 For example, the *Swadhin Bharat* pamphlets, SN14/1910, FN 1318 A/1910; SN 15/1910, FN 1318 B/1910, WBSA-IB.

69 *Swadhin Bharat* pamphlet in SN 56/1913, FN 1340/1913, WBSA-IB.

70 *Swadhin Bharat* pamphlet in SN 14/1910, FN 1318 A/1910, WBSA-IB.

71 *Khatriya, Kshatriya:* the Hindu warrior castes.

72 Pamphlet titled *Om Swadhin Bharat* beginning with words *Tomar desh, tomar swadhinata* (*Your country, your independence*), SN 56/1913, F.1340/1913, WBSA-IB.

73 *Swadhin Bharat* pamphlets, SN 56/1913, FN, 1340/1913 (*Tomar desh, tomar swadhinata* (*Your country, your independence*); SN 14/1910, FN1318A/1910; SN 38/1910, 13/8/1910 all In WBSA-IB.

74 For more on this theme see Mark Juergensmeyer, *The New Cold War? Religious Nationalism Confronts the Secular State* (University of California Press, Berkeley and Los Angeles, 1993), especially Chapter 6.

75 Ashis Nandy has expressed this view of revolutionary terrorism in *The Intimate Enemy: Loss and Recovery of Self under Colonialism* in *Exiled At Home* (Oxford University Press, Delhi, 1998), p. 26, 52. See also, C. A. Bayly, *Origins of Nationality in South Asia* (Oxford University Press, Delhi, 2003), p. 109. On the larger question of the 'derivative' nature of the discourse of Indian nationalism, see Partha Chatterjee, *Nationalist Thought and the Colonial World: A Derivative Discourse* (Zed Books, London, 1986).

76 For an excellent account of the foreign influences on revolutionary nationalism see, Hiren Chakrabarti, *Political Protest in Bengal,* p. 72–77.

77 Peter Heehs, 'Foreign Influences on Bengali Revolutionary Terrorism' in *Nationalism, Terrorism, Communalism,* p. 84–85.

78 J. E. Armstrong's report, 'An Account of the Revolutionary Organization in Eastern Bengal with Special Reference to the Dacca Anushilan Samiti', Parts I and II, Volume I in Samanta ed. *Terrorism in Bengal* (Government of West Bengal, Calcutta, 1995), Vol. II, p. 333–346.

79 Suresh Deb's confession recorded by H.C. Hunt on 17/9/1917 in WBSA-IB, SN 148/16, FN 132/16.

80 *Sedition Committee Report,* 23.

81 SN 84/16, FN 183/16 in WBSA-IB, C. Ezekiel's Report of 5-3-16. For details of the case see next chapter.

82 Amitabha Mukherjee, 'Revolutionary Nationalist Activities in Bengal (1902–1913)' in *Militant Nationalism in India, 1867–1947* (Institute of Historical Studies, Calcutta, 1995), p. 57–98.

83 See, for example, the *Swadhin Bharat* pamphlet beginning with the words, *Na jani janani* (*We do not know, Mother*) in P.T.S. Collection, 18-A-15, Police Museum Kolkata.

84 Hiren Chakrabarti, *Political Protest in Bengal*, p. 74.

85 Ramsay Macdonald quoting Bipin Chandra Pal in his *The Awakening of India*, cited in the report 'An account of the Revolutionary Organization in Eastern Bengal' in *Terrorism of Bengal*, Vol. II, p. 336.

86 For example, Bhupendranath Dutt, *Bharater Dwitiya Swadhinata Sangram* (Nababharat Publishers, Kolkata, 1983), p. 32; Nalinikishore Guha, *Banglay Biplabbad* (Mitram, Kolkata, 2012), p. 41. Some of the pamphleteers too refer to the example of Bankim's *Anandamath*, for example the *Swadhin Bharat* pamphlet of 5/3/15 in the Police Museum Collection.

87 From the pamphlet titled *Yugantar – Chaturtha Barsho – 1317 – sankhya 1* (*Jugantar, 4th issue, no.1*), National Archives of India.

88 Aurobindo, 'The Morality of Boycott', in *Sri Aurobindo, On Nationalism*, p. 363–364.

89 From the Official English translation of a *Swadhin Bharat* leaflet in WBSA-IB, SN 38/1910, FN 1318/1910.

90 SN 84/16, FN 183/16 in WBSA-IB.

4

The Battle for Domination
State Repression of Revolutionary Pamphlets

Revolutionary propaganda struck at the very heart of the normative world order of colonial India. The colonial world order was enshrined in law and underwritten by appeals to so called universal values of truth, justice and righteousness. The revolutionary propagandists attacked the colonial edifice by rejecting the moral and legal foundations of the claims to legitimacy of colonial rule over India. Revolutionary propaganda sought to persuade the public of the illegitimacy of colonial rule in India by arguing that its foundations rested on chicanery and force and its function was to drain India of its resources. If colonial rule could be demonstrated as resting on illegitimate foundations, revolutionary resistance through violence to colonial rule could then be represented as legitimate and just. To the colonial authorities, the attempt of the propagandists to de-mythicize colonial rule constituted an act of subversion of the established state-order, which was upheld through the rule of law. In India, the rule of law served to strengthen the foundations of empire through both practical and ideological means. Practically, the law served as a weapon of colonial extraction of labour, wealth, produce as well as of regulation and control, while ideologically it served to legitimize colonial rule by claiming that the British system of justice upheld peace and liberty, thus advancing the cause of Britain's civilizing mission in India.[1] But then, as scholars have pointed out, 'the function of ideology is much more significant in justifying an order to those who principally benefit from it and who must defend it than it is hiding the nature of the order from those who are its victims.'[2] For the colonial order to function smoothly and British rule to secure legitimacy, the proclamations of the colonial administrators regarding the enlightened nature of colonial administration and the impartial exercise of colonial law would have to be accepted and ratified by public opinion in the colonized territories. The revolutionary terrorists rejected the ideological suppositions that went to uphold the rule of colonial law, mocked its operations and defied it in practice. As a result they had to face the full blast of state violence that was unleashed through the operations of the law. The state utilized the category of 'sedition' in order to give meaning to those events that justified its own use of violence. The colonial order was sought to be protected by suppressing revolutionary propaganda and meting out the harshest punishment to the revolutionary propagandists by charging them with sedition. The two prevailing discourses on revolutionary violence in early twentieth century colonial Bengal, first, the revolutionary discourse that legitimized violence explored in Chapter III, and second, the state sponsored discourse on sedition which was used to justify the operations of colonial law against its opponents, the subject of this chapter, represented two diametrically opposed attempts to interpret revolutionary violence and violent behaviour within two alternative frameworks of meaning that were structured by clashes of political power and interest, conflicting social and cultural convictions and beliefs and racial stereotyping.

Scholars of colonial history have contended that it is the practice of power that provides the context within which colonial knowledge is configured. As George Balandier, the famous anthropologist pointed out long ago, the oppressive and exploitative policies of colonial governments were rationalized by propounding theories that pointed to the 'natural superiority' of the white races, the inherent childishness and lack of mental, cultural and material development of the colonized, the oppressiveness of indigenous governments and the moral need to bring civilization and progress to these backward peoples.[3] The empire 'imagined' was the 'other' of the British nation, a region of darkness that contrasted sharply with the centre of progress and civilization. In the words of Antoinette Burton,

> Staging Britain and its empire as dichotomous rather than as dialectic spaces was itself a technology of imperial rule – one of many 'grandiloquent displays' – which called upon Britons and others to recognize and hence to legitimate Britain's role as a *world* imperial power.[4]

The official archives of the colonial government bear ample evidence of the reactions evoked in governmental circles by the activities of the revolutionary nationalists. These reactions reveal contradictory tendencies. Government reports were quick to point out that the 'anarchist' or 'terrorist' movement was a limited one with an appeal that was restricted to a small section of the educated population. But often accompanying such dismissiveness were portentous comments on incipient conspiracies that could start a conflagration in the near future. Generalized fears of 'sedition' were a constant in the reports that poured out in voluminous proportions from the colonial offices during the disturbed years 1908–18. These reports sought to understand the causes, nature and extent of sedition in Bengal and suggested measures for its eradication.

One such report, drawn up in 1910, was sent from the office of Sir Harold Stuart, Secretary to the Government of India to that of the Chief Secretary to the Government of Bengal.[5] The report began by acknowledging the 'spirit of disaffection' that undoubtedly existed in many parts of India but hastened to add that a very inconsiderable part of the population was affected by this spirit which was confined 'with a few exceptions' to the literate middle classes. Within the literate classes again, the group that was especially susceptible to be overcome by this spirit and therefore liable 'to advocate and practice the methods of terrorism' were 'youths who are still at school and college,' and 'young men who have not long passed that period of their lives.' As to the causes of such disaffection, the report insisted that sedition was not 'the expression of revolt against excessive taxation or oppressive laws. It may have some slight economic basis, but in the main it is an intellectual sentiment and not founded on any material grievance, though those engaged in sedulously propagating the nationalist views are quick to seize ephemeral circumstances of that character to advance their cause.' The real cause of sedition, according to this report, was the 'ignorance and misapprehension of the motive and consequences of British rule in India.' Such mistaken opinions of colonial rule resulted from a misunderstanding of the lessons to be learned from history and economics. 'Lessons drawn from the History of the West are misapplied to the present circumstances of India; the broad generalizations of European writers on political science are stated without mention of their important reservations; and students are left to believe that what is approved in the case of Switzerland or Italy must necessarily be good for India.' What the report presumably meant to convey was that independence, nationalism and liberal-democratic government, political ideas that were much cherished in contemporary Europe, were totally inappropriate for application to Indian conditions and the sooner the nationalists were disabused of such unrealistic expectations for their own country and made to accept the reality of colonial rule, the better it would be for all concerned. Moving on to the domain of economics, the report branded the theory that India was being drained of her wealth by her connection with England as 'crude' and 'mischievous' but one that was believed in by 'young graduates' because they had never heard it controverted. Reports drawn up in later years to study the causes of sedition did not vary much in their essentials, though they did sometimes grudgingly admit that there might have been some material causes for discontent in Bengal. Thus, according to one such report,

> The general expansion of English education in this presidency is most marked in East Bengal. It has there produced a very large class of educated and half-educated youths whose ambitions and desires for a more civilized standard of existence have been excited and who have developed vague aspirations for political freedom, as yet unrestrained by any knowledge or traditions of discipline. For these no corresponding avenues of employment have been opened, and poverty and discontent are very prevalent amongst them. Among older schoolboys and students generally, and amongst numbers of the lower class of teachers who were very recently students themselves in East Bengal, there is a very strong anti-government feeling.[6]

The report went on to suggest ways in which sedition could be tackled and the list of measures, concentrated entirely on strengthening the administration, particularly the police force and had nothing to say on eradicating the increasing poverty and frustration of the educated classes. This was not surprising, considering that they emanated from the pen of a bureaucrat and a colonial bureaucrat at that. For the colonial administration revolutionary nationalism or the 'anarchist movement'[7] as it was referred to in government circles, was not an ideology but a pathology which corrupted the minds of inexperienced youth. Responsible for the spread of the disease were the unhealthy social conditions in Bengal for which, it was implied, the government could not be held responsible. 'Indeed,' commented a police officer, 'considering the neurotic and decadent conditions under which Bengal students live and are educated, it is a matter of surprise that the movement has not gone deeper and spread more widely in the productive soil which the schools offer for the growth and spread and fanaticism.'[8] Over the years, the police reports built up a model of sedition based on these assumptions, a blueprint on which to act in order to stop the spread of the contagion. Disloyalty to the government and the desire to overthrow it, according to the police reports, was the direct result of 'half-educated youth' imbibing western ideas that were ill-suited to application as far as eastern conditions were concerned. It bred unrealistic expectations of the government and led a people whose intelligence had been stunted by natural conditions to misunderstand its intentions. This half-educated section among the Indians then 'mischievously' set out to pervert the minds of a strangely imitative and gullible people, particularly students whose minds were poisoned by 'vituperative' and 'fanatical' writings which, in turn, led them to act in totally misguided ways. The solution was to make the seditious elements see the error of their ways while protecting the students from being corrupted by the 'contamination'.

By 1913, government circles were convinced of a widespread and carefully organized conspiracy existing in Bengal that aimed to bring about the violent destruction of British rule. The situation was dangerous enough, but there was a potential for greater danger for the 'bad example set by these men in an unwarlike Province like Bengal may, if it continues, lead to imitation in Provinces inhabited by fighting races, where the results would be disastrous.'[9] The administration was conscious from an early date of the dangers posed by 'anarchism' though the methods considered to deal with the problem in the earlier stages differed from those adopted in later years. Thus the earlier report on sedition drawn up in 1910 said clearly that 'remonstrance may often be a better remedy than prosecution [for sedition] and it should always be borne in mind that the Government desire to prevent rather than to punish.'[10] In line with this policy, the report laid down that district officers should try to nip seditious movements in the bud by trying to convince those who participated in seditious activities of the mischievous consequences of their conduct. Seditious propaganda was to be countered by governmental propaganda that would presumably succeed in removing ignorance and misunderstanding on the subject of British rule in India. The report expressed confidence that 'the great body of the people are entirely loyal and prepared to join with the officers of government in their mission against disaffection.'

In the course of the next few years, this confidence of the colonial administrators in successfully rooting out the 'spirit of disaffection' was severely undermined by the turn of events. Not only did the seditious sections of the population successfully resist the efforts of the government to disabuse their minds of all misapprehensions regarding the nature of colonial rule, worse, the general population did not participate quite as enthusiastically as had been anticipated in the 'mission against disaffection.' Though the colonial administrators put down this apathy to the fear of retribution from the 'anarchists', one government officer, in a rare moment of honesty, admitted in a confidential letter to his colleague that there was a large and increasing class of educated Bengalis 'who realize that revolutionary ideas are becoming widespread. They have a faint interest in the matter and generally approve of talk about Bengal being ruled by Bengalis or of the need for reform etc. They regard with the greatest suspicion all activities of the Police and are therefore on, the whole, pleased when they are unsuccessful and consider that they have in all likelihood behaved unjustly when they succeed.'[11]

In the course of the years 1908 through 1918, the government thus moved increasingly from the path of persuasion to repression and prosecution, for if sedition could not be prevented, it had to be punished in order to preserve the proper order of things and demonstrate the power of colonial rule in India. This trajectory in governmental policy with regard to sedition can be traced through the study of governmental attempts to deal with seditious writings in the press. All of the political reports that were prepared during this period on the subject of press legislation repeatedly emphasized the need for exercising an unremitting vigilance over the Press for the Government of India believed that the surest way of bridling sedition was by restraining the press from disseminating sentiments of hostility and disloyalty to the Government. No less a personage than Andrew Fraser, the Lieutenant Governor of Bengal, expressed his august opinion that it 'was known to all that there is in this country a terrible want of moral sense in regard to the conduct of the press.' Like the members of the colonial bureaucracy, he was convinced that the publishers of seditious writing 'are not giving expression to existing discontent, but are doing their best to produce discontent.'[12] Another official expounded on length along these lines when he compared the contrasting situations prevailing in England and India.

> In England the press has grown out of the endeavour of public opinion to find expression, and it now represents various and opposing sections of that opinion. In India, on the other hand, the views expressed in the Indian papers emanate from a small educated class in no way representative of India as a whole, and instead of representing public opinion, they form it, for the most part in a manner that is deliberately misleading and malevolent. Their views are addressed to a people who are qualified neither by education nor political training to assess them at their true value while their credulity renders them prone to be led astray by any allegation, however outrageous, which appeals to their prejudices and their passions.[13]

In the foregoing passage the official appeared to be referring, in the context of England, to an ideal public sphere, along the lines to be found in Habermas's work, where a public, educated and enlightened, engaged in informed discussion and formed their own opinions on debatable matters on the basis of a reasoned understanding of public affairs. In India, by contrast, the mass of the people, because of their lack of education and an unfortunate absence of the faculties of reasoning and understanding, were totally misled by an 'immoral' press that was controlled by a wholly unrepresentative section of the population and which led them into making misinformed judgments. The colonial authorities thus felt themselves morally bound to reign in the malevolent native press by formulating a suitable policy towards the press, more specifically towards those sections of the press that appeared to be inveterately disloyal towards the government and obdurately opposed to reforming their tone.

From 1907 a spate of governmental reports began to complain of the growing licentiousness of the native, particularly the vernacular press that seemed determined to spread 'misinformation' and 'calumnies' against the government and spoke of the necessity of firmer press laws to control this press. In the early twentieth century, sedition came under the purview of Act IV of 1898 which was an amendment of section 124A of the Penal Code. This amendment had been the result of a growing realization among the colonial rulers that the English laws on seditious libel on which section 124A of the Penal Code was modeled was quite unsuited to colonial conditions. As the Lieutenant–Governor of Bengal, Sir Alexander Mackenzie pointed out, 'a sedition law which is adequate for a people ruled by a government of its own nationality and faith may be inadequate, or in some respects unsuited, for a country under foreign rule.... No Government such as ours in India can afford to allow the minds of an ignorant and credulous oriental population to be gradually poisoned and embittered by persistent calumny of the Government and all its measures.' Not only were the minds of the oriental population especially susceptible to such calumny, but the vernacular press was also prone to spreading such calumny being unable to distinguish between liberty and license. Sir Griffith Evans, member of the Legislative Council expressed the view that:

> [A] free press is an exotic in India, and indeed in Asia, and like plants and animals transplanted into new surroundings is liable to strange developments. For many years a portion of the Native Press, and particularly of the Vernacular Press, has devoted itself to pouring forth

> a continual stream of calumny and abuse of the British Government in India and to teaching its readers that all their misfortunes, poverty and miseries arise from a foreign Government, which draws away their wealth and is callous to their miseries, and from whom they can expect neither justice nor sympathy.
>
> [T]his is the work of a small minority who have partaken of the cheap education of our schools and who distil and sell the poisonous product of the ferment in their heads of ill-assimilated and misapplied western ideas.[14]

These ideas were to be repeated ad nauseum in the years that followed, as justification for the institution of extensive controls over the Indian press.

The new provision introduced into the Indian Penal Code by Act IV of 1898 was as follows:

> 124 A. Whoever by words, either spoken or written, or by signs, or by visible representation, or otherwise, brings or attempts to bring into hatred and contempt, or excites or attempts to excite disaffection towards Her Majesty or the Government established by law in British India, shall be punished by transportation for life or any shorter term, to which fine may be added, or with imprisonment which may extend to three years, to which fine may be added.

The net was cast wide, perhaps with the hope that the fear of governmental prosecution might reign in the seditious sections of the population and the all-pervasive scope of the provision led a newspaper to comment that it was comparable with a fire 'which eats up everything. You will make the mouth of the pit very wide and yet blame people for falling into it.'[15] But with the growing radicalization of the Indian, including the Bengali Press, in the early twentieth century, it was increasingly felt in official circles that a law that dealt specifically with the transgressions of the Indian Press was the need of the hour. [16] Initially the government hesitated to act, because 'it was hoped that, as time went by and the agitation against the partition tended to die out, the papers would become less violent: and partly because it was recognized that a prosecution would bring the papers concerned into greater notoriety, and that unless really deterrent sentences were imposed and upheld on appeal, a prosecution would do more harm than good.'[17] But the hopes of the government were not realized and by mid 1907, the government was seriously contemplating steps to put a stop to the persistent campaign of 'misrepresentation and vituperation and open incitement to the people to resist the law and prepare for the time when the British rule can be thrown off' that was carried out through the columns of the newspapers.[18] Particularly targeted was the vernacular press led by newspapers like *Jugantar, Sandhya, Vande Mataram, Navashakti, Charu Mihir and Rangpur Vartabaha.* Vernacular papers had a much larger readership than the English newspapers whose readership was restricted to small, highly educated groups. Though a large section of the Bengali population could not read or write, they could nevertheless access the current political news through various channels. Thus one high placed government official summed up the administration's viewpoint when he expressed concern that the 'imperfectly educated clientele' of the newspapers, made up mainly of railway clerks and village schoolmasters had their news presented to them from one particular perspective and had no means of getting at the truth from other sources. The report went on to say that 'it has now become an almost universal phenomenon of Bengal rural life for the school-master in the evening to read out the newspaper to a circle of villagers, and in this way the poison is conveyed to wider circles and to strata of society whose attitude towards the government is more really important than that of the partially educated classes'.[19] The newspapers referred to here were most likely vernacular newspapers that found their way to the far flung villages, there to make mischief with their contents in the minds of the gullible classes.

After the Muzaffarpur Bomb Attack early in May 1908, followed by the discovery of a revolutionary hideout in Muraripukur Garden, Maniktala in Calcutta 'it was proved to the satisfaction of government that certain papers were not only morally responsible for the crimes already committed, but that their very existence was one of the constituent parts of an extensive revolutionary propaganda intended as the means by which the enterprising few were to be recruited for deeds of violence while the minds of the many were being prepared for a change in government.'[20] In an effort to intimidate the vernacular press the government not only launched a series of prosecutions against the above mentioned newspapers, but also passed the *Newspapers Incitement to Offences Act* of June 1908 as an emergency measure with which to tackle the press. The Act threatened with prosecution any newspaper that offered incitement to any act of murder and violence or to any offence under the *Explosives Substances Act* that had been passed concurrently in 1908. Speaking on the First Bill of the Act, the Viceroy, Lord Minto blamed seditious writing for the spread of the revolutionary movement, claiming that,

> The seeds of the wickedness have been sown amongst a strangely

> impressionable and imitative people – seeds that have been daily nurtured by a system of seditious writing and seditious speaking of unparalleled violence, vociferating to beguiled youth that outrage is the evidence of patriotism and its reward a martyr's crown.[21]

This Act was invoked to prosecute the *Jugantar*, *Sandhya* and *Bande Mataram* and close down their printing presses, thereby leading to the collapse of these papers. But in the course of these proceedings, the government came around to the view that only a comprehensive wide ranging law that would have the effect of preventing the publication of seditious writing rather than a law that prosecuted after the act, could effectively muzzle the Indian press. *The Press and Registration of Books Act* of 1867 which regulated printing presses, newspapers and books in British India mandated only that the names of printers and publishers appear in all publications. Proprietors of presses and editors of newspapers were not similarly registered. Consequently, it became difficult to fix responsibility for the authorship of seditious articles that appeared in periodicals and newspapers. In course of the prosecutions of the *Jugantar*, *Sandhya* and *Swadhin Bharat*, the government was left red-faced when the editors and managers of newspapers were able to escape prosecution and only printers were punished for sedition. Still more embarrassing for the government was the fact that teenage boys declared themselves to be the printers of newspapers and had to be proceeded against. Moreover, newspapers like the *Jugantar* were repeatedly prosecuted but continued to publish in defiance of the government's anger. A seditious newspaper could not be shut down even after being convicted for sedition. These prosecutions, the government felt, also gave a gratis advertisement to the papers concerned which became a much more valuable property allowing them to obtain facilities for being printed. To overcome these difficulties in prosecuting seditious writing, the government passed the *Press Law of 1910* by which proprietors of printing presses and the publishers of books, periodical and newspapers had to register their names with the government and also furnish security deposits. The *Press Act* gave the government the power to confiscate the deposits and further, in case of repeat offenses, to close down the printing presses and newspapers if they were found guilty of seditious writing. The aim of this Act was to 'restrain the Press within the limits of legitimate discussion'[22] by fixing responsibility for public writing and threatening offenders with drastic consequences in the event of transgressions.

The expectation that the *Press Act* would give government the power to effectively stop the spread of sedition and help maintain the peace, thus allowing them to continue with 'their strenuous efforts to advance the progress of India towards the highest stages of civilization'[23] were soon belied. This was because newspaper propaganda, which had been the primary target of the *Press Law of 1910*, was then outflanked by another form of propaganda that proved to be much more difficult to control. This was pamphlet propaganda. Government officials were keenly aware of the connections between newspaper and pamphlet propaganda. Even before 1910, the Chief Secretary of the Government of Bengal drew attention,

> [T]o the dangers which may arise from the circulation of leaflets which are not regular newspapers, but which may be made to take their place. It is quite probable that upon the suppression of a newspaper, by annulment of the declarations and forfeiture of the press, an attempt may be made to bring it out surreptitiously and to sell it or circulate it in the form of a leaflet, probably unauthenticated by the name of the printer or publisher. Something of the sort happened quite recently in the case of the *Yugantar*, although it is impossible to say whence and by whom the leaflet under that title was issued.[24]

The official went on to say that no responsibility could be enforced (and hence no prosecution was possible) because, unlike in the case of newspapers, leaflets came with no prior declarations from the publisher, editor or printer. He suggested therefore, that in order to put a stop to the sale or distribution of such leaflets that were printed or published in contravention of the proposed Press Act, police officers should be empowered to seize them when they were found in possession of any person in circumstances that gave rise to the suspicion that they were intended for sale or distribution.[25]

Despite the best efforts of the British government, most attempts to trace the origins and means of production of these pamphlets, ended in failure. The production and distribution networks of these underground pamphlets were highly decentralized. Individuals in their private capacity could procure printing materials from native and European firms and have pamphlets printed in presses by bribing compositors or printers.

The press-owners, in the unlikely event that they were implicated, would try and disclaim all responsibility for the matter. The revolutionaries would travel between various districts of the province or regions of the country making use of the services of shadowy presses for the printing of different editions of pamphlets or different consignments of the same pamphlets. Thus, tracking down the source of one consignment of pamphlets did not ensure that it would not surface again. The distribution networks were equally shadowy, with pamphlets being mailed from the post offices of various districts of Bengal and other provinces and sometimes even abroad. There were cases where individuals, particularly schoolboys, were prosecuted for copying pamphlets by hand and then mailing the manuscripts to friends and acquaintances. The police desperately tried to crack the underground information networks but seemingly met with little success. The police files are replete with cases when leads provided by informers led to frustrating dead ends. Nevertheless, despite limited success, the administration kept up its relentless efforts to suppress the production and distribution of pamphlets. Each edition of the offending pamphlets was declared seditious soon after its appearance, which meant that production, distribution and possession of these pamphlets with intention to publish or distribute made a person liable to prosecution by the government. The police followed leads, spied on individuals and on institutions like schools, government offices and post offices, made arrests, prosecuted offenders, bribed, persuaded and intimidated in order to elicit information, in other words did their best to win the war of words that was being waged by the revolutionary nationalists alongside their revolutionary activities. But not any of this led to much success in stamping out the propaganda.

The government's concern with pamphlet propaganda became glaringly evident from the time of the Alipore Court case of May 1908 when the revolutionary terrorists who had been rounded up in Muraripukur Garden were brought to trial together with their leader Aurobindo Ghose. Government reports uneasily record the fact that anarchists were winning the support of the population in the province, especially that of the young, educated classes among the Hindus and that the vernacular press was singing the praises of the spirit and courage shown by the 'criminals in their self-sacrificing patriotism.' They also mention in this connection the increasing distribution of virulently seditious pamphlets and confess that it was extremely difficult to obtain any information as to where and by whom they were published and how they were disseminated. The *Jugantar* leaflets which were issued after the collapse of the newspaper, were disseminated in large numbers from Calcutta by post to all corners of Eastern Bengal and Assam. They were addressed to Magistrates, Subdivisional officers, Postmasters, Secretaries of the Bar Libraries, Headmasters of Schools and others.[26] In Calcutta, Kiran Mukherjee, author of the 'virulently seditious pamphlet' *Pantha* (*The Way*), was suspected of having printed the early *Jugantar* pamphlets from a house at No. 28 Shampukur Road where the press which was formerly at No. 68 Maniktala Street from where the *Jugantar* newspaper was issued, was found. Certain papers and letters were also found which indicated that a number of members associated with the *Jugantar* gang and newspaper, like Kartik Dutt, Nikhileswar Ray, Kiran Mukherjee and Jagojiban Ray had set up mess in this house.[27] In February 1909, a number of lithographed *Jugantar* leaflets were received by various people in Calcutta and its mufassal (suburb), among them large numbers of students of colleges. The post marks were from Tunespet (Rajamundry) or Pondicherry. From the quality of the paper and the watermark of the wrappers it appeared that the leaflets had been sent from London and distributed from South India.[28] These were isolated nuggets of information and the general lack of success in controlling the spread of pamphlet propaganda greatly punctured the self-worth of the bureaucracy prompting one official of eastern Bengal to write in frustration that seditious writings that promoted violence were giving Bengalis inflated notions of their military superiority. The British had only to send in troops, preferably mounted troops into the province to disabuse them of their illusions.[29] This statement was indicative of a strand of thinking among colonial officials who hated to be outsmarted by the Bengalis and held that colonial masters should deal with rebellious subjects with overt violence rather than through the due processes of the law. This attitude was summed up by a military man who wrote in to the Calcutta Police offering advice on tracking down the propagandists and concluded, 'it is galling to any Englishman to see Bengali youths trying to scare us.'[30]

The result of the *Press Act* was to drive much of the seditious press underground. There was a corresponding increase in the number of seditious pamphlets that circulated both in eastern and western Bengal, thus increasing the pressure on the police. In a few cases informants provided some leads but most of them led to dead ends. For example, an informant provided the Superintendent of the Calcutta Police with the manuscript original of the leaflet *Hatya noi Jagna* (Not Murder, Sacrifice) in March 1910 and followed this up with the printed proof. The informant stated that he believed that the leaflet had been printed in a hand-press by Bibhuti Bhusan Ray and Abinash Sarkar who worked as compositors in the *Nayak* Press. But a search of the press precincts yielded no leaflets. Nor did searches of the homes of all the persons said to be connected with the production and distribution of the leaflet prove to be any more successful. Neither could the police make much headway in tracing the source of the *Swadhin Bharat* leaflets, of which three editions had appeared by

May 1910. But a breakthrough was made in the case concerning the issue of a new edition of a *Jugantar* leaflet that had appeared on 11 July 1910. The police received a tip from an informer that he had received 12 copies of the new *Jugantar* pamphlet from a certain Prabash Deb. The police arrested Prabash Chandra Deb, Gyanendra Kumar Basu, Ashutosh Sarkar and Mahendra Nath Chaterjee and prosecuted them under Section 124 A, IPC for printing and publishing the leaflets. Prabash had earlier been implicated in an alleged plot to assassinate the Viceroy at the Tollygunje Races on New Year's Day. Two letters of Prabash that fell into the hands of the police also showed that 'he was actively engaged in trying to obtain arms and ammunition and incite young impressionistic youth in acts of violence'. Gyanendra had served for sometime as editor of the seditious *Sarathi* Magazine and was a member of the *Sarathi Jubak Mandali* gang and so the two of them had been on the police radar for a while. Ashutosh Sarkar, a small time compositor, who had been paid by Gyanendra to have the leaflet set up in type and printed at a press owned by Mahendra Chaterjee testified against the others. Prabash Chandra Deb, who had actually written the leaflet, was sentenced to two years' rigourous imprisonment in September 1910, while Ashutosh, Gyanendra and Mahendra received lighter sentences.[31] Reports in police files indicate that the government also tracked the movements of individuals suspected to be connected with the production of pamphlets. Thus the police maintained lists of the names of printers of proscribed publications in Bengal. When the *Swadhin Bharat* pamphlets began to appear in large numbers in eastern Bengal in 1911, the police instituted inquiries regarding individuals who had once been employed on the staffs of seditious papers published from Calcutta in western Bengal like the *Jugantar* and *Sandhya* but had then moved to Dacca in East Bengal.[32]

But it was not enough to punish only the authors and publishers of the pamphlets. The government also kept an eagle eye on those who were suspected of distributing seditious material and drew up history sheets to check their political loyalties and antecedents.[33] The distributors of the pamphlets were usually young boys who did not know who the printers and composers actually were. Only a select few among the revolutionary terrorists who had the confidence of the leaders were placed in charge of the production process.[34] So the arrest of distributors often had little impact on the actual production process, as a case in Malda town demonstrated. In September 1910, the Headmaster of the Malda Zilla School handed over to the Malda police four *Swadhin Bharat* pamphlets, with a covering letter addressed to a boy named Durjadhan Das. As there was no boy named Durjadhan Das in the school, suspicion fell on a boy named Durjadhan Shah, and he was produced before the District Magistrate, who issued a warrant for a search of the boy's belongings in the town. In a locked trunk, belonging to the boy, a picture of the revolutionary martyr, Khudiram Bose was found. Their suspicions strengthened, the police launched an enquiry that led to the arrest of Surendra Narayan Adhikari, a keen volunteer and follower of the extremist leader Bipin Chandra Pal. Evidence indicated that Surendra had copied and tried to circulate the *Swadhin Bharat* pamphlets and so he was prosecuted Under Section 124 A, found guilty and sentenced to two years rigorous imprisonment for distributing seditious pamphlets amongst students in the Malda Zilla School. The matter appears to have ended there, though the supply of pamphlets to the school continued unabated, making Malda a notorious den of revolutionary activity.[35] What emerges repeatedly from the records is the nebulous character of the whole enterprise, with the names of distributors making fleeting appearances in police records and then disappearing beyond the radar of police surveillance. [36] The distributors were rarely caught red-handed. More often, the police had to painstakingly compare the handwriting on the envelopes that were mailed to different addresses with those of suspected revolutionaries (whose names were most often supplied by informers), a process that was made even more cumbersome by the fact that different batches of the same edition of a leaflet were addressed by different hands and mailed from different post offices.

Police officials often staked out post offices from where seditious pamphlets were posted in large numbers. Suspicious parcels were secretly opened and then sealed to avoid suspicion, raising uncomfortable questions in some quarters about the legality of such procedures.[37] In this game of cat and mouse, the propagandists began to use false names for both consignors and consignees and often had a third person pick up parcels that contained leaflets. Acutely sensitive to the public support for 'anarchism' the government also blacklisted those who received seditious material and did not promptly hand it over to the police. Even in the early days of revolutionary terrorism, the government had drawn up lists of subscribers to the *Jugantar* newspaper, keeping a particularly close watch on those subscribers who worked in government offices and quasi-government institutions. The subscribers included clerks employed in various government departments such as the Accounts Department of the Alipore Collectorate (24 Parganas) and the District Engineering Offices of Jalpaiguri and Kharagpur, in post offices and munsiff courts, teachers of schools and colleges, a Sub-Deputy

Collector, a Sub-Deputy Magistrate, the Officer in charge of Railway Police, Srimongol, Sylhet and in an interesting twist, postmasters and employees of postal services including the railway mail service.[38] This practice was kept up in the following years with police reports diligently recording the names of all those who had received seditious pamphlets and trying to trace their political affiliations, if any.[39] Students in schools and colleges were the objects of special attention. Headmasters of schools and principals of colleges were specifically instructed to hand over all seditious leaflets together with the names of students who had received them to the Director of Public Instruction.[40] One report commented in the context of the distribution of a particular *Jugantar* pamphlet that the extent to which the principals and headmasters produced the leaflet 'will be an index of the extent to which these instructions have been carried out, and to a considerable degree of the spirit by which the administration is animated.'[41] The results were disquieting for the police administration. Schools and colleges were not very conscientious in following such instructions and the police despaired of the seditious character of institutions like the Sonarang High School and the Jagannath College in Dacca and the Brojo Mohan Institution in Barisal where instructors supposedly matched their students in supporting sedition.[42]According to a police report,

> The systematic endeavour to secure recruits from the ranks of school boys is being steadily maintained and from the statements lately recorded we find that several of the most desperate characters in the organization have been working on various occasions as teachers in the schools throughout Bengal. The ease with which these persons secure teacherships in the schools is, I consider one of the most disquieting features in the situation. It may be safely assumed that in such schools the great majority of the students have imbibed the poison of sedition and have become active sympathizers, if not potent actors in the movement.[43]

The students were even more difficult to control. Leaflets were smuggled into schools, slipped insides the books of students, posted on blackboards or walls of classrooms and thrown into the rooms of students and masters with authorities at a loss to control their distribution.[44] Sometimes they were accompanied by notes baiting the police. The authorities of the *Zilla* (District) School in Birbhum received a *Swadhin Bharat* leaflet on 7 April 1910 accompanied by a pencil note which ended thus:

> Show the *Swadhin Bharat* leaflet to all and see only that it may not fall into the hands of the police *salas*.[45]

So paranoid was the government about the 'poison of sedition' infecting the students that merely reading pamphlets that had been posted in public places was enough to arouse suspicion. In March 1913, *Swadhin Bharat* leaflets were found posted at Cornwallis Square, Beadon Square and College Square in Calcutta. When the police visited these places to seize these leaflets they took down the names of several youths who were found either reading the leaflets or even loitering in the vicinity. A report drawn up by a Sub Inspector of Police about finding such a leaflet posted on a lamp post on the northern side of College Square mentions that 25 boys were reading it earnestly (some reading it aloud) and appeared to be enjoying the exercise immensely. After recording the names of some of them, the Sub Inspector took the help of a constable for taking the leaflet off. While doing so he 'was subjected to various sorts of ridicules by the boys and was obliged to put some of the boys to fear of arrest with a view to prevent their interference.'[46]

Even though the *Swadhin Bharat* leaflets were issued in large numbers, particularly in eastern Bengal and Calcutta and its vicinity, the police had absolutely no success in cracking the underground production and distribution network.[47] Matters were compounded when the *Liberty* leaflets began to appear in large numbers in eastern Bengal and Calcutta from 1913. The Raja Bazaar Bomb Case afforded proof of the close links between the revolutionary action and propaganda once again when Kalipada Ghosh, who was wanted in the Bomb Case was arrested on the 6 December 1913, with ten copies of the *Liberty* leaflets. It transpired that he was, until recently, employed in the Loke Nath Yantra Press at No. 11–1, Nawabdi Ostagar's Lane, the owner of which was Surendra Nath Basu who also had links with the revolutionaries. The press was searched and the investigations of the Superintendent of Government Printing, Bengal, helped to establish that at least two of the *Liberty* leaflets had been set up and printed at the Loke Nath Yantra Press[48]. Despite these important successes, there was no appreciable change in the situation. *Liberty* leaflets continued to appear in 1914 even though the Loke Nath Yantra Press was confiscated by the police in 1913.[49]

As pointed out earlier, the leaflets were printed in different presses, including hand presses, of which there were thousands in Calcutta alone and many more so throughout the districts and tracing leaflets to specific presses proved to be a herculean task. Nor did the police receive much help from the general population in suppressing seditious leaflets. For example, a police report of 1916 said that though the *Liberty* leaflet appeared in large numbers in various parts of the Dacca District, including Dacca town, Naraingunj, Sonarang, Bajrajogini, Manikgunj, particularly in schools and colleges, not a single student handed over any leaflet to the administration, although it was certain that many of them had received them.[50] This last point is important, for it indicated that in the battle between the colonial state versus the propagandists, the administration was on the losing side. The propagandists were targeting the students in recruiting for their cause and their efforts seemed to be paying off. C.A. Tegart, Special Superintendent of Police, Intelligence Branch, had this to say on the subject,

> We see how patiently the organizers have worked for years, sedulously implanting the seeds of hatred of the British government in the minds of the students. The seed falls on fruitful ground --- the Bengali student is frequently of a hysterical type.

Tegart's opinion was that in view of the drudgeries of the life of a typical Bengali student, which consisted only of studying for exams 'without any of the refining influences of education as imparted in English schools', the prospects held out to them by the astute revolutionary organizer could only appeal. 'A life of adventure is offered them. The glamour of work for the "mother", oppressed under a foreign yoke is depicted in glowing terms and the examples of those who have already died for their country are held up for imitation.'[51]

In the early years of the revolutionary movement the government of India had considered the idea of carrying out counterpropaganda as an antidote to the propaganda carried out by the revolutionaries. Government officials exhaustively discussed the pros and cons of the matter over a number of months. One report, like all similar government reports on this question, identified the schools and colleges as the crucible of the incipient revolution and emphasized the need to inculcate sound views among both teachers and students regarding both history and economics.[52] An effective way to counter seditious propaganda was to encourage 'the production of suitable text-books adapted to Indian conditions, and by the appointment of scholars of distinction to give special courses of lectures.'[53] Thus seditious propaganda was to be countered by governmental propaganda that would presumably succeed in removing ignorance and misunderstanding on the subject of British rule in India. Similarly district officers and their subordinates were asked to make special efforts to open lines of communication with the general population. Public servants and especially young European officers who were prone to 'err through ignorance' were urged to be courteous and considerate towards Indian gentleman.[54] More importantly, in order to counter the 'vicious calumnies' about British rule that were spread through the seditious press, the government seriously considered publishing newspapers of its own in the vernacular for circulation in the villages, or as an alternative, patronizing loyal Indian papers or educational journals in the provinces. The aim was to 'prevent the entire field of vernacular journalism from being occupied by the disaffected.'[55] These government sponsored vernacular journals would be encouraged to publish articles on a wide range of social and economic issues and the 'main object would be to teach the people that there are more interests in life than politics.' [56] The last idea did not take off because, as the Chief Secretary of the Government of Bengal pointed out,

> Indians of all classes are prone to suspicion; the panics which periodically spread among the ignorant and sometimes among classes not supposed to be ignorant are usually accompanied by distrust and suspicion of some sort of governmental action, and prove that, although the people may be submissive they are capable of crediting Government with the most Machiavellian intentions. It is not impossible that the knowledge that a paper is encouraged or subsidized by government may be an instrument in hands of the malignant sections of the press which will enable it to distort the aims and actions of Government even more effectively than at present.[57]

This statement is an expression of the awareness among one section of colonial bureaucrats who worked closer to the ground that, on the question of sedition, the government and the opposing public were locked on both sides of an unbridgeable mental divide that made a compromise impossible and a confrontation inevitable. Consequently, as the same government official pointed out, propaganda could not be a substitute for press legislation along the lines of Lord Lytton's *Press Act*.[58] As the minds of disloyal Bengalis could not be controlled, the only solution was to stop them from speaking their minds through threats and intimidation enshrined in the law. The question of sedition was framed in very different terms in revolutionary propaganda, making starkly clear the unbridgeable gulf between the rulers and the ruled.[59] The *Jugantar* article 'Sedition and the Foreign King' pointed out that since the English were foreign rulers, they could not charge the Indians with sedition, since the wishes of an entire nation could not be termed seditious. What was sedition under colonial law was the 'sacred urge for freedom' in the eyes of the Indians. Since the colonial government had no legitimacy in the nation's eye, it followed that colonial law carried no authority and sanctity.[60] The same point was made in the pamphlets.

The government's stand on sedition becomes clear from a perusal of the judgments handed out in sedition cases relating to pamphlet propaganda in the colonial courts. Of the two cases that will be considered here, one relates to the distribution of seditious pamphlets and the other to the murder of a headmaster who had become unpopular for stopping the distribution of seditious pamphlets in his school.

On the night of 20 January 1916, Superintendent of Police, J. A. Goldie was informed that *Swadhin Bharat* leaflets were being circulated in Pabna town by being pasted on the walls of houses, lampposts etc.[61] The Superintendent then sent out police patrols in various directions and joined one of the patrols himself. Soon, two arrests were made. The arrested were two young men. Manindra Chandra Bhattacharya, aged twenty, was a resident of Chittagong District and was a student of the First Year Class of the Pabna Edward College. The other was Sureshwar Bhattacharya, aged eighteen, a student of Pabna Institution, a High English School of Pabna Town and the son of a *kabiraj* (practitioner of indigenous medicine) of Pabna Town. Both were found to be carrying *Swadhin Bharat* pamphlets and had paste on their hands. It was also discovered that Sureshwar was carrying a dagger in his waist cloth under his coat. The two were prosecuted and were charged in the case with an offence under Section 124 A, Indian Penal Code, and abetment of the same, for having circulated or aided in the circulation of a seditious leaflet *Swadhin Bharat* and thereby having attempted to excite disaffection towards the Government established by Law in British India. The Judge, G. C. Chatterjee, District Magistrate of Pabna found that the leaflet *Swadhin Bharat* not only intended to bring into hatred and contempt and to excite disaffection towards the government established by Law in British India, but that it was also revolutionary in its character and openly advocated assassination, murder and armed resistance to the British government. The judge cited the leaflet in full, emphasizing the lines that had directly influenced his judgment. The sentence 'There is no second method of undoing the crooked method of English rules and their Policy of oppression – it is by resort to this active resistance that we shall destroy the authority of English rule' showed that the object of the leaflet was to excite feelings of disaffection and also to throw the British government by force. The leaflet praised *anarchists* like Amar Chand, Basanta Kumar, Paramananda and others who had been convicted in connection with the Delhi and Lahore Conspiracy cases. It censured and mocked police officers like Nanda Lal, Nripendra and others who had been shot by *anarchists* for doing their duties as Police Officers. The Judge cited the last section the leaflet which ran '[H]ark to the mother's reassuring message. In the same way whenever there will be oppression committed by the demons, I shall reincarnate myself and destroy the demons' as being significant. The demons were obviously the English men used here in a sense synonymous to the British government which, according to the leaflet was committing oppression upon the people. All the High officials of the government from the Viceroy to some important police officials were referred to defiantly.

The defense for the accused referred to a sentence in the leaflet 'but not to expel the English' as evidence that the accused did not want to bring about the end of English rule in India. This sentence was part of a paragraph that ran thus:

> Finally we shall say one word to the English. The English government leaving the responsibility of ruling the country in the hands of the police - imagine that it can now free the country of the thorns. But does it not see that some day or other, the country will be inundated with the blood of every Englishman (here). We ask no unreasonable demands. What we want we have clearly stated and in order to make this thing quite clear we are rending the heavens with the noise of repeated discharges of bombs, revolvers, and guns – but not to expel the English. If without conceding even a small part of our demand, you continue improperly committing brutal oppression on us like this, we shall make the life of every Englishman insecure....

Characterizing the defense's argument as a 'drowning man clutching at a straw', the judge declared that the leaflet when read as a whole, could only leave the impression that it was not only seditious but was also revolutionary. On the basis of the evidence the judge concluded that Manindra Chandra Bhattacharya and Sureshwar Bhattacharya had taken part in circulating the highly seditious *Swadhin Bharat* leaflet and were therefore guilty of the offence under section 124 A IPC.

In inflicting punishment on the accused, the judge took into consideration the following facts: (1) Several seditious leaflets of the nature of the *Swadhin Bharat* had been previously circulated and Pabna and other towns but this was the first instance when the culprits had been caught. (2) The present condition of the country, especially in Bengal, where a large number of assassinations and murders had taken place, and, where a comparatively large number of young men had been affected by sedition.

The Judge's message was clear. The government was not willing to tolerate any threats to its power and authority. The two young men, having dared to defy the government, were to be meted out exemplary punishment so that those so who were considering seditious action along the same lines were deterred by these examples. The High Court reiterated the same arguments when Manindra and Sureshwar appealed, maintaining, 'we have to consider not only the two accused who have been sentenced but we have also to consider others who might be tempted to become tools of others…' The tenor of the Judge's arguments appeared to indicate that the colonial state was feeling threatened by the emergent national community that was making its opposition clear to what it considered to be an alien state. The state, in turn, was bringing its power to bear against the wishes of the incipient nation. The case thus bore all the signs of a classic confrontation between the State and the Nation, or the National Community.[62]

The second sedition case was more sensational. It concerned the murder of the headmaster of Malda Zilla School, Nabin Chandra Basu, on the evening of 21st January 1916.[63] The Headmaster was returning home from school on a Friday afternoon when he was stabbed to death by four assassins. Two policemen, who happened to be near the spot managed to arrest one of the assassins when he tripped and fell. This was Mohendra Nath Das, son of Krishtodhan Das of Alal, Police Station Gajole, District Malda, who turned out to be a student of the Malda Zilla School. The murder was especially shocking because it followed the shooting death a year earlier of Sarat Babu, the headmaster of Comilla Zilla School who had earlier been headmaster for some time of the Malda Zilla School. Investigations revealed that Babu Nabin Chandra Basu was thirty five years of age and was a native of Bakarganj district of eastern Bengal. He had been headmaster of the Donough School at Jamalpur in Mymensingh where as 'loyal supporter of the Government and a determined foe of the anarchist party'[64] he had helped the authorities maintain discipline in his school during the riots and subsequent troubles in Mymensingh district in 1907. He had also appeared as a witness for the prosecution in 1911 during the Dacca Conspiracy case. 'As a recognition of his political services' to the government, he was appointed Assistant Headmaster of Malda Zilla School in 1912 where he became Head Master in 1914.

Malda had come into the news lately with several connections with revolutionary activity and Malda Zilla School had quite a reputation as a hotbed of sedition. A letter from a police official stated 'The Malda students are a bad set and did not improve by the influence exercised on them by Bireswar Bose. This man was the headmaster of the Bogra Zilla School from which he was dismissed from sedition. He then went to Malda and became Head Master of the National School there, and after the Barrah dacoity was taken in by the National School in Comilla.' [65]

In Malda, Nabin Babu was extremely unpopular among his students and assistant masters and also among the parents and guardians because of his open loyalty to the government and his efforts to curb 'seditious' activities among his students. As headmaster at Jamalpur, Nabin Babu had reported to the authorities about seditious leaflets being sent to the school. He was then warned through the post that he would pay for his attitude with his life. At Malda too, the threats, accompanied by seditious leaflets continued to pursue him. On the 8th April, 1915, Nabin Babu found in the School Post Box, a cover addressed to the 'Students of the Malda Zilla School' which had been posted at Berhampur. Inside was a copy of a *Swadhin Bharat* leaflet, the reverse of which contained in Bengali a threat to the effect that 'his soul would be blended with that of Sarat' (the murdered headmaster of Comilla) unless he stopped acting the spy. Quite unfazed, Nabin Babu reported the matter to the Superintendent of Police, Malda, C.Ezekiel, turning down at the same time the police offer of a personal guard.

Over the following months Nabin Babu continued to make himself 'obnoxious to those who sought to propagate the doctrines of anarchy and sedition among his pupils.'[66] So great was Nabin Babu's unpopularity that a series of articles appeared against him in a local weekly the *Gaur Duta* (Messenger of Gaur) in 1915 which claimed that Nabin Babu had managed to convert the Malda Zilla School into a 'Criminal Court' and asked 'that the extremely notorious and arrogant teacher' whose 'conduct will fill every Bengali with shame' be transferred from Malda.[67] Matters came to a head when, on the afternoon of the 25th January, 1916 the headmaster opened the Zilla School Post Box and found a cover posted at Rajshahi, another centre that had earned notoriety among the authorities as a centre of revolutionary activity, which was addressed to a Matriculation Student named Jatindra Narayan Ray. Inside the envelope were two seditious leaflets, *Swadhin Bharat* and *Liberty*. Nabin Babu duly turned over the leaflets to the authorities. Since

Nabin Babu made it clear that Jatindra Narayan Ray was the monitor of Hindu Hostel and one of the best behaved boys of the school, it appeared that the leaflets had been intended to fall into into Nabin Babu's hands. Three days later, the Head Master was dead.

The investigations that followed indicated that Mohendra 'had anarchist sympathies and tendencies.' As early as November 1913, Mohendra's name had come up in the course of the searches that had led to the institution of the Raja Bazaar Bomb Case. The correspondence seized in 296/1 Upper Circular Road[68] included a list in cipher of sixteen names, one of that being Mohendra's. Police suspected that these names were of men who were the correspondents in North Bengal of the Raja Bazaar bomb gang. A subsequent search of Mohendra's home in Mukdumpur, Malda turned up two manuscripts in Bengal, one entitled *Om Mahasakti Sadhana* (*The Worship of the Great Power*) that emphasized the value of self-sacrifice and another entitled *Ahvan* (*The Call*), where there was an exhortation to liberate oneself from *paradhinata* (subjection to foreign rule), two letters, one which urged Mohendra to do all within his power for the country and a book titled *Brahmacharya* (*Celibacy*). Mohendra's name was then included in the list of political suspects of Malda (*The Red Book*). After his arrest in 1916, a search of Mohendra's house in Mukdumpur once again led to the finding of some incriminating literature,[69] all of which emphasized the need for the country's independence. An anonymous letter sent from Rajshahi, dated 9 June 1916, addressed to Mohendra in English Bazaar but redirected to his father's home was also discovered in the course of another search in his father's home in Gajole. In it the writer inquired how and to what address and how many copies of *Shongbad Patra* (Newspapers) he would send to Mohendra and his associates. It was highly probable that *Shongbad Patra* referred to leaflets. On the basis of this accumulated evidence, a case was instituted against Mohendra in the Court of the Sessions Judge of Malda in June 1916. Mohendra was found guilty of the offenses of abetment of murder and murder in furtherance of common intention (Sections 302, 109 and sections 302, 34 of the Indian Penal Code) and sentenced to transportation for life on the 29 July 1916. Mohendra appealed against this sentence in the High Court but the sentence was upheld. A few years later, Mohendra died of consumption in jail.[70]

The find of pamphlet literature in Mohendra's residence proved to be damning for Mohendra's defense that had aimed to prove that Mohendra had no prior connection with the revolutionary nationalist movement. The defense had aimed to prove that the books, manuscripts, and the citations in the note books were 'examples of, or extracts from, religious and philosophical literature inculcating praiseworthy ideals and ambitions', and were in fact, evidence of Mohendra's moral standing and goodness which precluded the possibility of his being mixed up with the revolutionary nationalists. But language like:

> Thou impart devotion into our hearts and give strength to our arms – we will then be able to worship thee with our own blood – No longer shall we try to offer you flowers from the gardens which are foreign – but we will worship thee with flowers plucked up from the garden of our own hearts ...

merely strengthened the conviction of the Judges that Mohendra was an anarchist. The judges therefore declared that the literature only revealed that the appellant had 'anarchist sympathies and tendencies' because they were 'rhapsodies all couched in the metaphysical and mystic language apparently characteristic of anarchist propaganda.'[71] While on this theme, we may mention the judgment of the High Court in the Rajabazaar Bomb Case, dated 25 February 1915. The meaning of the words 'Mayer Lila' which occurred in a *Liberty* pamphlet that had been presented as evidence in the case, became the object of much scrutiny of the judges. The words literally meant 'the inscrutable ways of Mother' but the judges were more concerned with the metaphorical meaning of the words and declared

> At the same time there can be no question but that by a grievous and perverse misapplication of language, an act of sacrilege, which merits the strongest condemnation of all right minded people – revolutionaries have applied the expression (Mayer Lila) to describe anarchical outrages as if they were deeds sanctioned by the great mother of the universe.[72]

The language of propaganda caused incomprehension, repulsion and fear in the colonial masters because they found in it not the passionate attachment of impressionable young minds to the mystical abstraction called the motherland, but as the *Sedition Committee Report* put it, an example of 'perverted religion and equally perverted patriotism.'[73]

In pronouncing his sentence the Sessions Judge, J. Cornes, concluded with the following remarks:

> Some slight notice also might be taken of the fact that accused is a very young man, aged about 20, who has borne an exemplary

> character apart from this and who might have been a credit instead of a disgrace to his family if his mind had not been poisoned by the mischievous and abhorrent doctrine of anarchism as preached in Bengal. I cannot close this judgment without paying a tribute to the deceased Head Master, Babu Nabin Chandra Bose. ... Undeterred as lesser men would have been, by all kinds of scurrilous abuse, calumny, threats of his life (which he knew, full well were no vain ones), he has maintained, as we know from the evidence for the last 5 or 6 years and probably for much longer, a firm and steadfast loyalty to the British Government. ... Such a man is a true hero."[74]

The views held by the colonial administration were contested by the revolutionary nationalists who inverted the colonial categories to present a mirror image of the political situation then obtaining in India. The very actions that made Nabin Babu a favourite with government officials caused him to be regarded as a figure of hatred by the revolutionary terrorists. The leaflets like *Swadhin Bharat* that Nabin Babu had handed over to the authorities referred contemptuously to informers and collaborators of the British government and contained powerful warnings of the fate that awaited them. One *Swadhin Bharat* leaflet had this to say:

> We and the English have conflicting interests in India. Just as we regard loyalists as traitors to the country, similarly the English look upon patriots as disloyal. The enemies are representing us to the world as murderous blood-thirsty creatures. But we are not sorry for it.[75]

In the revolutionary discourse it was the colonial rulers who were portrayed as the sinners – immoral predators whose actions had reduced to ruin the inhabitants of a great nation and who were therefore deserving of punishment. The pamphlets questioned the wisdom of the judgment of those who refused to recognize this simple truth:

> Of those who judge of demerits and merits with the help of arguments and reasoning and who bless or curse accordingly, we ask, whether or not those people whose oppressions are leading *lakhs* and *lakhs* of breadless men and women to advance, every moment, on the path of ruin.... assassins? Are they not blood-thirsty whose ceaseless suckings have deprived a great nation of its life-blood and reduced it day by day to a mere skeleton? Are not those people robbers who loot others' wealth in order that may indulge in luxuries themselves? Have those who are moved by sudden blood-shed ... discussed these

questions for once before allowing themselves to be drowned in the ocean of grief caused by the sight of the *feringhi's* bloody form?[76]

Finally, the colonial discourse on the civilizing mission in India was neatly reversed in a *Liberty* pamphlet thus:

> You speak of National Development and of co-operation. When good institutions are started and attempts are made to educate the people on national lines and teach them the needs of Freedom and Patriotism – the only thing needful for National Development and Self-Government – you come with your Risley Circular, Defence of the Realm Act, sedition and such other engines of oppression – the only offensive and defensive weapons of self-protection of the usurping tyrants. By our money (Revenue) you beguile our weak-minded countrymen and twin them into a host of spies and informers and by all foul means, ensnare the noble youths by false evidences, and call them Anarchists. You hang our patriots and preach in the same breath about peace, tranquility and love! How long can such fraud be tolerated![77]

And so the battle went on between the ruler and the ruled, pitting the two in an antagonistic relationship in which both struggled to gain the upper hand. The colonial discourse, condescending and contemptuous of the ruled, was countered with a revolutionary discourse that painted the rulers as deceitful, unjust and undeserving of loyalty. These two alternative discourses, representing fundamentally different images and perceptions of the 'self' and the 'other' structured the worldviews of the rulers and ruled, providing the rationale behind and justifying their actions in the fractured world of a colonial society.

Endnotes

1 Elizabeth Kolsky, *Colonial Justice in British India. White Violence and the Rule of Law* (Cambridge, Cambridge University Press, 2010), p. 1–5, 232.

2 For the ideological assumptions implicit in the operations of 'Law' see Robert M. Cover, 'Violence and the Word' in Bruce B. Lawrence and Aisha Karim, editors, *On Violence: A Reader* (Duke University Press, Durham and London, 2007), p. 294–313.

3 George Balandier 'The Colonial Situation: A Theoretical Approach' in Stephen Howe ed. *The New Imperial Histories Reader* (Routledge, London and New York, 2010), p. 23–40.

4 Antoinette Burton, 'Rules of Thumb: British History and "Imperial Culture" in Nineteenth and Twentieth- Century Britain', ibid. p. 41–54, esp. 42. See also J. Mackenzie (1984) *Propaganda and Empire: The Manipulation of British Public Opinion, 1880–1960* (Manchester University Press, Manchester, 1984), p. 254.

5 *Reviewing the Present Political Situation in India, the Causes of Sedition and its Remedies, Calcutta, 4th March, 1910.* From the office of Sir Harold Stuart, Secretary to the Government of India, Home Department, Political Branch, to the Chief Secretary to the Government of Bengal, in West Bengal State Archives (hereafter WBSA), Intelligence Branch (hereafter IB), Serial Number (hereafter SN) 40/1914, File Number (hereafter FN) 9/1914.

6 From the Hon'ble Mr J. G. Cumming, Officiating Chief Secretary to the Government of Bengal to The Secretary to the Government of India, Home Department, Political Branch, dated Calcutta, the 30 August 1913, 7186 P. – in WBSA-IB, SN 65/1914, FN 258/1914.

7 The revolutionary nationalists were usually referred to in official documents as 'anarchists' during this period, though the terms 'nihilists', 'extremists' and 'terrorists' were also variously used.

8 From R. B. Hughes-Buller, Inspector General of Police, Bengal, to the Chief Secretary to the Government of Bengal, dated Calcutta, the 6 January 1914 in WBSA-IB, SN 65/1914, FN 258/1914.

9 From the Secretary to the Government of India, Home Department, Political Branch to the Chief Secretary to the Government of Bengal, dated 27 May 1913, in WBSA-IB, SN 65/1914, FN 258/1914.

10 *The Present Political Situation in India,* 1910, op cit.

11 'Regarding Revolutionary Movement in Bengal', letter written by G. W. Dixon, Special Superintendent of Police, Intelligence Department, to J. G. Cumming, Officiating Chief Secretary to the Government of Bengal, on the 18 December 1916, from Ramna, Dacca, Political Department, Political Branch (Confidential) No File No. – 1916 – *Revolutionary Movements in Bengal,* WBSA-Writers Building (hereafter WB).

12 Note drawn up by A. H. L. Fraser, Lieutenant Governor of Bengal, dated 29 June 1907 in Government of Bengal, Political Department, Political Branch, File No. 132 0f 1908 in WBSA-WB.

13 From Sir Harold Stuart, Chief Secretary to the Government of India, Home Department to the Chief Secretary to the Government of Bengal, dated 1 July 1909 in Government of Bengal, Political Department, Political Branch, File 172 of 1909, Serial No.2, WBSA-WB.

14 Walter Russell Donogh, *The History and Law Of Sedition and Cognate Offences In British India: Penal and Preventive* (Thacker, Spink and Company, Calcutta, 1914), p. 56–8.

15 Comment in the newspaper *Nayak* in the context of the *Hitavadi* Sedition Case of December, 1910, translated and reproduced in the *Annual Report on Indian Newspapers and Periodicals Published in Bengal during the year 1910* in Government of Bengal, Political Department, Political Branch, File No. 83 of 1911, WBSA-WB.

16 There are extensive collections of reports dealing with the Indian and

particularly the Bengali Press in the West Bengal State Archives, Writers Building. See particularly Government of Bengal, Political Department, Political Branch (Confidential), File Number (hereafter FN) 132 of 1908 (*Press Legislation*) and Government of India, Political Department, Political Branch, FN 176 of 1909 (*Proposal for Improving the Tone of the Native Press.*) See also the various *Annual Reports of Newspapers and Periodicals* published in Bengal, all in WBSA-WB.

17 *Proposed Prosecution of Certain Native Newspapers in Bengal* – Note from E. A. Gait, Officiating Secretary to the Government of Bengal to Sir Herbert Risley, Secretary to the Government of India, Home Department, dated 19 May, 1907, National Archives of India, Home Department, Political Branch (Confidential), Deposit – July 1907, No. 66.

18 Ibid. Also see *Violence Exhibited by the Native Press in Calcutta and the Districts of Eastern Bengal and Assam,* Note from H. Le Mesurier, Officiating Chief Secretary to the Government of Eastern Bengal and Assam to the Secretary to the Government of India, Home Department, dated 4 June 1907, National Archives of India, Proceedings of the Home Department, Political Branch (Confidential), Deposit July 1907, Nos. 17–18.

19 Letter from F. W. Duke, Chief Secretary to the Government of Bengal to the Secretary to the Government of India, Home Department dated 18 September 1909, in Government of Bengal, Political Department, Political Branch (Confidential), File No. 176 of 1909, Serial Nos. 1–2, WBSA-WB.

20 *Annual Report on the Newspapers Owned by Indians Which Were Published in Bengal during the Year 1908,* WBSA-WB, Home Department, Political Branch, FN, 139/1909.

21 Quoted in *Sedition Committee (Rowlatt) Report* (New Age Publishers, Calcutta, New Print, 1973), p. 193.

22 *History and Law of Sedition,* op.cit., p. 237.

23 Note of A. H. L. Fraser, Lieutenant Governor of Bengal, dated 29 June 1907, arguing for the enactment of a Press Law that would allow the government 'effectively and promptly to suppress the publication and dissemination of writings of a seditious character or with a tendency to promote a breach of the peace', Government of Bengal, Political Department, Political Branch, File No. 132 of 1908 in WBSA-WB.

24 Ibid., from F. W. Duke, Officiating Chief Secretary to the Government of Bengal to the Secretary to the Government of India, Home Department dated 14 July 1908. Also see A. H. L. Fraser's note, dated 29 June 1907, in the same file.

25 Ibid.

26 *Fortnightly Reports on the Political Situation in the Province of Eastern Bengal and Assam,* Proceedings of the Home Department, Political, Part A in National Archives of India, Report for the first half of month of July, dated 31 July 1908, No. 38. The comment in quotes is from the report on the second half of the month of May, dated 8 June 1908, No. 29.

27 *Intelligence Branch, C.I.D. Bengal, Weekly Reports on the Political Situation and Enquiries of a Political Nature in Bengal, October 1908–December 1909,* See especially report of the week ending 31 October 1908, WBSA-I.B.

28 Ibid. *Report of the Week Ending 20th February, 1909.*

29 *Fortnightly Reports on the Political Situation in the Province of Eastern Bengal and Assam,* Home Department, Political, A. National Archives of India, Fortnightly Report for the second half of the month of July, dated 11 August 1908, No. 42.

30 Enclosure in WBSA-IB, SN 14/1911, FN 105 A/1911. The letter, dated 4 August 1911, was written to the Editor of the *Statesman* from an individual in Dinapore Cantonment (signature illegible) in response to an article in the *Statesman* that reported the appearance of a new *Sandhya* leaflet in August 1911.

31 C.I.D. Bengal, *Weekly Reports of 1910.* Also see handwritten police notes in SN 3/1908, FN 699/1908. The quote is from this file.

32 For the list of printers see SN 38/1910, FN 1318/1910. For the second report, Ryland's note dated 20 July 1911, ibid.

33 Several such cases of police surveillance of suspected individuals are recorded in, SN 38/1910, FN 1318/1910, WBSA-IB.

34 See Confidential reports on the *Jugantar* leaflets dated 1 March 1913 and 12 March 1913 in SN 45/1913, FN 380/1913, WBSA-IB.

35 All reports relating to this case may be found in SN 35/1910, FN 191/1910, WBSA-IB. See especially police report dated 2 October 1910.

36 For example, Nalini Kanta Mukharjee was suspected of circulating *Swadhin Bharat* leaflets that circulated in the Serajgunj subdivision in 1911 but could not be traced. Nalini Kanta's father, Akshay Kumar Mukharjee claimed that he had not heard from his son in years. The inability of the police to track down suspects in this case provoked the Superintendent of Police to remark that the Serajgung police were not handling the case with particular intelligence. An idea of the floundering helplessness of the police in tracking down suspects in the Serajgunj case may be formed by consulting the records in SN 38/1910, FN 1318/1910 in WBSA - IB.

37 'Interception of Revolutionary Correspondence', SN 104/1918, FN 237/1918, WBSA-IB.

38 Postmasters and railway police were to play a very important role in the governmental plan to stop the flow of seditious material between provinces and from outside the country. See Report in file mentioned in last footnote. The list includes forty four names and may not be a complete one. Note headed *Calcutta Police Office, 18th July 1907,* SN 19/1911, FN IV/278/1911, WBSA-IB.

39 There are a large number of files in the WBSA-IB dealing with the dissemination of *Jugantar, Swadhin* Bharat and *Liberty* pamphlets beginning from 1910 that diligently record the names of all locations where the pamphlets appeared, the post offices from which they were posted, and the names of individuals who received these pamphlets and handed them over to the police for example SN 35/1910, FN 191/1910; SN 38/1910, FN 1318/1910; SN 36/1910, FN V/94/1910 all in WBSA-IB.

40 SN 38/1910, FN 1318/1910, WBSA-IB. A large number of reports in police files that relate to the 'seditious' activities in the National Schools are indicative of the concern in ruling circles at the rapid spread of revolutionary ideas in both parts of the province. See *Report on the National Schools in the Province of Eastern Bengal and Assam (from 1st October, 1908 to 30th June, 1909)*; *Report on National Schools*

in the Province of Eastern Bengal and Assam (from 1st July 1909 to 31st December, 1911); Report on the National Schools of Bengal, 1910–11; Statement showing the Participation of Masters and Students of Schools and Colleges in the Bengal Presidency in Political Agitation, all in Amiya Samanta ed. *Terrorism in Bengal: A Collection of Documents*, (Government of West Bengal, Calcutta), Vol. IV, p. 751–1088.

41 Calcutta Records, 2, 1910, Government of India, Home Department, Political A, Proceedings, April 1910, Nos. 1–2, National Archives of India.

42 Particular mention may be made of Jyotish Ghose, who planned the bomb outrage in Dalhousie Square, Calcutta on 2 March 1911. Jyotish Ghose was a professor of Hoogly College, a brilliant scholar, an MA from Calcutta University and an intimate friend and admirer of Aurobindo Ghose. The Police Report on the investigations into the outrage mentioned the Jyotish was 'a man of extreme views who frequently mixed with students and apparently exercised an unwholesome influence on them.' Police Report dated 11 March 1911 SN 11/1911, FN 1950/1911, WBSA-IB.

43 Note drawn up by R. B. Hughes Buller, Inspector General of Police Bengal, dated the 24 December 1913 in WBSA-IB, SN 65/1914, SN 258/1914.

44 SN 35/1910, FN 191/1910, WBSA-IB.

45 Police Report dated 7 April 1910, SN 38/1910, FN 1318/1910, WBSA-IB.

46 Report submitted by Sub Inspector S. C. Mukherjee on 2 March 1913, SN 45/1913, FN 380/1913, WBSA-IB.

47 F.C. Daly, The Deputy Inspector General of Police in charge of the Special Department, Calcutta, wrote to H. T. Cullis, the Under-Secretary to the Government of Bengal on 3 May 1911, saying 'I think the Eastern Bengal and Assam Police are, like ourselves, waiting for some definite clue on which to make a start. They always inform us when copies of the leaflets come into their hands, but they have not been able to obtain any clue as to the authors or distributors of them', SN 35/1910, FN 191/1910, WBSA-IB. On another occasion, he commented, 'I am afraid that I must admit that the revolutionaries have succeeded far better than we have in organizing and carrying on their work with secrecy…', letter written to Stevenson Moore (Commissioner of Police) on 7 March 1911, SN 11/1911, FN 1950/1911, WBSA-IB.

48 Secret Note sent by R. B. Hughes Buller, Inspector General of Police, Bengal to the Chief Secretary to the Government of Bengal, dated 6 January 1914, SN 65/1914, FN 258/1914, WBSA-IB.

49 Extensive enquiries were carried out to track the underground propaganda network after the sensational findings at the Loke Nath Yantra Press in December 1913. Numerous names are mentioned in the files as suspected authors of the *Liberty* leaflets (including that of Aurobindo Ghose as author of the *Liberty* leaflet titled *Solemn Declaration Liberty*) and many more as distributors, but despite the strenuous efforts of the police, success in following up on these leads was severely limited. See especially the files SN 8/1914, FN 1266/1914; SN 39/1914, FN 1021/1914; SN 70/1916, FN 467/1916 in WBSA-IB.

50 First Report dated 17 April 1916 regarding the distribution of seditious leaflets, Superintendent of Police, Dacca, SN 70/1916, FN 467/1916, WBSA-IB.

51 'The Revolutionary Movement in Rangpur', Confidential Note drawn up by C. A. Tegart, dated 1 March 1913, SN 21/1915, FN 323/15, WBSA-IB.

52 The government also tried other, more repressive means, to keep the students in check. For example, the *Carlyle Circular* of October 1905 placed upon the heads of colleges and schools the responsibility of preventing students from actively participating in the *swadeshi* movement, while the *Seditious Meetings Act* of November 1907, gave the government considerable powers to prevent the holding of public meetings.

53 *Present Political Situation*, dated 4 March 1910, op.cit.

54 Ibid.

55 From Sir Harold Stuart, Chief Secretary to the Government of India, Home Department to the Chief Secretary to the Government of Bengal, dated 22 July 1909, Government of Bengal, Political Department, Political Branch, File 176 of 1909, WBSA-IB.

56 Ibid.

57 Ibid., letter sent from F. W. Duke, Chief Secretary to the Government of Bengal to the Secretary to the Government of India, Home Department, dated 8 September 1909.

58 Ibid.

59 See Chapter III and below.

60 '*Sedition o Bideshi Raja*' (*Sedition and the Foreign King*), in the *Jugantar* issue of 30 July 1907 reproduced in *Agnijuger Agnikatha*, p. 615–16. Also see *Conspiracy or Desire for Freedom* – Official translated version of *Jugantar* article of 9 May 1908 in *Report on Native Papers in Bengal* for the week ending 16 May 1908.

61 This incident has been reconstructed on the basis of the documents compiled in SN 72/1916, FN 133/16, 'Arrest of Manindra Chandra Bhattacharjee and Sureshwar Bhattacharjee for circulating in Pabna a seditious leaflet entitled *Swadhin Bharat* ', WBSA-IB. See especially the *Judgment* against the two accused, dated 11 April 1916, 11-4-16, by the District Magistrate of Pabna as well as the *Judgment* in the High Court of Judicature at Fort William in Calcutta, dated 20 July 1916. 20-7-1916.

62 For another account of the relationship between rulers and the ruled, see Robert Darnton, 'Literary Surveillance in the British Raj. The Contradictions of Liberal Imperialism,' *Book History* 4 (2001), 133-176; Also see Vinay Lal, 'The Rhetorical and Substantive Basis of the "Rule of Law" under Colonialism; A Study of Colonial Perceptions of Terrorism in Colonial Bengal', *The Calcutta Historical Journal* (vols, XIX and XX combined: 1997–98), p. 141–72.

63 The murder of Babu Nabin Chndra Basu and the events that followed have been reconstructed from the voluminous reports compiled after his death which are to be found in, SN 84/16, FN183/16 'Murder of the Head Master of Maldah Zilla School', WBSA-IB.

64 Ibid. From 'Trial No. 2 of June 1916, Malda. The King Emperor versus Mohendra Nath Das. In the Court of the Sessions Judge, Malda'.

65 Ibid. Extract from F. F. Kemp's letter dated the 6 February 1916.

66 From the judgment rendered in the High Court of Judicature at Fort William in Bengal, dated the 8 January 1917.

67 *Gaur Duta* of 26 July 1916.

68 296/1 was the place in Upper Circular Road where the explosives used as evidence in the Raja Bazaar Bomb Case were discovered in December 1913.

69 For details of this literature see, Chapter III.

70 Additional Notes from 1924 on Mohendra's case, SN 84/16, FN 183/16, WBSA-IB.

71 Sentence passed in the High Court of Judicature at Fort William in Bengal by Justices Teunon and Chaudhuri, 1–2 . Ibid.

72 Annexure (I). 'Summaries of some Bengal Judgments' in *Sedition Committee Report* (Calcutta, Bengal Secretariat Press, 1918), p. 9.

73 *Sedition Committee Report,* p. 31. The above quote is from the English translation of a pamphlet *Mahasakti* (*Worship of the Goddess of Spiritual Strength*) which was found along with other literature in Mohendra's house at Alal, SN 84/16, FN 183/16, WBSA-IB.

74 Judgment in the Malda Murder Case, Trial No. 2 of June 1916, p. 20. Ibid.

75 Official English translation of excerpt from *Swadhin Bharat* leaflet in WBSA-IB, SN 38/1910, FN 1318/1910.

76 Ibid. *Lakh*: Hundred thousand.

77 Excerpt from *Liberty, A Review,* which made its first appearance in Barisal Town in March 1916. Included in Amiya Samanta ed. *Terrorism in Bengal: Collection of Documents,* Vol. IV, p. 501.

5

Summing Up
An Identity Forged in Battle

The revolutionary pamphlets offer us fascinating glimpses into the narrative construction of a 'revolutionary nationalist identity' at the turn of the twentieth century. The revolutionaries were born and grew to manhood in a colonized world that was structured by unequal power relations between the colonizers and the colonized. The colonial environment had an immediate impact on their everyday existence by setting limits on and defining the parameters of the ways in which they could choose to lead their lives as colonial subjects. It generated powerful emotions of alienation from the colonial state and the desire to foster an identity alternate to that of the colonial subject. These emotions became embedded in the consciousness of the revolutionary nationalists and also contributed to their collective sense of self. As the earlier chapters have demonstrated, this collective sense of self involved a voluntary subscription to certain shared values and ideals that delineated the political community which the revolutionary nationalists identified with. This chapter explores aspects of this definition of self that were specific to the revolutionary nationalists. The distinctive feature of the revolutionary identity was that it was constituted in battle against the colonial rulers and drew sustenance from the shared passions of fellow revolutionaries which, in turn, bred a sense of solidarity among them. This identity also acquired legitimacy from the terms in which the conflict between the state and the brotherhood of revolutionaries was framed. This identity was the crucial element in revolutionary political culture as it defined the role of the revolutionary nationalists in the struggle for nationhood and demarcated the boundaries of their political community. The revolutionary political community, with its shared ethos, experiences and practices, was represented as distinct from those of other political communities that shared space with the revolutionary nationalists in the public political realm at the turn of the century.

It is in the formation of this revolutionary identity that the fusing of the public and the private spheres becomes most apparent. The personal emotions and convictions, aspirations and frustrations of the revolutionaries played a critical role in molding their political subjectivities.[1] The subjectivities of individual revolutionaries influenced their relationships with fellow political actors and also accounted for their emotional investments in and identification with the discourses of the public sphere. Revolutionary pamphlet rhetoric absorbed components from the discourses then prevalent in the public sphere but molded them in accordance with the emotional and ideological proclivities of the pamphleteers. A study of pamphlet rhetoric reveals that revolutionary nationalist identity was deeply rooted in time and place, yet distinctive in concept and expression.

The members of the revolutionary secret societies were mostly educated, idealistic, sensitive and impressionable young men and boys who shared an intensely emotive bonding with the land of their birth that found expression in veneration for the territorial space and physical environment of the country. Nalinikishore Guha, one of the first generation of revolutionary nationalists, described this form of affective nationalism with these words,

> In every country are born some individuals who literally consider each speck of dust of the land to be flecks of gold. The sky and the wind, moon and stars, planets and stars – the trees, birds and animals, rivers and mountains of the nation fill their beings with happiness; every object in their land constitute their life blood. [2]

From this mystical adoration of the land of their birth, it was a logical progression on the part of the revolutionaries to humanize and sacralize the territorial space of the nation. Emblematic of this form of affective nationalism was the figure of the mother-goddess – part earthly mother, part divinity who had to be both protected and obeyed. Scholars have argued that somatic representations of nationhood help to transform abstract geographical territory into a living enchanted nation-space capable of provoking passionate emotions of devotion and desire for the imagined geo-body of the nation.[3] It may be added that iconic representations of the nation as mother also served as a unifying mechanism within the nationalist imagination. This image, which figured in the visual imaginary as a collective embodiment of the love and reverence of individual revolutionaries towards their mothers, helped to bring the revolutionaries closer together in emotional communion. Filial emotions, which ordinarily operated within the sphere of the family were redirected towards the nation-mother and the revolutionary community was imagined as an extended family with the revolutionaries joined together in a fraternal bond. Nalinikishore Guha, quoted above, dedicated his memoirs to the mothers, both living and dead, of the revolutionary nationalists because it was the mothers who had had to bear in silence the pain and the sorrow that followed from the activities of their revolutionary sons. Bhupendranath Dutt tellingly remarked in one of his essays that the smaller (birth) mother had to be sacrificed for the larger (nation) mother in the revolutionary cause.[4] The close association between the two figures – the birth mother and nation-mother – in the political imaginary of the revolutionaries becomes evident from the two instances cited above. Pain, sorrow and sacrifice, tropes that defined the relationship between the revolutionary community and the nation-deity in pamphlet rhetoric, are deployed in both cases to define the relationship between the individual revolutionaries and their birth mothers. Pamphlet rhetoric also cast the relationship among the revolutionaries as a fraternal bond with the latter bound in an oath to sacrifice their lives to defend the honour of the mother-nation.

The revolutionary enterprise would exercise an obvious attraction for youth who were rebellious or adventurous in disposition and not easily cowed by fear of arrest, torture and imprisonment. In their memoirs, several of the early revolutionaries recall with admiration the great bravery and courage with which young recruits faced danger and the stoicism and even irreverence with which they received sentences of long jail terms. Even though official records sanctimoniously attributed the appeal of revolutionary nationalism for young men to the frustrations arising out of poverty and unemployment, it is to be noted that a sizeable number gave up profitable careers, comfortable homes and happy family lives to embark on the revolutionary enterprise.[5] Bhupendranath Dutt, an important member of the early *Jugantar* society and the first editor of the newspaper, often pondered the question of revolutionary mentalité or that unconscious psychological dynamic that impelled individuals to become revolutionaries, knowing the tremendous sacrifices in family life and career that such a choice would entail. He wrote that the revolutionary nationalists were often described as *deshpagla* (crazy for love of the country) by their compatriots, and Bhupendrananth's choice of term indicates that the decision to become a revolutionary could not be explained in rational, cold-blooded terms. A sign of the strength of character of the revolutionary nationalists, according to Bhupendranath, was their ability to stand steadfastly by their ideals even when they were uncertain of their basic material wants being met while living the life of a revolutionary.[6] Analysing the character traits of the revolutionary nationalists in his memoirs, he wrote that flippant or dissolute types could not become members of the secret societies because of the emphasis placed within the societies on hard physical activity, learning and moral restraint. Idealistic young men were drawn to these associations precisely because of the quality of training involved in becoming a revolutionary.[7] It was only after four to five years of dedicated training that the revolutionary aspirants could take their vows and become full-fledged members of the societies.[8] Upendranath Bandopadhyay has described in his memoirs the absolute penury in which the revolutionary nationalists who had gathered at the Maniktala Gardens in 1907 lived and worked and the hard grind that was a part of their daily existence. Those who were unable to tolerate the conditions quit early on.[9] Revolutionary nationalists have written frequently about their experiences while under arrest and in jail. The horrific descriptions of prison life and torture in police custody constitute evidence enough that those who were willing to suffer such conditions, not once, but repeatedly, in the course of their lives, possessed rare reservoirs of strength and courage with which to face and overcome hardship in the service of their beloved motherland.[10]

Lessons in economics, history, politics and the religious texts constituted an integral part of the revolutionary education. Learned works like Dadabhai Naoroji's *Poverty and Un-British Rule in India* and R. C. Dutt's *The Economic History of British India* had already informed educated Indians about colonial expropriation and the progressive agricultural and industrial impoverishment of India under British rule. But it was Sakharam Ganesh Deuskar's *Desher Katha* (*The Story of the Country*) that was published in 1904 and went through five editions by 1908 that took educated Bengalis by storm. Marshalling evidence from official records and statistical tables, yet written in simple uncluttered language, *Desher Katha* touched a deep emotional chord among the Bengalis in its depiction of the economic degradation of the country under colonial rule. One reviewer wrote that while he had known about the present condition of the country in an abstract way, it was this book that brought the facts home to him in clear and lifelike fashion.[11] Deuskar's influence on the young revolutionaries was especially profound. Hemchandra Qanungo was to write later in his memoirs of the emotions that reading *Desher Katha* evoked in him. He wrote that though there was nothing in the book to arouse a *sense of nationality*, yet anyone who read it could not but become deeply anti-British. He went on to say that there was no other instance in Bengali literature of a book that offered such proof of the depredations carried out by the British. He characterized *Desher Katha* as an early example of revolutionary propaganda literature.[12] Bhupendranath Dutt has also written about the encouragement provided by Sakharam Ganesh Deuskar to the young writers of the *Jugantar* newspaper.[13] In a similar vein, Jadugopal Mukhopadhyay and Hemchandra Qanungo have written about the impact on young recruits of Jogendra Nath Vidyabhushan's writings as well as of classics like *Neel-Darpan* and *Coolie-Kahini* that dwelt upon the sufferings of Indians under colonial rule.[14] The revolutionary recruits learned from these books about the conditions in their country and this intellectual grounding had a sufficient intellectual and emotional impact for them to try and disseminate the knowledge that they had gained from such readings among the population at large through the medium of newspapers and pamphlets.

Not only did the recruits learn from books, but their personal experiences of colonial rule instilled in them a deep sense of anger at the egregiously unjust fashion in which relations between the rulers and the ruled were regulated in colonial India. Racial insults and humiliations which were an everyday experience under colonial rule increasingly bred a sense of rebelliousness in the youth of Bengal. Almost all the revolutionary nationalists recall, in their memoirs, incidents of racial abuse and the revengeful impulses that such incidents provoked. Reacting to incidents of racial abuse became the mark of the true patriot and in the closing decades of the nineteenth century, incidents of Bengalis brawling with Europeans occupied pride of place in newspaper reports. Saraladevi Choudhurani, a member of the Tagore family and an immensely talented woman of many accomplishments, introduced a new feature in the periodical *Bharati* that she edited whereby she invited Bengalis to send in accounts of their run-ins with Englishmen. Her intention in publicizing incidents of Bengali men retaliating when subjected to humiliation by Englishmen in public places such as in steamers, trains or roadways was to instill self-confidence and racial pride among Bengalis.[15] Ullaskar Dutt who joined the revolutionaries at the Maniktala Gardens was thrown out of Presidency College and the boy Sushil Sen was sentenced by the Presidency magistrate, Kingsford, to fourteen lashes, both for beating up Europeans, the first an abusive Professor, and the second, a physically aggressive European sergeant.[16] The revolutionaries learned to interpret not only their personal experiences, but world events as well, through this veil of racial difference. Thus Japan's victory over Russia in the Russo-Japanese war of 1905 was an event for celebration and a cause of hope among the revolutionary nationalists who reasoned that if a small Asiatic country with limited resources could defeat a great European imperial power, then Bengalis too, could take the fight to the British through the secret societies and gradually overpower them![17]

The founding of the secret societies in the closing decades of the nineteenth century was one among the many early signs of the growing impulse among a section of the Bengalis to get organized for battle against the British. The early attempts at such political organization were more a testimony to hope than to effectiveness. In his memoirs, *Jibansmriti*, Rabindranth Tagore has pointed out with his usual insight that the early secret societies were expressions of the desire to celebrate the heroic that is latent within every culture.[18] This desire to cultivate the heroic and manly was a defining feature of the cultural nationalism that had swept over Bengali society from the closing decades of the nineteenth century. At the level of the individual, it found expression in the cultivation of bodily strength through physical exercise. This emphasis on masculinity and virility was a response to the colonial stereotyping that branded Bengalis as 'effeminate' and lacking in masculine vigour. As Mrinalini Sinha has pointed, in the late nineteenth century, this stereotype of the 'effeminate babu' was used by the colonial administration to characterize the politically conscious, educated middle class Indians, a large majority of whom were Bengali Hindus.[19] Middle class Bengalis, in turn, internalized such stereotypes and the causes of Bengal's decline in the nineteenth century were closely associated in the middle class imagination with such notions of effeminacy and degeneracy. Bankimchandra, in his essay, *Bharat Kalanka* (India's Shame) connected such effeminacy with the loss of nationhood and the consequent loss of national consciousness among modern Indians for, in his view, it was the resolve to defend their national sovereignty against invading foreigners that had contributed to the martial vigour of ancient Indians.[20] The programme of nationalist regeneration in late nineteenth century Bengal incorporated a somatic ideology with the individual body representing in microcosm the geo-body of the nation. The individual body, virile and healthy, became the symbol of a strong and glorious nation. This form of somatic nationalism found concrete form in the *akharas* or gymnasiums where training in bodybuilding, weightlifting and wrestling was imparted. Middle class Bengalis, who had traditionally looked down upon physical exercise as an activity properly belonging to the domain of the working classes, began to show an active interest in cultivating bodily strength, because nationalist ideology had brought about a transformation in the way the body was viewed. From being a mere repository of labor power, the body now crystallized into a political metaphor. The martial and virile body became the fundamental element in the composition of the geo-moral order constituted by the nation state, a receptacle of the virtues necessary for building up the nation.[21] Saraladevi Choudhurani took the lead in organizing the *Birashtami* and *Pratapaditya* festivals in which exhibitions of swordplay, wrestling and fighting with staves (lathis) took pride of place. A novel feature of the *Birashtami* festival, organized on the third day (*Mahashtami*) of the festival of the goddess Durga was the worship of a decorated sword in place of the image of the goddess, together with the chanting of hymns eulogizing brave historical characters.[22]Somatic nationalism brought within its ambit even the institution of the circus with its gravity defying gymnastic displays and feats with wild animals and ringmasters like Shyamakanta Bandopadhyay, Motilal Bose and Krishno Basak became symbols of this newfound martial prowess of the Bengalis. Wrestlers like Ghulam *Pahalwan*, Gama *Pahalwan* and Karim Bakhsh emerged as unlikely cultural icons because of their victories over famous foreign wrestlers.[23]

The *samitis* or voluntary associations that were founded in the late nineteenth and early twentieth centuries in Bengal were also conceived in accordance with this ideology. For example the *Anushilan Samiti*, established in Calcutta in 1902 had initially been founded as a gymnasium attached to Scottish Church College by its founder Satishchandra Basu. The *Anushilan Samiti* became the model of many such *samitis* that were founded throughout Bengal. Bankimchandra Chattopadhyay had used the term *anushilan* in his novel *Anandamath* to mean the cultivation of physical, mental, ethical and spiritual qualities in order to attain perfection of character and the *samiti* leaders adopted this ideal as their goal in the training that they imparted to the young recruits. Consequently, cultivation of bodily strength went hand in hand with the inculcation of spiritual values. Thus the recruits were required to practice *brahmacharya*, or celibacy which was looked upon not only as a marker of a virtuous life but as a means of conserving physical energy. The *Gita*, as mentioned earlier, played a central role in the spiritual training of the revolutionaries, inspiring them to work selflessly for the motherland, without hope of any immediate gain, which was the idea underlying the concept of *Nishkama karma*, expounded in the *Gita*. The religious underpinnings of the movement led to the ritualization of acts of violence. The revolutionary nationalist enterprise was conceptualized as an elaborate religious sacrifice with individual revolutionaries cast in the role of sacrificial victims who were being dedicated to the nation-deity. As Wendy Doniger has pointed out, the paradigmatic sacrifice in Vedism and in all sacrificial theory is self sacrifice, because while sacrifice ordinarily operates on a principle of substitution, in self-sacrifice the human who is considered to be the closest counterpart and therefore the most valuable to the creator god is being sacrificed. The act of self-sacrifice (*atma-bali*) or martyrdom was foundational to the whole revolutionary nationalist endeavour because it served to bestow an ethical and moral dimension to acts of violence and so to legitimize the movement. [24] From contemporary reports and revolutionary memoirs it appears that not only did the young revolutionaries themselves aspire towards martyrdom, but it was this element of heroic self-sacrifice associated with acts of revolutionary terrorism that appealed most to the sentiments of the public. The last moments in the life of Khudiram Bose, who was hanged on 12th June, 1908 were widely reported in the newspapers and his martyrdom was celebrated in song and verse throughout Bengal. Even the solidly pro-government newspaper, the *Empire* reported,

> Khudiram Bose was executed this morning. ...It is alleged that he mounted the scaffold with his body erect. He was cheerful and smiling.[25]

The public frenzy that surrounded the funeral procession of Kanailal Dutta, who had assassinated the informer Naren Gosain and was hanged on 10 November 1908, led the government to refuse permission for the public cremation of Satyen Bose, Kanailal's co-conspirator. The hangings of Kanai and Satyen acquired a symbolic meaning in the public mind. It was as if the perfect life, achieved through *anushilan*, had climaxed in the perfect death, and ordinary mortals were swept along in the wake of this extraordinary moment. It was this ideal and practice of martyrdom that gave the revolutionary nationalist its distinctive identity, and it was the foregrounding of this principle of martyrdom that enabled the revolutionary nationalist movement to cross its elitist barriers and make a lasting impact on the wider public life of Bengal.

The *swadeshi* movement marked the moment when many among the Bengali youth were roused to patriotic consciousness. As contemporary writings make clear, it was as if a people that had resigned itself to the shamed existence of the colonized subject awoke to the happy realization that achievement of the identity of the free citizen was not only desirable but possible. Vivekananda's exhortation of *Manush Hoyo* (Be A Man!) found new meaning in a new context and Rabindranath's call for *atmashakti* reverberated throughout the public political sphere, arousing intense feelings of pride and achievement among Bengalis. In the words of Ullaskar Dutt,

> During this period our inner selves too, as if infused by the novel spirit of patriotism gradually forgot their insignificance, their worthlessness and tried to advance towards a particular goal with a view to achieving an overall realization of life.[26]

The *swadeshi* movement infused new life into the secret societies whose attempts to mobilize fresh recruits began to show results and thus enabled them to prepare seriously for the revolutionary mission. The search for the new identity among the revolutionary nationalists began from the time of *swadeshi* and the first step was the awareness that a new age had begun in the life of Bengal. The pamphlets often recalled with pride the time of the *swadeshi* movement when an emasculated population had sought to regain national pride after suffering through decades of humiliation.

The pamphlets may be read as thumbnail sketches of the pamphleteers' perception of their lives under colonial rule. The pamphleteers focused on certain aspects of life under colonialism that their readers could immediately identify with and showed how such conditions had led to a loss of self-respect and subsequent loss of national identity. Once such conditions were reversed, the pamphleteers argued, the dignity of the nation could be recovered. The all enveloping degradation of life under colonialism which had led to a loss of self-esteem and a crisis of identity was summed up by one pamphleteer with these words

> *Firinghi purushanukrame tomar hitakangkhir chhadyobesh dharon koriya, chhale bale kaushale, tomar sharbonash shadhon koritechhe – khudhar anno, trishnar jwal hoite tomake bonchito koritechhe, tomar samaj-bandhan dharma-bandhan shithil koriya ditechhe. Tomar shiksha-diksha, ruchi-prakriti firinghir swarthanujayi gothito koriya loitechhe, durbhikkho, mahamari aniya sonar bharat ke swashan koriya, felitechhe, tobu o shei khal jatir nyay-nishthar upar bishwas korite probritti janmitechhe?*[27] (Translation: For generations, the *firinghis*, posing as your well-wishers, have brought about your ruin by treachery and by force. They are depriving you of the food to assuage your hunger, water to slake your thirst; they are weakening the ties of your society and religion. They are molding your education and character to suit their own interests; unleashing famine and plague

to convert golden India into a cremation ground, and yet you are inclined to place your trust in this treacherous race.)

The sorrowful state of affairs was a source of great shame for the revolutionaries, for in negating their sense of manhood, it destroyed their sense of self. This is evident from the reproaches that the revolutionaries heaped upon their readers...

> *Shato shato batshorer dashyotto-pirhone tomar monushyotto ki ekebare lupto hoiyachhe? Souchohin, acharhin, strijeeto, kamonmatto feringhee baniker nishthur dahane tomar khatrotej ki ekebare bhoshyibhuto hoiachhe?*[28]
>
> (Translation: Has the oppression of bondage over centuries caused you to lose your humanity? Has the cruel oppression of the unclean, irreligious, womanizing, lustful feringhis totally destroyed your manhood?)

Or

> *Tomar atmashakti – te abishwas ashiyachhe?*[29]
>
> (Translation: Have you lost belief in your power of self?)

The message that was preached by the pamphleteers was that this negated self could only be reclaimed by taking up battle with the English in order to restore the dignity and honour of the Motherland. It was this metaphor of the motherland that connected the individual selves of the revolutionaries with their collective self. The love and admiration that individual revolutionaries bore for their biological mothers was displaced on to the nation-mother who encompassed within her earthly body the collectivity called the nation.

One such pamphlet that began with the words *abar ghumaile* (*Have you fallen asleep again*) and was devoted almost entirely to summoning the Bengali youth to rally around the revolutionary cause, reminded them that barely a few years ago, during the *swadeshi* age, the youth of Bengal had abandoned their lives of pleasure and contentment to devote themselves to the service of the Motherland. This had instilled in those patriots a sense of pride and achievement that the pamphlets celebrated.

> *Desher shei shumohan muhurte bangalir, gyan, karma, bhakti, deshcharjyabhimukhe probahito hoite lagilo. Kobi o gayak bharatlakhshmir bandana gahite lagilo, karmi deshshebake – i karma*

boliya grahan korilo, bhabuk desher katha bhabiya i pulakito hoilo, banik swadeshi drabyo sambhare tahar bipani sajaite lagilo, jatiyo bidyalaye poriya balokera gaurab bodh korite lagilo, ar jalasthal byom kampito koriya mahakashe mahadhwoni uthilo 'Bandemataram!'[30]

(Translation: At that momentous point of time, the knowledge, activity and faith of Bengalis flowed towards the service of the country. The poet and singer began to sing the praises of the goddess of India's fortunes, the activist took up service for the country as his only vocation, the thinker gloried in thoughts of his country, the trader began to stock his shop with indigenously manufactured (*swadeshi*) goods, the young boys joined national schools and felt proud of it and the earth and skies rocked at the sound of the great cry of *Bande Mataram*!)

The proud moment had become a distant memory, because the terror unleashed by the government and its police had caused fear to enter the hearts of the Bengali youth, who had retreated to the safety of a depoliticized and therefore, meaningless existence. The pamphleteers sought to rally Bengali youth to the cause of revolutionary nationalism by seeking to instill in them self-confidence and dignity as well as pride in their own culture, all virtues on which the experience of being colonial subjects had taken its toll. Years of colonial stereotyping had done their work and the Bengali youth had come to believe, perhaps despite themselves, in all the degrading and humiliating myths about their intellectual shortcomings, physical cowardice and cultural degeneration that the discourses, practices and institutions of colonialism promoted. The pamphleteers were acutely aware that the internal battle over the minds of Bengali youth had to be won before the external battle could be waged.

Emon ekdin chhilo jakhon aneke bolito, 'He Bidhatoh amake abonoto bharoter bangladeshe bangalir ghare janma dile keno?' She atmaglanir din choliya giyachhe. Barindra ar Jatindrer nyay deshbhaktoganer jibane nabojibon labh koriya aj amra boli 'He Bidhatoh, tomake shato shahosro dhanyabad je ami bangali; je bharot achire obhyuday o muktir shamonyoye jagater shikshaguru hoibe, shei bharoter shikshaguru je Bangladesh, shei bangalay ami jonmiyacchi.[31]

(Translation: There was a time when many said 'O God why did you let me born into the home of a Bengali in the Bengal of a dependent India?' Now the time for the self hatred has gone. Inspired by the

> lives of patriots like Barindra and Jatindra, we proclaim today, 'O God, thank you a million times that I am a Bengali; that India, gaining from both power and freedom will soon become the educator and guide of the world and that Bengal which is the guide and educator of India is where I was born.')[32]

The pamphleteers repeatedly reminded their readers of their distinctive and proud identity as Indians that even the long experience of living as colonial subjects had been unable to extinguish.

> *Mone rakhite hoibe – amra paradhin hoileo amader ekta swatantra shatta achhe – she bharotiyo bhab shahosro batsharer, shato atyachare shotrur kathor nishpeshone dhwangsho hoy nai – kakhon je hoibe erup asha o nai. Ihar ki kono karon nai ? – Achhe boi ki. Ei bharotiyo bhab amor boliya – i bharot abar swadhin hoibe.*[33]
>
> (Translation: It has to be kept in mind – even though we are not independent we have a distinctive Indian identity – that Indian identity has not been destroyed despite thousands of years of oppression and torture by the enemy – there is no hope that it will be ever extinguished. Is there no reason for this? Of course there is. Because this Indian identity is eternal, India shall be free again.)

The pamphleteers then set about constructing an alternative narrative within which they sought to define the essence of the Indian identity.

> *Tomader desh, ekdin swadhin chhilo, ekdin tomader deshe birputra janmogrohon korto, ekdin dhane, punye, jashe, gaurabe o biratwe tomader desh abar swdhin hoibe – abar shei desher biratwe, shei desher dharma gaurave, jagat stambhito hoibe. Ekatha bhabteo je atul anondo. He murkho bango santan, e katha tumi keno bujhitechho na?*[34]
>
> (Translation: Our nation was once free, brave sons were born in this land, one day your nation shall once again be free in wealth, virtue, fame, glory and courage – the world shall again be stupefied by that nation's courage and the glory of it *dharma*. To think these thoughts bring immense happiness. O you foolish sons of Bengal, why do you not understand this?)

The qualities of courage, righteousness and patriotism were projected as the defining characteristics of the citizens of an independent land and these qualities were evoked in the hope that it would inspire the youth to join in the revolutionary nationalist movement.

The same effect was sought to be achieved by contrasting the vital life power of the revolutionaries that stemmed from their passion to fight for independence with the listlessness and lethargy of the general population which was itself symptomatic of a deep-seated malaise – the absence of freedom in their lives.

> *He mahan gouraber kankal! Mahajagnyer bhashma! Re pranheen manushatyaheen dharma karmaheen hrito sarbashyo hatobhagyo jati, ekbar nijer dike chahibe na? Ekbar o ki bhabibe na ki chhile, ki hoiyachho? Bhabibe na – keno aj shonar kamal chhinno-bhinno. Keno Bharater shadhonar dhan Sita aj apohrita? Ar parish jadi, re swadhinatar shukh borjito hatabhagyo jat, ekbar nijer dike drishtipat kar, ar oi dekh swadhinatar lilaniketaner santan, swadhinatar sevak ki mahiyan, pabitra. Swadhinatar garbo-mukh bimandito badan mandale ki swargiya jyoti ki mahimmoy bibha, taha tumi parapad dalita, kemon kariya bujhibe? Hay! Taha kalpanay aniteo tumi akkham.*[35]
>
> (Translation: You, the skeletal remains of past glory! The ashes of a grand sacrificial ceremony! You lifeless, dehumanized, hapless race, bereft of work and *dharma*, will you not cast a look at yourself? Will you not think even once, what you were and what you have become? Will you not think why has the golden lotus been torn to pieces? Why has the object of India's adoration, her Sita, [36] been abducted? And if you can, you hapless race, bereft of the happiness of independence, cast a look at yourself and then look at the children of the paradise of independence, the devotees of independence, how pure and glorious! Their faces luminous with a heavenly light, with the pride born of independence, how will you appreciate that, crushed as you are under the heels of a foreign race! Alas you are incapable of even imagining that!)

The pamphlets equate the loss of independence with the loss of manhood. It followed logically that if the youth of Bengal were to recover their manhood, they had to devote themselves to the cause of independence. To embark on the mission of gaining independence was a daunting task but it could be achieved by adopting the right outlook and behaviour.

> *Esho bhai, amra manush hoi o desher janyo prokrito manushyo kormi gorite shikhi. Jodio amader montrer dharona kashtoshadhyo tathapi ashadhyo nahe. Charitroban o porisromi hoiya amra jodi abhishto shadhone broti hoi swadhinata amader karayotto hoibe o shamogro bharote ek dharmorajya protishthito hoibe.*[37]

> (Translation: Come, my brothers! Let us become human beings and prepare true workers for the cause of the country. Though working for the cause is difficult, it is not impossible. If we work with grit and fortitude, we shall be independent and a *dharmarajya* will be established in India.)

The nature of the sacrifices involved in working for the independence of the country was also described in the pamphlets.

> *He jubakmandali, tomader karjya baro kothin. Tomader sharbotyagi hoite hoibe – jatodin na bharotbarsho swadhin hoy tatodin mayer molin mukh dekhiya protigya korite hoibe tomra kaminikanchan porityag koribe. Putro-kalatrer mukh dekhile amra bhagobaner karjya bhuliya jai – sheijanyo sharboprokar bhog tyag koriya tomader mayer deule ashiya daraite hoibe. Mone rakhiyo jei din aboshyok, tomader prano-o dite hoibe.*[38]

> (Translation: O Youth, your task is very difficult. You have to be all sacrificing – look at the sad face of the mother and take a vow to stay away from women and wealth the till the day that India is independent. We forget our duty to God when we look upon the faces of our sons and wives – therefore you have to give up all self-indulgences and enter the temple of the mother. Remember that when the time arrives, you shall have to give up your life for your mother.)

As the last line of the passage makes clear, all the sacrifices that the revolutionaries would make for the motherland were but preparatory steps for the ultimate self sacrifice. For, as the pamphlets pointed out, the righteous state could only emerge when the corrupt old order had been destroyed and the country had been cleansed of its sins.

> *Ekhon chai shudhu bali, chai shudhu atmadan, chai shudhu jibanahuti, chai ekhon rakter ganga, dridhotar pashandurgo, bishshaswer atal bhudhar, chahi kebol nabin shadhok*[39].–

> (Translation: What is needed now is only sacrifice, self-sacrifice, self-immolation; what is needed now are rivers of blood, nerves as strong as fortresses of stone, belief as unshakeable as mountains, what is needed now are only courageous, young devotees.)

In the pamphlets, the revolutionaries are portrayed as warrior heroes, whose task is to emulate their glorious ancestors who have, time and again, laid down their lives in the service of the motherland. The past is read as a history of struggle, in which is inscribed the figures of martyrs, the examples of whose sacrifice should serve as a lesson to the freedom-fighter warriors in the present.

> I read the history of my past which revealed to me the might, the glory, the martyrdom of my ancestors! [40]

The idea of martyrdom lay at the heart of the revolutionary enterprise. The revolutionaries knew in their own minds that theirs was an impossible enterprise, for a band of ill-prepared and ill-trained young men could hardly hope to dent the might of the colonial state. But the point of the revolutionary enterprise in the early twentieth century was not that it would be able to defeat the colonial state, but that it would put an end to the power of the state to colonize the Indian mind. Hence the intense identification between the pamphleteers and the martyrs, that is evident in the following passage.

> They [the martyrs] are mine, essentially mine, and so they by their martyrdom, have breathed a divine immortality into my nation not only by infusing the love of liberty, which the foreign histories could have done, but by proving even the present capacity of my people to pass through the fiery ordeal required. Born of my mother, brought under the same enervating shadow of the tyranny, speaking the same language, products of the same civilization, inspired by the same Bhagavat Gita and Upanishads; if these martyrs' spirits did nothing else, yet this message of the intact vitality of the Indian Nation that they have delivered is nothing short of a Napoleonic battle won, the song that nerves a nation's heart is in itself a deed.[41]

The revolutionary pamphlets also point to an eclectic gallery of martyrs of different nations who were all depicted as examples to be emulated by the revolutionaries.

> *Ekbar, Mazzini, Garibaldi'r jiban-kahini manosh pate ankito karo, Robert Bruce er adamya adhyabashaer katha bhabiya dekho, Greekbir Leonidas er apurbokirti smaran karo, Pratap Singh er biratwer bhab hridoye dharon karo, bujhite paribe – deshbhakti jahar hridoy ke adhikar kariyachhe, deshcharya jahar jibaner broto boliya gyan koriachhe ... . biruddho paksher dando-niti ki kokhono tahar utshaho udyam mandibhuto korite pare?*[42]

> (Translation: Etch the life stories of Mazzini and Garibaldi in

> your minds, think about the indomitable spirit of Robert Bruce, remember the remarkable achievements of the Greek warrior, Leonidas, take to heart the courageous example of Pratap Singh and you will understand – those whose hearts are full of love for their nation, those for whom service for the nation is the only goal – can the oppressive policy of the opposition ever crush their enthusiasm and enterprise?)

But it is to the example of their compatriots that the pamphleteers returned repeatedly. Almost all of the pamphlets contain references to the martyred revolutionaries who had died under torture, been hanged on the gallows or exiled to foreign lands, all for selflessly taking up the cause of the motherland. The pamphleteers pointed out that their countrymen owed a special debt of gratitude to the martyrs for leading them on the path to freedom and that it behooved them to avenge their martyrdom. One pamphleteer celebrates the martyrdom of the boy Khudiram with these words,

> Khudiram stands in the prison as fresh as a morning rose and as bold as Abhimanyu of old. He is asked 'Are you sorry for what you have done?' He answers, 'Not a bit. If you let me go, I shall do the same thing again.' The death sentence is pronounced, and it is inquired of him, 'Are you afraid of death'. He smiles, 'Why? Have I not read the *Gita*?'[43]

This attainment of martyrdom marked the climactic point of an inspiring journey on which the revolutionaries had embarked upon with a mission to fulfill. In the revolutionary imaginary, this journey was fated to end in death. But it was not an end to be feared for it was the end that made the journey worthwhile.

> *Tomra amriter santan, tomader mrityu nai. – bhay porityag karo. Bedanter sharbosreshtho shabdo abhi, arthath bhayshunyo hoyo.*[44]
>
> (Translation: You are sons of immortality, you cannot die – overcome fear. The greatest word in the Vedanta is *abhi,* which means be fearless.)

It was by transcending their momentary existence in mortal time that the revolutionaries finally found an identity. The identity was that of a martyr who had gained immortality by laying down his life for the motherland –

> *Swadhinatakangkhya amrito bhando haste desher odhishthatri debike*

> *abolokon koro. Shei amritapane tumi chirokal amor hoiya prithibite bash karo.*[45]
>
> (Translation: Look upon the founding mother of the land carrying the vessel full of the nectar of the desire for independence. Drink that nectar and become immortal on earth.)

And again

> *Matripujay aj sharboshreshthho dan ongikar karo, tuchho pran diya mahapran paibar e sujog chhario na.*[46]
>
> (Translation: Pledge the greatest gift of all in the worship of the Mother, do not give up the chance to attain the great life in exchange for the petty life.)

The identity that had escaped them in life as subjects of a colonized land was ultimately achieved, be it only in death. It was as if the spirit of the martyrs became one with the eternal spirit of the nation and in the process achieved immortality.

The call to arms, the vision of apocalyptic violence resulting in the birth of a new nation, the glorification of martyrdom, were all part of the revolutionary scheme of things. But the revolutionary ideology was not shared by other political communities. One part of the revolutionary project therefore, was to point out the fallacies of the ideas of their political rivals and, in the process, legitimate the revolutionary enterprise.

The pamphleteers mocked the moderate policy of 'prayers and petitions' that like the other political radicals they dismissed as mendicancy. They pointed out that the nation could hope to gain nothing from such a policy. However much the moderates protested their devotion to the British Raj, they would always be treated dismissively. It was only through bloodshed that a defeated nation could hope to win back its lost independence from the conquerors. The pamphleteers looked to history to make their case and pointed out that the English had refused to grant independence to the Americans without battle, despite the fact that the latter were the coreligionists of the English and belonged to the same race. This was because the English were a race of merchants and the systematic looting of other nations was a national trait. The pamphlets went on to maintain that it was sheer foolishness to hope that the Indians could get back their independence from the British without bloodshed. One pamphlet referred to the words of

Valentine Chirol, journalist, diplomat and spokesperson for imperialism, who had proclaimed that since there was no community of historical traditions, social mores, customs and beliefs between the British and Indians, no sentimental bonds could be forged between the two races, making it impossible to grant to Indians the right of self-government that had willingly been conceded to other communities of their own race. It followed, the pamphleteers pointed out, that it was the fear of revolutionary violence that had forced the government to make the meager concessions that they had in the course of the past few years.[47]

A leaflet of the *Swadhin Bharat* series comments thus upon this achievement:

> *Nabo preronay udbuddho atmahara Narendrar durbalatar sandhan paiya kutabudhhi banikraj shamagra desher upar jakhan bhimbajra prayog koribar ayojan karitechhilo shaktishadhonay siddhilabh koriya bharater abhaboniyo shaktir parichay dibar janyo mahabir Kanailal swechhay British karagare shurakhhito louhanigar karabeshtito Alipur jail er pratyek kakhho kampannito koriya mahasadhaker bhimbajra jakhan swadeshdrohir bakhhe raktopat korilo takhonoi ingraj bujhiyachhilo je bange je agun jwalioachhe ihar mule ek adbhut shakti protishthhito achhe.*[48]
>
> (Translation: When, coming to know of the weakness of Narendra, who roused by a new impulse, had lost his self-control, our crooked-minded merchant rulers were preparing to hurl a terrible thunderbolt upon the whole country, and when the great hero Kanailal, after having achieved success in the effort to acquire strength, in order to give an exhibition of India's unexpected strength, wielding the terrible thunderbolt of the great magician, and making every chamber in the Alipore Jail quake, drew blood from the breast of the traitor to his country, safe in a British prison, in iron chains, surrounded by the walls of a prison, then indeed the English realized that the flame which had been lit in Bengal had at its roots a wonderful strength in store.)

The only reason that people continued to support the colonial administration and expect good to accrue from colonial rule, the pamphleteer continued, was fear of the English. It was only a matter of time when the people woke up to the real truth about colonial rule and rejected the loyalists as well as the calumnies they spread about the revolutionary nationalists. In a particularly notable passage one pamphlet rejected the portrayal of the revolutionary nationalist cause as one of destruction and instead emphasized that it was an act of creation that was intended to bring a new nation into existence. Further, in an interesting twist, the legitimacy of the colonial state was challenged and the label of 'anarchist' was displaced onto the colonial rulers, to whom the pamphleteer rhetorically posed the following question.

> Now let the tyrant answer what word or act is here in these divine characters that they want to term 'anarchical?' Yes, anarchists they all are. For when the great political lie dances hideous over the earth, when the truth is driven to dungeons and dens, and when the Platform and the Press can preach nothing but the satanic twin of Tyranny and Treachery, if then, under these conditions to organize secret societies is anarchism, when the tyrant disarms you to rob you of your protection, then to fill up bombs to rob him of his triumph is anarchism; if to liberate a people, if to watch over the cradle of a nation's birth, if to reinstate justice among the downtrodden is anarchism, then Birendra and all of them are anarchists of the brightest type. If to build is to destroy, if to create is to kill, if an architect is an anarchist, then most assuredly Hem and Ullas and Khudiram are all anarchists, and so were Christ and Muhammad and Mazzini.
>
> But if to enslave one fifth of the whole human race and to reduce it to brute level is anarchism; if to utter the diabolical phrase 'liberty for us, slavery for the rest' is anarchism; if to kill five millions of souls in famines and plagues, without letting them utter even a groan, least the world might know and foam and revolt against the inhuman machine of death is anarchism; if publicly to profess and preach and act upon the gospel 'India must be bled' is anarchism; if first to disarm and then let the *gundas* [goons] violate the honour of the Indian homes simply for the pleasure of ridiculing the imbecility of the unfortunate victims is anarchism – then who are the real anarchists you or they?[49]

The colonial condition and the consequences that flowed from such a state of affairs were pithily summed by a pamphleteer with the following words.

> *Amra shoshito – uhara shoshak, amra bhakkhya uhara bhakkhak. E abosthay uhader shohit shotruta abashyambhabi. .....shutorang e abosthay biplaber ayojan karai amader ekmatro upay.*[50]
>
> (Translation: We are the oppressed – they are the oppressors, we are the devoured, they the devourers. Under the circumstances enmity with them is inevitable. .....In this situation preparing for a revolution should be our only plan of action.)

The figure of the revolutionary nationalist took shape and form in pamphlet literature and this figure became etched in the minds of the public through the medium of pamphlet propaganda. The revolutionary was above all a patriot, tied by strong bonds of emotion to the Motherland whom he wished to free from the chains of servitude. He would dedicate his entire life to the task, fully aware that his would be a life of privation and sacrifice and would end in a violent death in the service of the nation. Yet this death would be the pathway to an eternal life for the martyrdom would be forever memorialized by the nation. Thus it was through martyrdom that the patriots would finally achieve the recognition and the identity that they had yearned for during their lifetime, an identity that had been denied them as colonial subjects. The revolutionary nationalist of pamphlet literature was a heroic figure, of great physical courage and mental strength, a figure that was likely to impress and appeal to the imagination of the public. While their dedication to some common ideals bound the revolutionaries together in a strong fraternal bond, it also helped to demarcate the political community that they had forged from that of their opponents. The revolutionaries saw themselves in the mirrors of their Others, their political opponents and the self-image of the revolutionaries was drawn in diametric opposition to that of their political enemies. The political Others were counterposed to the revolutionaries, their stereotypical figures constructed by broad strokes of the pen and lined up along a spectrum of political opposition to the revolutionary nationalists. At the extreme end of the political spectrum were the British rulers whose image was the polar opposite of the revolutionary nationalists – hedonistic, cruel, degenerates, who had to be eradicated so that the body politic could be nurtured back to a state of health and happiness. Situated very near to the British rulers on the political spectrum were the collaborators – the spies, informers and policemen, portrayed in the pamphlets as self serving and fawning minions of their political lords, deserving of the same fate that awaited the political masters. Located a little higher in the hierarchy of the fallen were the political loyalists, cowardly creatures who were deceiving themselves willfully in desperate efforts at political survival. The propagandists laid out the political choices very clearly before their readers, exhorting all self-respecting, righteous and courageous youths to embrace the right choice and join the revolutionary political community.

This political community was a gendered formation, conceived as an armed brotherhood of young men, who would not only dedicate their lives to the achievement of national independence but also take a vow of to remain celibate till this task was achieved. The masculine public sphere was constructed by attributing to men alone the qualities necessary for the task of attaining independence for the nation – physical strength, courage and moral righteousness – and consequently assigning to them alone the responsibility of carrying out this task. This idea was presented metaphorically in the pamphlets which bestowed upon the sons, but not upon the daughters, the duty of rescuing the mother-nation from the depredations of the invaders. Even the construction of the iconic image of the nation-mother in the pamphlets bore traces of this mental outlook.[51] In Bankimchandra's *Anandamath*, the mother–goddess in her various representations is a supremely powerful awe-inspiring figure who even in her state of deprivation, inspires fear in the beholder. This glorious image is evoked in the following passage.

> *Jnahader ma shareisharjyashalini, dashopraharanadharini, padatale harjyakhhyaraj shatrudalane niyojito, jnahar shangi balarupi Kartikeya, jnanarupi Ganesh, jnahar pashe Lakshmi ebong bidyadayini Saraswati, jnahar rupe bhuban alokito, tumi ki shei mayer santan, tnahar shebak?*[52]
>
> (Translation: Are you children of that Mother, her devotee, the Mother who is possessed of six kinds of wealth, ten kinds of arms, who has the lion-king fighting the enemy at her feet, who is accompanied by the epitome of strength, Kartik, the epitome of wisdom, Ganesh, at whose side is Lakshmi and the giver of learning Saraswati, the one whose beauty lights up the world?

Closely associated with the above image is that of the mother-goddess as *shakti* or primal force that recurs throughout the pamphlets, where she wields power over her sons, the revolutionaries, who are portrayed as obedient sons dutifully carrying out her command to shed the blood of her desecrators. As one of the earlier *Jugantar* pamphlets, which called upon its readers to revenge themselves for the wrongs inflicted upon the motherland, put it,

> The *Bhairabi* (i.e., the dark demoness of revenge) is thirsting after blood. Gratify her thirst by offering blood. There is no time to wait.[53]

But the pamphlets, especially the *Swadhin Bharat* pamphlets dating from 1911 frequently incorporate another image – of a birth mother, weak and defenseless, who has suffered utter humiliation at the hands of the oppressors and is mournfully looking to her sons to restore her dignity by righting the wrongs that have been committed against her. The adjectives used to describe the nation-mother, *jeernodehochhinnobashona, asru-molinbadona, rukkho kuntala, paradhina janmobhumi* (emaciated, dressed in rags, mournful, with unkempt hair, the enslaved birthland), in one such pamphlet, conjure up an image that is a far cry from the figure of the goddess who gloried in her strength while commanding her sons to battle.[54] Sometimes the two images are juxtaposed, bringing into sharp relief the contrast between the two, as in the following sentence,

> *Oi dekho Andamane nirbashito Barindropromukh birgon jnahara danob-rakto pipashu chandidebir pujarthe bharatjananir srinkhol mochonarthe jatheshto ayojon koriyachhilen tnahadiger proti ingrej ki bhishon atyachat koritechhe.*[55]
>
> (Translation: Look how the English are fiercely torturing brave men like Barindra who have been exiled to the Andamans for organizing the worship of the bloodthirsty goddess *chandi* and attempting to free Mother- India from her chains.)

The older, more traditional image of the Mother-Goddess variously addressed in her numerous manifestations as *Ranachandi, Bhairavi, Kali, Chandi* is overlaid by the more domesticated, pliable image of the mother-nation, dependent on her sons for protection, an image that became increasingly familiar to Bengalis from the time of the *swadeshi* movement, when it was much celebrated through verse and song. In the pamphlets, the sons are addressed as *santans,* which literally means children in the Bengali language but the context leaves no doubt that the pamphleteers have in mind only the sons and not the daughters of the nation-mother. For closely coupled with the image of the defenseless mother is another one, that of helpless women being violated in public places by the colonial rulers who are described as those who 'humiliate your sisters, your mothers, who violate the chastity of the women of your country in their trains and steamers....'.[56] Failure to protect their womenfolk was a reflection on the manhood of the readers, who, the propagandists maintained, ought to be shamed out of their cowardly existence by such a state of affairs and rush to the defense of their sisters. Thus, to the many other character attributes required of the revolutionary nationalist was added another one, gallantry. The chivalric ideal was a central component of masculine subjectivity in several revolutionary movements and the revolutionary nationalist movement was evidently no exception.[57] It is noticeable that this construction of a masculine public sphere involved the transference to the public arena of normative codes of social conduct according to which private life was ordered. Thus men, who were held accountable for policing and protecting the chastity of women within the home, were also given the responsibility of avenging the outraged honour of mothers and sisters in the public sphere.

Though women were not portrayed as active agents in the revolutionary struggle by the pamphlet propagandists, they were not represented as passive onlookers either. They too were required to consciously make tremendous sacrifices, though of a different kind. Thus the pamphleteers urged their women readers to give up their sons and husbands to the revolutionary endeavour, and invoked the example of Kunti, the proud and courageous mother of the Pandavas,[58] which could also be interpreted to imply that women should actually encourage their men folk to enter the fray rather than simply accept the decisions that the men should choose to make.[59] The idea that the revolutionary movement should have a more inclusive and active role for women was promoted in a pamphlet titled *Sandhya, second edition, fourth year* and headed '*Sadher e ghoom ghor kobhu ki bhangibena*' (Will this fond slumber never end?) which appeared in August 1911. [60] The pamphlet began by expressing familiar sentiments but gradually became more radical in tone. Thus in a passage where it exhorted the youth of Bengal to end their slothful existence and join the revolutionary fray, even while it echoed sentiments expressed in the other pamphlets , there was a different slant to the language.

> Ye, Aryan Heroes you [at] one time used to offer your first born child to the mother Ganges, you have had your wives burnt in the same pyre as their husbands against their will. Though that self immolation and self-denial on the part of women are no longer in vogue, can you not revive this spirit in another shape? Can you not sacrifice one of your children for '*Desher Kaj*' (Nation's work)? Can you not teach the women to assist their husbands. Just a paralytic man cannot move about without the help of a stick, so the national life cannot be developed without the assistance of women.[61]

The pamphlet then goes on to cite several historical examples from around the globe of the contributions of women to the glory of their husbands. The pamphlet ends, however, by appearing to assign to men and women an equally important role in the revolutionary struggle even while the language remains ambiguous because it does not categorically affirm for women an active role in the movement.

> Through the union of *Prakriti* and *Purush* (i.e., nature and power)

> this world was created and is now working out its destiny. Come, ye brothers and sisters. Let us unitedly offer floral offerings at the feet of the mother.

The emphasis that the pamphlet laid 'on the important part which women must play in the liberation of India' led the Commissioner of Police, F. L. Halliday to suspect that the pamphlet was the handiwork of Miss Kumudini Mitter, a relative of Aurobindo, who was also suspected of writing the first of the *Sandhya* leaflets that appeared in July 1910.[62] But the Commissioner also mentioned in his letter that the pamphlet was badly printed and contained a lot of mistakes as regards punctuation and spelling, which makes it suspect as the handiwork of an established writer like Kumudini Mitter. But the expression of such sentiments is the exception rather than the rule and in pamphlet propaganda, for the most part, the role of women was envisaged as dedicated but secondary supporters of the revolutionary movement. But it should also be pointed out that unlike some western revolutionary movements such as the French Revolution, the revolutionary nationalist movement in Bengal did not express hostility to the participation of women in the public sphere.[63] In fact, Bhupendranath Dutt in his later years recognized the important role that women had played in the early revolutionary movement and acknowledged with humility that services rendered by women revolutionaries had been overlooked in the early accounts of the movement.[64] Therefore, the presence of sentiments which unexpectedly surfaced in public as in the case of the pamphlet mentioned above, indicated new possibilities for the construction of a democratic public sphere in the future and opened up the way for the participation of women as equal members of the revolutionary movement in its later phases.

Appendix I

Excerpts from the History Sheet Number 226 of Makhan La Sen of Sonarang, Dacca

Makhan Lal Sen is the son of Guru Nath Sen, Assistant Surgeon, Sibpur Engineering College, Calcutta.

He is about 28 to 29 years of age (1910) of medium height and strongly built. His complexion is of a medium blackness…

He has studied upto and passed the BA Examinations of Calcutta University and resides at Sonarang village in the Dacca district, where he is proprietor of a national school said to be the most flourishing in the district and a menace to the Government School in the same place. Although the school had not been long at work, yet by June 1909 it had, in the short space of little less than a year met with great success and had 175 boys on its role.

...

He was strongly suspected of having been one of the distributors of inflammatory leaflets in the Dacca District and was reported to have invited discussions for assisting the accused in the Rajendrapur train dacoity and murder. Taking the above facts into consideration, he must be regarded as one of the most dangerous and unscrupulous characters in the district. His zeal in the cause of national education with all that it signifies in the propagation of extremist views and anarchy must bring him into close touch with leaders of the movement.

Excerpts from the History Sheet Number 727 of Dr Jnanendra Nath Mitra alias Muni Babu alias Brahmananda Swami

Compiled in Intelligence Branch, CID Bengal

43 years (1913)

F.A. of Calcutta University and an L.M.S. of the Calcutta Medical College. Lived at Rue-de-Fosse, French Chandernagore.

After obtaining his degree from the Medical College, Dr Mitra established himself at Bankipur where his brother Binode Bihari Mitra was a pleader. For some time he had a good practice which however gradually vanished as he exchanged it to play the role of a *sanyasi,* a cloak to further the anarchical movement in Bengal. This however, could not be done with a poor purse, and the doctor had to devise means for the accumulation of funds as well as the medium through which to propagate anarchical propaganda. To this end he established a newspaper called the *Motherland,* which published seditious matter from time to time. On the staff of the paper were Fanindra Nath Mitra, afterwards convicted for sedition in connection with the *Jugantar* and Satish Chandra Sarkar who figured in the Howrah Gang Case.

Before the establishment of the *Motherland,* the doctor was stated to have been a correspondent to the *Bengalee* and *Amrita Bazar Patrika* and in that capacity he wrote articles against officials and dealt with political and social matters.

Endnotes

1 In recent years, historians who study 'masculinity' within the field of gender studies have drawn attention to the question of political subjectivity, that is, 'in the emotional experiences of men as public actors, in the qualities and character of their relationships with others and in the place of unconscious motivation in human action'. Moving beyond an analysis of the normative discourses and ideological codes that operate in the public sphere and which are studied through their representations in political tracts, poetry, religious discourse and propaganda, they have moved into the realm of psychic and emotional states of political actors which are intimately connected to their material lives and lived experiences. For a theoretical statement on the subject of political subjectivities see, Michael Roper, 'Slipping out of View: Subjectivity and Emotion in Gender History', *History Workshop Journal*, No. 59 (Spring, 2005), p. 57–72 . The above quote is from Roper, 'Slipping out of View', p. 57. This chapter studies political subjectivities with a view to gaining insights into the personal investments of the revolutionary nationalists in the propaganda that they disseminated and into the reasons for their identifications with the discourses of the public sphere. The memoirs written by the revolutionary nationalists are an invaluable source for the reconstruction of their personal lives, emotions and experiences. These memoirs, even though they cannot evidently be read as providing direct pathways into the inner lives of the revolutionary nationalists do provide, as this chapter will show, some crucial pointers to their feelings and emotions that found expression in revolutionary discourses and practices.

2 Nalinikishore Guha, *Banglay Biplabbad* (First Mitram edition, Kolkata, 2012), p. 91, my translation. Also see p. 58–59 where he describes the idealism and character traits of the revolutionary nationalists. The section of the *Sedition Committee Report* that contained statistics of age, caste, occupation or profession of persons "convicted of revolutionary crimes or killed in commission of such crimes" reported that an overwhelming majority of such persons were young boys and men. Thus 126 out of the 175 persons whose ages were recorded (out of a total of 186 convicted or killed) were 25 years or below. 84 were students and teachers. See *Sedition Committee, 1918, Report*, (Bengal Secretariat Press, 1918), Chapter III, p. page 33 and Annexure 2. The report went on to say that "the persons committing these outrages are usually young men of the *bhadralok* class. They are often reported as speaking in English or in the vernacular as spoken by persons of *bhadralok* position in life."

3 Sumathi Ramaswamy has argued that mapping the territory of the nation – the nation-space, through the form of the female body helped to transform 'abstract territory into lived nation', thus personalizing it into 'an entity worth dying for.' She contrasts the rational and scientific practice of colonial cartography with the production of such "bodyscapes" that breathed life and emotions into dry, empty space and served to bind the beholder in an emotive bond with the mapped entity . See Sumathi Ramaswamy, 'Body Politic(s): Maps and Mother Goddesses in Modern India' in Richard H. Davis, *Picturing the Nation: Iconographies of Modern India* (Orient Longman, New Delhi, 2007), p. 32–50, esp. p. 35.

4 Bhupendranath Dutt, '*Bharatiya Baiplabiker Monostattva*' (*The Psychology of the*

Indian Revolutionary) in Sailesh Dey ed. *Agnijug* (Purna Prakashan, Kolkata, 1978), Part II, p. 12. Jadugopal Mukhopadhyay also recalls in his memoirs his mother's agonized reaction to incidents of rape and molestation of Indian women by British soldiers and her tearful entreaties to her sons to rid the country of the foreign invaders. See Jadugopal Mukhopadhyay, *Biplabi Jibaner Smriti* (*Memories of a Revolutionary Life*) Academic Publishers, New Delhi, 1956, p. 175.

5 See for instance, the conclusions arrived at in the Government report titled *Memorandum on the History of Terrorism in Bengal: 1905–33* (Calcutta, Bengal Government Press), p. 22.

6 Bhupendranath Dutt, '*Bharatiya Baiplabiker Monostattva*' (*The Psychology of the Indian Revolutionary*) in Sailesh Dey ed. *Agnijug*, Part II, p. 8–14.

7 Bhupendranath Dutt, *Bharater Dwitiya Swadhinata Sangram* (*India's Second Struggle for Independence*) Nababharat Publishers: Kolkata, 1983, p. 13.

8 Bhupendrakishore Rakshit-Ray, '*Banglay Bipabbad O Gita*' in *Agnijug*, 15.

9 Upendranath mentions that each day the duty of cooking for the entire group was assigned to two members, many of whom were young boys in their teens. Lacking even the basic utensils, the members ate out of coconut shells and earthen plates which they carefully washed and stored away after every meal. They washed their own clothes, though some, as Upen Bandopadhyay facetiously remarks, made do with the clothes that had been washed by others. See Upendranth Bandopadhyay, *Nirbashiter Atmakatha* (Basumati Corporation Limited, Kolkata, second edition, 1993), p. 6.

10 Ibid. The author's humourous and sometimes irreverent style of describing the everyday lives of those sentenced to deportation to the Andaman Islands and imprisonment in the Cellular Jail in the wake of the Alipore Conspiracy Case, lends a poignant edge to the events that he recounts. Some of the young revolutionaries paid a terrible price for their deeds. Ullaskar Dutt lost his mind and Indubhushan Ray committed suicide in Cellular jail. See also Barindra Kumar Ghosh, *Dwipantarer Katha* (*A Story of Exile*, Sagnik Books, Kolkata, 2012.) Horrific accounts of the torture that the revolutionary nationalists suffered while in police custody are to be found in Nalinikishore Guha, *Banglay Biplabbad*, p. 311–320. See especially, the petitions that were submitted to the authorities by Arun Guha and Jogesh Chandra Chatterjee which contain details of the ill-treatment they suffered at the hands of the police.

11 Dinesh Chandra Sen, quoted in Gautam Bhadra's '*Janaparisar–e Itihas: Desher Katha*' (*History in the Popular Sphere*), *Charchapad*, July, 2012, p. 48.

12 Ibid., p. 48.

13 Bhupendranath Dutt, *Bharater Dwitiya Swadhinatar Sangram*, p. 26 . Bhupendranath also mentions that Sakharam Ganesh Deuskar was inspired by the example of European revolutionaries to write his *Desher Katha*. The revolutionary nationalists learned about the intricacies of Indian political history from the classes held by Sakharam Ganesh Deuskar in the Kolkata *Anushilan Samiti*, ibid., p. 32. A chapter from Deuskar's *Desher Katha* that had itself been forfeited to government under the *Press Act*, was published and disseminated

in the form of a pamphlet entitled *Krishaker Sarbanash* (*The Ruin of the Peasants*) in 1911. There were two editions of this pamphlet. This pamphlet detailed the misery that was the life of the Indian cultivator under the colonial regime. In his analysis of the state of Indian agriculture, the author commented that the rulers after having destroyed the old industries in the country had made the country overly dependent on cultivation of land. The government had embarked on a policy of rack-renting with the result that the peasants, unable to pay their dues, were sinking deeper into debt. The author concluded that 'there is difference of heaven and hell between the subjects of an independent country and of a conquered country. Such miserable conditions are befalling us because the king is more mindful of looking towards the interests of the white subjects than of us.' For Sakharam Ganesh Deuskar's *Krishaker Sarbanash*, see, SN 23/1910, FN V/184/ 1910 in WBSA-IB.

14 Jogendra Nath Vidyabhushan's works on the lives of Mazzini and Garibaldi were sources of inspiration for Bengali youth. His patriotic teachings influenced many members of the *Jugantar* group. See Jadugopal Mukhopadhyay, *Biplabi Jibaner Smriti*, op.cit. p. 166. Hemchandra Qanungo, *Banglay Biplab Pracheshta* (Chirayoto Prakashan, Kolkata, 1928), p. 23.

15 Saraladevi Choudhurani, *Jibaner Jharapata* (Dey's Publishing, Kolkata, 2007), p. 120. Brahmabandhab Upadhyay, editor of the *Sandhya* newspaper also earned notoriety in government circles for advocating in his newspaper columns, a 'tit for tat' policy in dealing with European aggression.

16 Qanungo, *Banglay Biplab Pracheshta*, p. 147, 163. The harsh punishment meted out to the boy Sushil Sen in Kingsford's court was perhaps the first impulse behind the chain of circumstances that led to the Alipore Conspiracy case. The summary sentences handed out by Kingsford to *swadeshi* nationalists had already made him extremely unpopular among the revolutionary nationalists and the sentence of whipping handed out to fourteen year old Sushil was the proverbial last straw. The revolutionaries then embarked on the mission to eliminate Kingsford. A series of unsuccessful attempts culminated in the tragic expedition of Khudiram Bose and Prafulla Chaki to Muzaffarpur in April 1908. The bomb attack and the death of two innocent women in a case of mistaken identity, appear to have woken up the Bengal police to the gravity of the situation. The arrest of Khudiram was followed the next month by the raid on the Maniktala gardens and the institution of the Alipore Conspiracy case.

17 Nalini Kishore Guha, *Banglay Biplabbad*, p. 32.

18 Rabindranth had been deeply disturbed by the emergence of the violent streak within Indian nationalism as indicated by the founding of the revolutionary secret societies. He remained a lifelong critic of violent nationalism which, in his view, had bought into the worst cultural stereotypes of 'masculinity' fostered by western imperialism. In his view, the secret societies were evidence of the pathology that had gripped Bengali society as a result of having been doomed to a life of 'clerkdom' under colonial rule, which had stifled all outlets to celebrate its heroic side. The forceful suppression of the heroic aspects of Bengali society had resulted in it being forced underground and then finding perverted expression in the secret societies . In *Jibansmriti* (*Memories of my Life*),

Rabindranath Tagore has described with ironic humour, one such ineffective but idealistic attempt at organizing a nationalist secret society, of which he himself had been a member as a boy. This society, he says, was long on mysterious rituals but short on action. 'The only terrifying thing about this society was its secretiveness' wrote Rabindranath. This secret society, like so many others of its ilk, soon broke up without creating the slightest ripple on the political scene. See *Jibansmriti* in *Rabindra Rachanabali* (Collected Works of Rabindranath Tagore, Centenary Edition published by the Government of West Bengal, 1961), Volume IX, p. 67. Rabindranath's agonized criticism of revolutionary nationalism found voice in his novel *Char Adhyay*, published in 1934. For more on this theme see Ashis Nandy, *The Illegitimacy of Nationalism: Rabindranath Tagore and the Politics of Self* included in (*Return from Exile* (Oxford University Press, 1998).

19 Mrinalini Sinha, *Colonial Masculinity: The 'manly Englishman' and the 'effeminate Bengali' in the nineteenth century* (Kali for Women, New Delhi, 1997), p. 16–21.

20 *Bankim Rachanaboli* (*Collected works of Bankimchandra*, Sahitya Samsad, Kolkata, 1361 [B. E.] 1955), Vol. II, p. 234–41.

21 For an extended analysis of the same idea in a different context, see Joseph S. Alter, 'Somatic Nationalism: Indian Wrestling and Militant Hinduism', *Modern Asian Studies*, 28, 3 (1994), p.557–88.

22 Saraladevi Choudhurani, *Jibaner Jharapata* (Dey's Publishing, Kolkata, 2007), p. 132–34.

23 Jadugopal Mukhopadhyay, *Biplabi Jibaner Smriti*, p. 98–9.

24 For an analysis of the principle of sacrifice in Hinduism, see Wendy Doniger, 'Sacrifice and Substitution: Ritual Mystification and Mythical Demystification in Hinduism', *On Hinduism* (Aleph Book Company, New Delhi, 2013), p. 207–32. She writes 'One may view sacrifice in the history of post-Vedic Indian religion not so much as a ritual act or set of acts but rather as a category that acts to provide explanatory power, traditional legitimacy and canonical authority in Indian history.' ibid., p. 225.

25 The *Empire* dated 12 August 1908, reproduced in *Agnijug*, Part I, p.12. For an account that celebrates the bravery of young revolutionary nationalists during their last days and moments see, Bhupendra Kishore Rakshit-Ray, '*Banglay Biplabbad O Gita*' ('*The Revolutionary Ideology and the Gita*') in *Agnijug*, p. 14–34 .

26 Ullaskar Dutt, *Kara-Jiboni* (*Prison-Life*) (Sagnik Books, Kolkata, 2012), p. 80.

27 From *Swadhin Bharat* pamphlet in WBSA-IB, SN 35/1910, FN 191/1910 beginning with the words *Je paryanto bhayer karon uposthith na hoy* (*Till the cause of fear actually materializes*).

28 *Swadhin Bharat* pamphlet of April 1911, P.T.S. Collection, 18-A-15 in Calcutta Police Museum. The pamphlet was proscribed under Government Order, No. 228 P.D. dated 22 April 1911.

29 *Swadhin Bharat pamphlet*, SN 35/1910, FN 191/1910.

30 *Swadhin Bharat* pamphlet, PTS Collection, 18-A-17, Calcutta Police Museum.

31 *Jugantar* pamphlet titled *Shamay hoiachhe ki* (*Has the time come?*), SN 115/1916,

FN 2223/1916, WBSA-IB. The same kind of sentiments were expressed in the *Swadhin Bharat* pamphlets of 29 December, 1910 (*Abar ghumaile – Have You Fallen Asleep Again?*) and 15 April 1910 (*Na Jani Janani – I know not Mother*), PTS Collection, 18-A-17 and 18-A-15 in Calcutta Police Museum.

32 From *Jugantar* pamphlet titled *Shamay hoiacche ki* (*Has the time come?*'), SN 115/16, FN 2223/16 in WBSA-IB.

33 From *Swadhin Bharat* pamphlet beginning with the words, *Bharater mongol uddeshye* (*For the welfare of India*), SN 16/15, FN 347/15 in WBSA-IB .

34 *Swadhin Bharat* pamphlet beginning with words *Karmer tare bharate* (*In India, the call to work*), SN 45/1913, FN 380/1913 in WBSA-IB.

35 From *Swadhin Bharat* pamphlet beginning with words, *Dekhe, dekhe, hoilam stabdhapara* (*I fall silent on beholding*), PTS Collection 37(6), dated 21 September 1913 in Calcutta Police Museum.

36 Sita was the wife of Rama, the hero of the great Indian epic, the *Ramayana*. Sita was abducted by the demon Ravana, king of Lanka. Rama and Ravana then fought an epic battle at the end of which Sita was rescued from the clutches of Ravana. Here the pamphleteers are drawing an analogy between the abduction of Sita and the loss of India's independence with the intention of inciting their readers to battle.

37 From *Jugantar* pamphlet of 1912, proscribed on 16 December 1912, FN 17/1913, 37/1913, WBSA-IB.

38 *Swadhin Bharat* pamphlet of 5/3/15, PTS Collection, Calcutta Police Museum.

39 *Jugantar* pamphlet titled *Tora shabai manush ho* (*All ye, become Men*), SL 50, PTS Collection, Calcutta Police Museum.

40 From official English translation of the pamphlet titled, '*Jugantar. Prafulla*' in Amiya Samanta edited, *Terrorism in Bengal: A Collection of Documents* (Government of West Bengal, Kolkata, 1995), Vol. IV, p. 384.

41 Ibid. p.385.

42 From *Swadhin Bharat* pamphlet, FN 35/1910, SN 191/1910 in WBSA-IB.

43 From official English translation of *Jugantar* pamphlet titled *Prafulla* in Samanta ed. *Terrorism in Bengal*, p. 385.

44 From the *Jugantar* pamphlet titled *Yugantar – Chaturtha Barsho – 1317- sankhya 1* (*Yugantar, 4th Year- 1317, No.1*), National Archives of India, Home Department Political, Part B, January 1910, p. 34–51.

45 From *Swadhin Bharat* pamphlet beginning with words *Abar ghumaile*, PTS Collection, 18-A-17, Calcutta Police Museum.

46 From *Jugantar* pamphlet *Shamay hoiacche ki*, SN 115/1916, FN 2223/1916 in WBSA-IB.

47 Such sentiments were expressed, for example, in the *Swadhin Bharat* pamphlets beginning with the words, *Na jani janani* and *Bankimchandra Anandamathe*, both in the PTS Collection, Calcutta Police Museum, op. cit. Valentine Chirol is

quoted in the first pamphlet.

48 From official English translation of *Swadhin Bharat* pamphlet beginning with the words, *Ingrejer swashone thakiya* (*Living under the rule of the English*), in SN 56/1913, FN 1340/1913, WBSA-IB.

49 From the official English translation of pamphlet *Jugantar – Prafulla*, reproduced in Amiya Samanta ed., *Terrorism in Bengal*, op.cit. p. 385–86.

50 From *Swadhin Bharat* pamphlet beginning with words, *Na jani janani*, op.cit.

51 Also see in this context, Jasodhara Bagchi, 'Representing Nationalism: Ideology of Motherhood in Colonial Bengal', *Economic and Political Weekly*, 20–27 October 1990, p. 65–71 and Tanika Sarkar, 'Nationalist Iconography: Image of Women in 19th Century Bengali Literature', *Economic and Political Weekly*, 21–28 November 1987, p. 2011–15.

52 *Swadhin Bharat* pamphlet beginning with words *Dekhe dekhe hoilam stabdhapara* (*I am silenced on beholding*), op.cit. This is the Mother in her *Jagaddhatri* image, the first of the three manifestations of the mother as described in the *Anandamath.*

53 From official English translation of pamphlet titled *Jugantar (Salutation to Mother)* reprinted in Samanta ed. Terrorism in India, Vol. IV, p. 395 . The subscript to the pamphlet claimed that it was printed at the *Feringhi* Destruction Press and published by the bands of *Santans* for Liberty.

54 *Swadhin Bharat* pamphlet from PTS Collection, 18-A-15, Kolkata Police Museum. See also 18-A-16 from the same collection.

55 From *Jugantar* pamphlet of 1912, beginning with words, *Ranorangini deshmatar*, endnote 36.

56 See for example, The *Jugantar* pamphlet of 1914, beginning with the words, *Tora shabai manush ho* in PTS Collection, Serial Number 50, Calcutta Police Museum.

57 For the operation of the ideal of chivalric masculinity within the Irish revolutionary movement, see Catriona Kelly, 'A Gallant Nation: Chivalric Masculinity and Irish Nationalism in the 1790s', in Matthew McCormack ed. *Public Men: Masculinity and Politics in Modern Britain* (Palgrave, Macmillan: Hampshire, 2007), p. 73–92.

58 Pandavas: The band of five brothers who are the protagonists in the Indian epic, the *Mahabharata.* The great battle of Kurukhshetra, which forms the core of the epic, is fought between the two groups of cousins, the Pandavas and the Kauravas .

59 See, for example, the *Swadhin Bharat* pamphlet of March 1911 in PTS Collection, 18-A-16, Calcutta Police Museum.

60 SN 14/191, FN V/105A/1911 in WBSA-IB.

61 From official English translation of the same pamphlet. *Desher Kaj:* The nation's work.

62 Ibid., letter from F. L.Halliday, Commissioner of Police, to C. J. Stevenson Moore, Chief Secretary to the Government of Bengal, dated 3 August 1911.

63 Joan Landes has argued in *Women and the Public Sphere in the Age of the French*

Revolution (Cornell University Press, Ithaca, 1988) that the construction of the public sphere in revolutionary France was predicated on the assumption that the exclusion of women from the public realm and their relegation to the domestic sphere was part of the natural order of things. Consequently the public sphere in revolutionary France was deliberately exclusivist and directed against the participation of women.

64 '*Bharatiya Baiblabiker Monostattava*' in *Agnijug*, Part II, p. 12.

Conclusion

The revolutionary nationalist pamphlets may be described as clarion calls summoning the young men of Bengal to take up arms against the colonial rulers. The appearance of numerous editions of the pamphlets in large numbers and at frequent intervals and the alarm that their publication provoked in ruling circles, indicate that the pamphlets were perceived as an effective medium with which to build up support for the nationalist revolutionary movement. The pamphlets provided their readers information and perspective on the political events of the day, urged them to take a political stance and invited them to join in the impending revolution against colonial rule. The rhythm of the language, the urgency of tone and the richness of rhetoric convey even to the modern day reader a sense of immediacy and evoke feelings of identification with the political pulse of the times that go to demonstrate the power of the pamphlets as tools of political communication.

Further, an analysis of the language and the rhetoric adopted by the pamphleteers allows us access into the world of Bengali public opinion and political culture in the early twentieth century. These pamphlets, at first glance, appear to refer to only a cross-section of the political world of Bengal in the early twentieth century but since revolutionary nationalist ideas were an integral part of the mosaic of intellectual, political and cultural currents in early twentieth century Bengal, these pamphlets, as vehicles of these ideas, allow us an understanding of the overall political culture of the period. The pamphlets provide us important insights into the conceptual structures through which the terms of Bengali politics were defined and understood at the turn of the twentieth century and the symbolic and intellectual processes through which a national identity was being constructed during this period.

A reading of revolutionary pamphlet propaganda of the early twentieth century makes it evident that this period marked an important moment of transition in the political culture of Bengal when the meanings attributed to state and sovereignty, political legitimacy and authority were gradually changing. The experience of being the subjects within the colonial state for a century and a half had accustomed the people to the idea that the basis of sovereignty was force. This dependence on force was masked by an appeal to the civilizing mission that the colonial state had supposedly undertaken in the colonized world and upheld in law. But these assumptions were increasingly questioned with the rise of new ideas of nationhood, popular sovereignty and rule with the consent of the governed. These ideas found expression with the spread of national consciousness and its institutionalization in organizational forms in the later decades of the nineteenth century. The emergence of the idea of a single nation with a national culture was made possible by the growth of a print culture which gave rise to a national sphere within which public debate and rational discussion could be conducted on issues that transcended regional and local interests. The sense of a common identity and history that were disseminated through books, newspapers and pamphlets became the basis of the new idea of the nation-state. One pamphlet expressed the view that Bengal would take the lead in bringing about the formation of the new Indian nation.

> *Bangala aj ek bishal bharatiya jati sanghathita koribe.*[1]
>
> (Translation: Bengal shall bring about the union of an immense Indian nation.)

Concomitant with a questioning of the basis of colonial authority was the growth of the idea that the source of political legitimacy should derive from a national consensus and that the state and nation should be fused into a single entity. The idea that the population of India represented a sovereign homogenous people was a theme reiterated in the pamphlet literature of the period. The propaganda disseminated by the pamphlet writers threatened to counter the might of the colonial state with a revolutionary counterforce that would sweep away the colonial state and reveal it to be a house of cards that rested on very weak foundations. The pamphleteer – propagandists rejected the legitimacy of colonial rule and projected revolutionary violence as a countervailing moral force whose authority stemmed from divine sanction.

> *Prokando shorir dekhiya bhito hoiyo na – prithibir jatiyo itihas path karo; jekhane parokiyo rajshakti nyayer bidhan longhon kare, jekhane*

amanushik khamota baloboti hoy, shei khanei shamobeto jatiyo shaktir obhyudoy hoy; shei khanei Mahamayar ashurdalani shaktir abhirbhab hoy.

(Translation: Do not be frightened by looking at the huge body. Read the histories of the nations of the world; where ever the rule of law is flouted by alien imperial powers, where ever extraordinary power gathers strength, it is there that there is an upsurge of national strength, it is there that the demon destroying power of the *Mahamaya* (Great Power shows itself.)[2]

The political imagination of the pamphleteers was marked by a fusion of traditional sensibilities with a new political outlook and the programme and rhetoric of the pamphleteers give ample indication of the complexities of the historical conjuncture from which the pamphlets emanated. Thus, the pamphleteers made it appear that the national project consisted in rebuilding an ancient and glorious nation which had fallen on hard times and whose time for resurrection had finally arrived but they also emphasized that the national mission could only be achieved through an act of collective political will that had to be forged in the present. This is best brought out by referring to a passage from a pamphlet,

Gita ebong Chandir bhagobatshaktir bhobishyote je abotoroner katha shunite pao, taha kono byakti ba murti bishesh shambandhe projukto boliya mone koriona, uha desher shreshtho janamandalir jugpat jagoron. Shei jagoraner ayojon karo.

(Translation: Be informed that what you hear about the divine power of the *Gita* or *Chandi* descending to earth in the future does not apply to any specific individual or image but is concerned with the simultaneous uprising of the best sections of the population. Prepare for that uprising.)[3]

It is remarkable that the pamphleteers insisted that the moral and legal legitimacy of the new political order should be predicated on the consent of the ruled. This idea of people's rights was appropriated from a different context and indigenized. One such source of the idea of the sovereignty of the people is indicated in a pamphlet that rhetorically poses a question to the colonizers,

Tomader desher itihas' e Cromwell tomader raja prothom Charles er shirochhed keno koriachhilo?[4]

(Translation: In the history of your country why did Cromwell behead your king, Charles I?)

The revolutionary import of the words lay in the idea that the font of political power emanated from the people. It was the people who then delegated this power to its rulers, whose right to rule derived from the consent of the people. If the rulers violated the political covenant, the people had divine sanction to take back their rights, through violence if necessary. As one pamphleteer pointed out, the meagre political rights that the Indians had been able to secure in the recent past was not due to the condescending kindness of the British but because of the ability of the revolutionary nationalists to wrest from the rulers the political rights that were justly due to them — *iha Ingrajer dayay hoy ni, parantu amader nyajyo adhikar aday koribar shakti hoite hoiachhe.*[5]

Scholars like C. A. Bayly have written about the discourse of 'traditional patriotisms' in India which predated nationalist discourse and which laid emphasis on rational religion, useful knowledge and pious rule. Emerging nationalist discourse, according to Bayly, dovetailed with these old patriotisms and found resonance not only in the port cities but in the religious hinterland as well. It may be pointed out here that the crucial difference between the two discourses was the absence of the idea of an *empowered* citizenry in the older one. The old patriotisms were based on the idea of a political hierarchy, where power was concentrated at the top and ordinary people dependent on the beneficence of the powerful – an idea that the discourse of the nation-state did away with.[6] The pamphleteers no doubt appealed to the *dharma-rashtra* of yore, which according to tradition referred to an ethico-religious order which was based on the performance of right duty by each of its constituent groups. In this ethico/moral/spiritual universe, it was the rulers' duty to protect the interests of the people by ensuring them good governance but the concomitant idea of the people's right to good rule and to protest against misrule was not similarly emphasized. The appeal to the *dharmarashtra* did not mean that the pamphleteers wanted to return to the archaic but rather that they wished to utilize the authority of *dharma* to carve out a distinctive public sphere strengthened by the sense of moral responsibility. *Dharma* in the sense of ethics was not banished from the sphere of politics because it was ethics that would provide a map for the correct conduct of politics. Religious authority was invoked to make new political ideas appear traditional and venerable rather than to sanction a retreat into the past. Thus, it was a past that was not frozen in time but a past infused with the concerns of the present, a past that was, in Walter Benjamin's words, 'charged with the time of the now'.[7] Though the pamphleteers did not speak the language of democracy, the association of the idea of political consent with legitimate government marked an important breakthrough to the emergence of the concept of a democratic polity. The idea of the citizen-subject was clearly emerging, although the category of citizenship was thoroughly masculinized. Yet even this masculinized and virilized concept of citizenship left room for flexibility because the categories of thought, although gendered, had not hardened into implacable hostility towards the idea of female participation in the public sphere. Similarly the call to all castes to unite in political revolution against the foreign invaders which was couched in the sanskritized *sadhu bhasha*[8] favoured by the upper castes also brought into relief the tension between the newly emerging political ideas which were straining against the constraints imposed by the old conceptual structures. The sophistication of the language indicated that political ideas were being exchanged among the elites who appeared to remain blissfully unaware of any necessity of including the ordinary people in the political dialogue.

The sources of the new political ideas that entered the public domain during this period were varied but there was a commonality of themes and an overlapping across the boundaries of conceptual frameworks as different groups went about fashioning a national identity according to their own vision of what the nation was or should be. This commonality was as striking as the distinctiveness of the various versions of the nationalist project. The commonality of themes stemmed from the engagement between the past and present as particular aspects of the supposed past of the putative nation were brought into play in accordance with the needs of the present in order to structure a national identity and shape a national culture. Turning to the revolutionary pamphlets of the early twentieth century, we find that national identity began to be shaped around certain traditional icons, symbols and memories and myths that gained new meaning in the present. Imagining the birth land as mother gave a mystical dimension to the idea of the nation and created a sacred space within which the idea of the nation was carved out. The Hindu religion, imagined in new ways to suit the needs of the present, became a cementing factor in national identity. 'Religionized' politics that valourized the idea of a unitary political culture became a way of providing a viable political identity for some (but repelled others who imagined a nation constituted on plural and even non-religious foundations) in the circumstances of the times. But just as national identities are not transhistorical entities but cultural constructs that mutate with changing circumstances[9] so also the language used to shape nationhood assumes different meanings and valences in different contexts. The revolutionary nationalists did make use of Hindu 'tradition' while weaving the narrative of the nation but their effort has to be understood differently from subsequent efforts by other groups who resurrected historical myths in order to fashion political ideologies with narrow sectarian goals. This is because the conceptual structures within which apparently similar terms and languages were conceived and interpreted in order to be utilized towards the achievements of political goals were radically different in the two cases.

The view of the revolutionary nationalists that the idea of the nation had to be translated into reality through the use of violence also marked a paradigmatic shift in the relationship between the rulers and the ruled. The discourse and counter-discourse of the revolutionary nationalists and the colonial authorities brought out into the open the fundamental antagonism that lay at the heart of the relationship between the rulers and the ruled. While the rulers looked upon the ruled with the complacent condescension born out of a deep belief in the innate superiority of their civilization and complete confidence in their power, the latter challenged these assumptions both through actions and words. The revolutionary pamphlets emerged as an important medium through which the claims of the colonial state were contested. The revolutionary pamphlets constituted a fundamental *critique*[10] of British rule and this critique destroyed the legitimizing assumptions of colonial rule by asserting that the power of the state could not be allowed to override the interests of the nation. The pamphlets, instead, went about constructing the alternate vision of a polity that would be free from the shackles of a colonial state that had no moral or legal rights over its subjects. This alternate vision was that of a nation-state within which a national community would, at last, fulfil its destiny.

Endnotes

1 From *Jugantar* pamphlet titled *Shamay hoiachhe ki*, SN 115/16, 2223/16, West Bengal State Archives (hereafter WBSA), Intelligence Branch (hereafter IB).

2 From *Jugantar* pamphlet of 1914, beginning with words *Tora shabai manush ho* (*All ye, become Men*) in PTS Collection, Serial Number 50, Calcutta Police Museum.

3 From the *Swadhin Bharat* pamphlet, *Dekhite, dekhite* (*Over the Years*) in SN 4/1913, FN 404/1913 in WBSA, IB.

4 From the *Jugantar* pamphlet, *Amader Asha*, (*Our Hope*), SN 115/1916, FN 2223/1916, WBSA, IB.

5 'This (acquisition of political rights) has not happened because of their kindness, but because of our power to acquire what is justly ours' – from *Swadhin Bharat* pamphlet beginning with words, *Ingrajer shashone thakiya,* (*living under the rule of the British*), SN 56/1913, FN 1340/1913 in WBSA-IB.

6 C. A.Bayly, 'Patriotism and Ethical Government, c. 1780–1860' in *Origins of Nationality in South Asia: Patriotism and Ethical Government in the Making of Modern India* (Oxford University Press, New Delhi, 1998), p. 63–97; 78–84.

7 Walter Benjamin, *Illuminations,* quoted in Terry Eagleton ed. *Walter Benjamin or Towards a Revolutionary Criticism* (Verso, London, 2009) p. 49.

8 *Sadhu bhasha* literally means chaste language. I am grateful to one of the anonymous readers of the manuscript for drawing my attention to this point.

9 For example, the concept of India that emphasized unity in diversity has been gradually replaced by the idea of a polity that celebrates diversity in unity.

10 If government is 'a social practice of subjecting individuals by mechanisms of power which lay claim to truth *critique* will be the movement by which the subject assumes the right to question truth on its effects on power and power on its effects on truth' – Michel Foucault, quoted by Colin Jordan in introduction to James Faubion ed. *Michel Foucault: Power* (New Press, New York, 1984), p. XXXIX.

Bibliography

I. Official Records and Publications

National Archives of India, New Delhi

Records of the Home Political Department of the Government of India, 1907–18

West Bengal State Archives: Writers' Building, Kolkata

1. Confidential Records of the Political Department (Political Branch) of the Government of Bengal, 1907–20
2. Confidential Miscellaneous Records
3. History Sheets
4. *Extracts Dealing with Revolutionary Crime from Articles in Various Newspapers in Bengal, with Prelude* (Compiled from the *Weekly Reports and the Annual Reports of the Bengali Translator to Government and from Judgments*)
5. Report on the Native Papers in Bengal

West Bengal State Archives, Shakespeare Sarani, Kolkata

1. Records of the Intelligence Branch of the Government of Bengal, 1908–20
2. Intelligence Branch, C.I.D. Bengal, *Weekly Reports: October 1908–December 1909, 1910*

Maharashtra State Archives, Mumbai

Records of the Judicial Department, 1906–18

Collections of Documents

Samanta, Amiya, ed. 1995 *Terrorism in Bengal: A Collection of Documents*, 6 Volumes., Government of West Bengal, Calcutta.

Trial Records

Trial Records of *Jugantar, Bande-Mataram, Sandhya* Sedition Cases in *Smaraniya Bichar Sangrahlaya* (Museum of Memorable Trials), Alipur Sessions Court, Calcutta.

II. Non-official Primary Sources

Collections of Documents, Books, Complete Works

Chaudhuri, Kamal, ed. 2005. *Bangabhanga O Samakalin Bangasamaj*. Documents on the Partition of Bengal and contemporary Bengali Society. Kolkata: Dey's Publishing.

Ghose Aurobindo. 1996. *On Nationalism: Selected Speeches and Writings*. Second edition. Pondicherry: Sri Aurobindo Ashram Trust.

———. 1997. *Bande Mataram: Early Political Writings*. Pondicherry: Sri Aurobindo Ashram.

———. 1995. *Bankim Chandra Chatterji*. Third edition. Pondicherry: Sri Aurobindo Ashram.

———. 2006. *Bankim, Tilak, Dayananda*. Sixth edition. Pondicherry: Sri Aurobindo Ashram.

———. 1992. *Karakahini* (*The Prisoner's Story*). Seventh edition. Pondicherry: Sri Aurobindo Ashram.

Bandopadhyay, Angshuman. 2001. *Agnijuger Agnikatha: 'Jugantar'* [*A Collection of Jugantar Files*]. Pondicherry: Sri Aurobindo Ashram Publications Department.

Bandopadhyay, Sandip. 2004. *Nathipatre Swadeshi Andolan* [A Collection of Documents on the Swadeshi Movement]. Kolkata: Granthamitra.

Mukhopadhyay, Ashok Kumar. 2006. *Mukti Kon Pathe* [A Collection of Articles Published in the *Jugantar*]. Kolkata: Punascha.

Vivekananda, Swami. 1983. *Swami Vivekanander Bani ar Rachana* [The Sayings and Writings of Swami Vivekananda]. Fifth edition. Kolkata: Udbodhan Karjalaya.

Newspapers and periodicals

Amrita Bazaar Patrika.

I have consulted stray files from the *Bande-Mataram*, *Jugantar* and *Sandhya* newspapers in the *Smaraniya Bichar Sangrahalaya* collection.

Memoirs

(There exists a considerable collection of memoirs penned by revolutionary nationalists. Listed below are the works that I have read and referred to in the book.)

Bandopadhyay, Upendranath. 1993. *Nirbashiter Atmakatha* [Autobiography of an Exile]. Second edition. Kolkata: Basumati Corporation.

Chaudhurani, Saraladevi. 2007. *Jibaner Jharapata* [The Fallen Leaves of a Life]. Kolkata: Dey's Publishing.

De, Sailesh ed. 1978. *Agnijug* [Age of Fire]. Kolkata: Purna Prakashan.

Dutt, Bhupendranath. 1983. *Bharater Dwitiya Swadhinatar Sangram* [The Second Indian Struggle for Independence]. Kolkata: Nababharat Publishers.

———. 1999. *Biplaber Padachinha* [The Footsteps of Revolution]. Kolkata: Sahitya Samsad.

Dutt, Ullaskar. 2012. *Karajibani* [The story of Prison-Life]. Kolkata: Sagnik Books.

Ghose, Barindra Kumar. 1972. *Barindrer Atmakahini: Dhar-pakorer Jug* [The Memoirs of Barin: The Age of Arrests]. New edition. Kolkata: D M Library.

———. 2012. *Dwipantarer Katha* [The Story of Exile]. Kolkata: Sagnik Books.

Guha, Nalinikishore. 2012. *Banglay Biplabbad* [Revolutionary Ideology in Bengal]. New edition. Kolkata: Mitram.

Qanungo, Hemchandra. 1928. *Banglay Biplab Pracheshta* [The Revolutionary Endeavour in Bengal]. Kolkata: Chirayata Prokashoni.

Mukhopadhyay, Jadugopal. 1956. *Biplabi Jibaner Smriti* [Memories of a Revolutionary Life]. New Delhi: Academic Publishers.

Pal, Bipin Chandra. 1932, 2004. *Memories of My Life and Times*. New Delhi: UBSPD.

Rakshit-Ray, Bhupendrakishore. 1966. *Shabar Alakhye*. Kolkata: Bengal Publishers Private Limited.

III. Secondary Sources: Books and Articles

Anderson, Benedict. 1983. *Imagined Communities: Reflections on the Origin and Spread of Nationalism*. London: Verso.

Bagchi, Jasodhara. 20–27 October 1990. 'Representing Nationalism: Ideology of Motherhood in Colonial Bengal', *Economic and Political Weekly*, XXV(42–43) : 65–71.

Baker, Keith Michael. 1990. *Inventing the French Revolution: Essays in French Political Culture in the Eighteenth Century*. Cambridge: Cambridge University Press.

Bayly, C. A. 2003. *Origins of Nationality in South Asia*. Delhi: Oxford University Press.

Bhattacharya, Sabyasachi. 2003. *Vande Mataram: The Biography of a Song*. New Delhi: Penguin India.

Bose, Sugata. 2007. 'The Spirit and Form of an Ethical Polity: A Meditation on Aurobindo's Thought', *Modern Intellectual History*, 4: 129–144.

Bose, Sugata and Ayesha Jalal, eds. 1997. *Nationalism, Democracy and Development: State and Politics in India*. Delhi: Oxford University Press.

Broomfield, J. H. 1968. *Elite Conflict in a Plural Society: Twentieth Century Bengal*. Bombay: Oxford University Press.

Chakrabarty, Dipesh. 2001. *Provincializing Europe: Post Colonial Thought and Historical Difference*. Oxford: Oxford University Press.

———. 2002. *Habitations of Modernity*. Delhi: Permanent Black.

Chakrabarty, Hiren. 1992. *Political Protest in Bengal: Boycott and Revolutionary Terrorism, 1905–1918*. Kolkata: Papyrus.

Chatterjee, Partha. 1986. *Nationalist Thought and the Colonial World: A Derivative Discourse?* London: Zed Books.

Chattopadhyay, Bankimchandra. 1955. *Bankim Rachanabali*, Vol. 2. Kolkata: Sahitya Samsad [Bengali Era, 1361].

Chisick, Harvey.1993. 'The Pamphlet Literature of the French Revolution: An Overview', *History of European Ideas*, 17(2/3): 149–166.

Darnton, Robert. 1996. *The Forbidden Best-Sellers of Pre-Revolutionary France*. New York: Norton and Company.

———. 2001. 'Literary Surveillance in the British Raj: The Contradictions of Liberal Imperialism', *Book History* 4: 133–176.

Das, Veena and Ashis Nandy, eds. 1986. *The Word and the World: Fantasy, Symbol and Record*. New Delhi: Sage.

DasGupta, Uma.1977. 'The Shackling of the Vernacular Press', *Rise of an Indian Public: Impact of Official Policy, 1870–1880*. Kolkata: Riddhi.

Davis, Richard H. 2007. *Picturing the Nation: Iconographies of Modern India*. New Delhi: Orient Longman.

De Baecque, Antoine. 1997. *The Body Politic: Corporeal Metaphor in Revolutionary France, 1770-1800*, tr., Charlotte Mandell. Stanford, California: Stanford University Press.

Deshpande, Prachi. 2007. *Creative Pasts: Historical Memory and Identity in Western India*. Ranikhet: Permanent Black.

Donough, Walter Russell. 1914. *The History and Law of Sedition and Cognate Offences in British India: Penal and Preventive*. Calcutta: Thacker, Spink and Company.

Ellul, Jacques 1965. *Propaganda: The Formation of Men's Attitudes*. New York: Knopf.

James Faubion ed. Robert Hurley translated. 2001. *Michel Foucault: Power. Essential Works of Foucault, 1954-1984*. New York: New Press.

Girard, René. 1977. *Violence and the Sacred*, tr. Peter Gregory. Baltimore: Johns Hopkins University Press.

Greenfield, Liah. 2007. *Nationalism and the Mind*. Oxford: One World Publications.

Gruder, Vivian. April-June, 1992. 'Un message politique adressé au public: Les pamphlets "populaires" a la veille de la Révolution', *Revue d'histoire modern et comtemporaine*, 39(2): 169–97.

Guha-Thakurta, Tapati. 2007. *The Making of a New 'Indian' Art: Artists, Aesthetics and Nationalism in Bengal, c. 1850–1920*. Cambridge, Great Britain: Cambridge University Press.

Gupta, Swarupa. 2006. 'Notions of Nationhood in Bengal: Perspectives on Samaj, 1867–1905', *Modern Asian Studies* 40 (2): 273–302.

Habermas, Jurgen. 1989. *The Structural Transformation of the Public Sphere: An Inquiry into a Category of Bourgeois Society*, tr. Thomas Burger. Great Britain: Polity Press.

Hall, Catherine, Keith, McClelland and Jane Rendall, eds. 2000. *Defining the Victorian Nation: Class, Race, Gender and the Reform Act of 1867*. Cambridge: Cambridge University Press.

Heehs, Peter. 1993. *The Bomb in Bengal: The Rise of Revolutionary Terrorism in India, 1900–1910*. New Delhi: Oxford University Press.

————. 1998. *Nationalism, Terrorism, Communalism: Essays in Modern Indian History*. Delhi: Oxford University Press.

Hobsbawm, E. J. 1990. *Nations and Nationalism since 1780: Programme, Myth and Reality*. Cambridge: Cambridge University Press.

Howe, Stephen, ed. 2010. *The New Imperial Histories Reader*. London and New York: Routledge.

Juergensmeyer, Mark. 1994. *Religious Nationalism Confronts the Secular State*. Delhi: Oxford University Press.

Karim, Aisha and Bruce B. Lawrence, eds. 2007. *On Violence; A Reader*. Durham: Duke University Press.

Kaviraj, Sudipta. 1995. *The Unhappy Consciousness: Bankimchandra Chattopadhyay and the Formation of Nationalist Discourse in India*. New Delhi: Oxford University Press.

Kolsky, Elizabeth. 2010. *Colonial Justice in British India: White Violence and the Rule of Law*. Cambridge: Cambridge University Press.

Landes, Joan. 1988. *Women and the Public Sphere in the Age of the French Revolution*. Ithaca: Cornell University Press.

Lee, Mabel, and Michael Welding, eds. 1997. *History, Literature and Society: Essays in Honour of S.N. Mukherjee*. New Delhi: Manohar.

Mackenzie, J. 1984. *Propaganda and Empire: The Manipulation of British Public Opinion, 1880–1960*. Manchester: Manchester University Press.

Mazumdar, R. C. 1981. *History of Modern Bengal, Part –Two, 1905–1947*. Kolkata: G. Bharadwaj and Co.

McCormack, Matthew, ed. 2007. *Public Men: Masculinity and Politics in Modern Britain*. New York: Palgrave MacMillan.

Mukherjee, Amitabha. 1995. *Militant Nationalism in India, 1867–1947*. Calcutta: Institute of Historical Studies.

Mukherjee, Haridas and Uma. 2007, 1st edition: 1958. *Bipin Chandra Pal and India's Struggle for Swaraj*. Kolkata: Dey's Publishing.

———. 2004, First edition: 1961. *Swadeshi Andolan o Banglar Nabayug*. Kolkata: Dey's Publishing.

———. Second edition: 1996, First edition: 1972. *Bharater Swadhinanta Andoloney Jugantar Patrikar Dan ba SriAurobindo o Banglay Biplabbad*. Kolkata: Firma KLM.

———. 1957. *Bande Mataram and Indian Nationalism*. Kolkata: Firma KLM.

Mukherjee, Uma. 2004, First edition: 1966. *Two Great Indian Revolutionaries: Rash Behari Bose and Jyotindra Nath Mukherjee*. Calcutta: Dey's Publishing.

Mukhopadhyay, Ashoke Kumar. 2006. *Mukti Kon Pathe*. Kolkata: Punascha Publications.

Nandy, Ashis. 2003. 'The Intimate Enemy: Loss and Recovery of Self under Colonialism', in *Exiled at Home*. New Delhi: Oxford University Press.

O'Donnell, Victoria and Garth S. Jowett, eds. 2012. *Propaganda and Persuasion*. Fifth edition. New Delhi: Sage Publications.

O'Sullivan, Noel, ed. 1986. *Revolutionary Terrorism, Ideology and Revolution: The Origins of Modern Political Violence*. Sussex: Wheatsheaf Books.

Popkin, Jeremy. 1989. 'The Prerevolutionary origins of Political Journalism', in Jack Censer ed. *The French Revolution and Intellectual History*. Chicago: The Dorsey Press.

———. Spring, 1989. 'Pamphlet Journalism at the end of the Old Regime', *Eighteenth-Century Studies*, 22: 351–355.

Ray, Rajat Kanta. 1984. *Social Conflict and Political Unrest in Bengal: 1875–1927*. New Delhi: Oxford University Press.

———. 1988. 'Moderates, Extremists and Revolutionaries: Bengal, 1900–1908', in Sisson, Richard and Stanley Wolpert eds. *Congress and Indian Nationalism: The Pre-Independence Phase*. Delhi: Oxford University Press.

———. 1993. 'Land, Religion and Political Culture: The Militant Hindu Gentry of East Bengal, 1905–1917', Paper presented at the Bicentenary Evaluation Seminar on the Permanent Settlement Organized by *Bangladesh Itihas Samiti* in November 1993.

Ray, Tapti. 1996. 'Disciplining the Printed Text: Colonial and Nationalist Surveillance of Bengali Literature', in *Texts of Power: Emerging Disciplines in Colonial Bengal*. Kolkata: Samya.

Ray, William. 2001. *The Logic of Culture: Authority and Identity in the Modern Era*. Oxford: Blackwell Publishers.

Raychaudhuri, Tapan. 1988. *Europe Reconsidered: Perceptions of the West in Nineteenth-Century Bengal*. New Delhi: Oxford University Press.

———. 2009. *Prabandha Samgraha*. Kolkata: Ananda.

———. 2000. 'Shadows of the Swastika: Historical Perspectives on the Politics of Hindu Communalism', *Modern Asian Studies*, 34(2): 259–279.

Riches, David. 1996. *The Anthropology of Violence*. Oxford: Blackwell.

Robb, Peter. 2007. 'The Colonial State and Constructions of Indian Identity: An Example on the Northeast Frontier in the 1880s', in *Liberalism, Modernity and the Nation*. New Delhi: Oxford University Press.

Roper, Michael. Spring, 2005. 'Slipping out of View: Subjectivity and Emotion in Gender History', *History Workshop Journal*, 59: 57–72.

Sarkar, Sumit. 2010. *The Swadeshi Movement in Bengal: 1903–1908*. Ranikhet: Permanent Black.

———. 1997. *Writing Social History*. New Delhi: Oxford University Press.

———. 2004. *Beyond Nationalist Frames: Relocating Postmodernism, Hindutva and History*. Delhi: Permanent Black.

Sarkar, Tanika. November 21, 1987. 'Nationalist Iconography: Image of Women in Nineteenth-Century Bengali Literature', *Economic and Political Weekly*, XXII(47): 2011–2015.

Sartori, Andrew. 2010. 'The Transfiguration of Duty in Aurobindo's Essays on the Gita', *Modern Intellectual History*, 7: 319–334.

Schmidt, Bettina E., and Inge W. Schroeder. 2001. *Anthropology of Violence and Conflict*. London and New York: Routledge, Taylor and Francis Group.

Schudson, Michael. April, 2002. 'News, Public, Nation', *The American Historical Review*, 107(2): 481–495.

Sen, Amiya. 1993. *Hindu Revivalism in Bengal, 1872–1905: Some Essays in Interpretation*. New Delhi: Oxford University Press.

Sen, S. P. ed. 1975. *History in Modern Indian Literature*. Kolkata: Institute of Historical Studies.

Sengupta, Nandogopal 1984. 'Sambad Patra: Swadhinata O Sanskriti' in Rathin Chakrabarty ed. *Gano-Andolan o Sangbad Patro* (Peoples' Movements and the Press). Kolkata: Lokmat Prakashani.

Sharma, Mallikarjuna. 1987. *Role of Revolutionaries in the Freedom Struggle: A Critical History of the Revolutionary Movements, 1918–1934*. Hyderabad: Marxist Study Forum.

Sinha. Mrinalini. 1997. *Colonial Masculinity: The 'Manly Englishman' and the 'Effeminate Bengali' in the Nineteenth Century*. New Delhi: Kali for Women.

Smith, Ted J., ed. 1989. *Propaganda: A Pluralist Perspective*. London: Praeger.

Suny, Roger Grigor. 2001. 'Constructing Primordialism: Old Histories for New Nations', *The Journal of Modern History*, 73(4): 862–96.

Tagore, Rabindranath. 1961. *Jibansmriti* in *Rabindra Rachanabali*. Centenary Edition. Vol. 10. Government of West Bengal.

Thapar, Romila. 2000. *History and Beyond*. New Delhi: Oxford University Press.

Tripathi, Amalesh. 1967. *The Extremist Challenge: India between 1890 and 1910*. Calcutta: Orient Longman.

Index